A NEW EARTH

A
NEW EARTH

———

ELSPETH HUXLEY

1960
WILLIAM MORROW & COMPANY, INC
NEW YORK

Library of Congress Catalog Card No. 60-12634

916.7
H

Printed in Great Britain by
Ebenezer Baylis & Son, Ltd.
The Trinity Press
Worcester and London

Contents

List of Illustrations

Maps

CHAPTER 1

Keeping Deserts at Bay

1

ONCE, in a Nigerian town, I was shown a thin stone column which legend held to be a petrified staff belonging to an ancient giant who had prowled the earth conquering cities and laying waste the land with his heavy sword. One day he heard his own people calling him to their aid. He strode homewards, killing as he went, until he noticed that the vanquished at his feet were his own clansmen. In his blind progress he had killed the men he loved. Despairing, he thrust his staff into the ground where it still stands, and vanished.

There is Progress for you, I have often thought—except for the vanishing. Friend and foe, good and bad, strong and weak go down before him. Nothing can halt him, he does not pause to fuss over butterflies or vipers crushed under his feet.

This is a book about Progress striding through a part of Africa, where he is on the move at breakneck speed. Whether the giant is an angel or an ogre I shall leave readers to judge—or, rather, whether the results of his conquests are on the whole beneficial, or the reverse, to the human race. He himself is surely neither: an elemental force, like wind or sun or lightning, that doles out good and evil more or less impartially. One can neither halt Progress, nor be sure that because he is walking forward he approaches a goal. He may be going round in a circle, or back to camp.

The point is, he is on the move. Customs, habits and traditions ten thousand years old topple down, and in his wake new habits and ideas spring up: some no doubt better than the old ones, some worse, some about the same human blend of the two. It is a waste of time to make moral judgements about these things. They happen, that is all; they are a part of the continuous metabolism of history.

This giant Progress finds some places and people easier to

conquer than others. Like lesser fry, he moves the fastest in
fertile lands with good communications: wastelands and
deserts slow him down. They do not check him altogether, but
his footfalls make a light impression on lava rock or shifting
sand, and so his passage through a part of Kenya only is the
theme of this book. We shall see nothing of the big cities,
which appear sometimes as growing-points of civilization but
perhaps more often as foci of social disease; nothing of the
coast, that long, narrow strip along the Indian Ocean where
most of local history resides; nothing of the Northern Frontier
District with its great deserts and lava mountains, its camels
and ancient wells, its turbaned Somalis and armed raiders
from the Ethiopian border-lands—the most untouched, truly
African region that occupies over half of Kenya, whose total
size is about that of France.

Nor shall we travel through those regions where the conquest
of Progress has been most complete: the so-called white
highlands, an area about twice the size of Yorkshire embedded
in great tablelands and mountains raised some 5,000 feet or
more above sea-level between the ocean and Lake Victoria,
where a handful of European farmers has established a small
but thriving settlement and a nucleus of Western economy.

Since this book is about changes that are revolutionizing
the lives of African peasants, we shall explore only those
regions where nearly all Kenya's six million Africans live.
Although none of them is particularly remote or, thanks to
the Land-Rover, inaccessible, it is a strange fact that few are
visited by travellers, who either, if they are journalists, stick
to the cities or, if they hope to write travel books, invade the
dwindling privacies of the animals or seek the last survivors
of the noble savage with his photogenic pigtails and ornaments,
his natural indifference and his haunting air of doom. We
shall concern ourselves, therefore, with that section of Kenya,
slightly larger than the total area of England, whose inhabitants in the main pursue a settled life, in contrast to the
nomadic custom, either as cultivators or herdsmen, or more
commonly as a combination of the two: for most East Africans
are cattle folk at heart.

This region is administered in four provinces and twenty-five districts, all of which I visited, although of course I did not penetrate into every part. Each tribal group still holds jealously to its traditional region, even if it reached its present homeland only in the last few hundred years, or indeed within the last century. Kenya is honeycombed with land barriers, both of race and tribe: but whether people like it or not (and they seldom do) Progress in his headlong march is knocking them over. This year the practice which for half a century has reserved the white highlands for farmers of European descent has ended, and in this region no racial bar now inhibits the lease or sale of land.

But such a bar still prevents exchanges of land between members of one tribe and another. Whereas a Kikuyu, for example, may now buy land in the white highlands, if he has the money and can convince a local board that he also has the skill, he cannot do so in the country of the Masai or the Tugen, the Kamba or the Kisii. All the country I visited belongs to the people who live in it, and is recognized as their property by the Government; without their consent, no great changes can be made.

Tomorrow, if Progress is not to stumble, tribal barriers will have to go as racial barriers have gone, and land become, as in other countries, the property not of tribes but of individuals.

II

The Suam river forms a natural boundary between the deserts of the Northern Frontier District and the equatorial highlands through which the Rift Valley runs. It is not a wide or noble river and it reaches its destination, Lake Rudolf, only for about three months of the year. The rest of the time it peters out, or seeps underground where animals and humans can reach it only by scooping out the sand. Game animals know how to do this by instinct but cattle do not: men have to act for them. The game animals help each other. Not long ago a sad sight was discovered beside a dried-up water-hole: twenty-nine rhinos dead of thirst. Their armoured noses cannot dig in sand. Normally, elephants do the digging, drink first and leave the pool to other animals. In this case the elephants had been driven away by poachers and so the rhinos perished slowly, water within two feet of their parched mouths.

The tree-lined Suam lies at the foot of one of the mightiest escarpments in Africa. Down, down you twist along a writhing narrow road from the flanks of the wild and wooded Cherangani mountains, whose cold and mist-enshrouded crests rise to over 10,000 feet. At the bottom you are down to 3,000 feet in hot, dry, bare thorn-country typical of God knows how many thousand square miles of Africa. There is no proper soil left, just tawny red sand and mottled flaking rock. All is bare as a plank. Under rocks, in the thickest bush, there are plants of sorts, mostly with tendrils like wire or pale, thin twists of leaf that somehow live, with desperate resolution, in this dry furnace, in the rock, in the sand.

Bush is everywhere: hard as iron, tough as old boots, vicious with spikes. The struggle merely to exist is fierce and elemental, there seems no room for grace. And yet you may find a so-called desert rose, the bare *adenia* bush with its big bulbous root for water-storage and its gay pink flowers. And at the right season every acacia tree and shrub is dusted over with tiny white or yellow flowers that smell sweet and hum with bees.

On the flat, baking, spiky bank of the Suam stands a small trading-post consisting, like all its fellows, of a few squalid little tin-roofed, open-fronted shops kept sometimes by Indians, Somalis or Swahilis but more often, nowadays, by local talent. This is the country of the Suk, a tribe on whom Progress is only starting his conquest. The lean, hard young men still go about in warrior's attire, their hair matted with cow dung and grease into strange shapes, especially into a round plate-like appendage at the back which must be kept off the ground, during sleep, by a little neck-stool which every man carries, together with his long spear. In their lower lips they fix brass cylinders about the size of a cigarette, and on their arms and chests are rows of bumps, made in youth by rubbing ash and dirt into knife-holes until these fester and scar-tissue forms to make a studded pattern. Still spurning trousers, they wear a length of cloth in toga fashion, looped on one shoulder, stained with ochre, sometimes caught in with a bead belt.

They look proud and free, displaying the lithe action, the glistening healthy limbs, the loping stride of tribesmen who have so far kept Progress at bay.

As for the women, their shaven heads poke up through glinting ruffs of beads and wire that stand out a foot or more under chins and ears. Goodness knows how they sleep in them; so far as I know, they are never removed. These women look like walking flowers with black stalks and flat red, blue and copper heads. Coils of wire tightly bind plum-like upper arms, legs and ankles. Ear-lobes, heavy with beads and metal, hang down to the shoulder. Strong and tough as mules, these women do not cultivate, for here nothing grows.

III

We jolted over sand and thrust through thick bush that scraped the olive-green sides of our Land-Rover to find a *manyatta*, a rough circle of huts in a bush clearing. One of the scrawny mothers of the tribe, clad in skins, took me into her hut. It was made of withies twisted between upright sticks like a basket, with plenty of daylight showing through. The roof was of mud plastered over a cap of withies and it had an air of marked impermanence, for the Suk are nomads.

Possessions were down to the bone. A few hollow gourds stoppered with cows' tails in a woven bag hanging on a wall; a clay pot, upside-down on a stick, for milking into; a spear tucked into the side of the hut; a few hides in a corner. Nothing else. Two low platforms, perhaps a foot high, made of sticks bound with thongs, provided elementary beds. Sunlight dappled the floor as it probed chinks in the walls. A smell of wood-smoke, rancid fat and cow dung—rather pleasant. The old girl hawked and spat as she talked, and her neck coils twinkled in the sun and shadow.

What did she think of Progress—represented, in this instance, by a scheme to improve the grazing? She rubbed her skinny arms with claw-like hands. Her naked stomach was fretted all over with bumps, which had been made, she said, in her childhood to cure a great sickness.

'We have to move too much,' she complained. 'Why can't

we be left alone with our goats? Why do we have to trek from one place to another?'

It is the same everywhere: the old women are the strongest enemies of the giant. And as their ranks are filled from the age-grade below them, the minds of the new matriarchs harden into the mould of their predecessors. I said:

'The boys go to school at Kacheliba' (that little trading centre by the Suam). 'There are no girls there. Why not send them too?'

The old woman, and her cronies who were squatting in the doorway, buzzed like meat-flies. Several spat juicily. 'Schools? Girls? Who would agree to that? The place of girls is with their mothers. No schools. No, no, no.'

The fathers do not want to send them either, lest they slip away and out of control. It is women who hold the tribe together. If they go, all goes.

No cooking-stones in this hut, such as you find in all the huts of cultivating people. There is no need to cook. Curdled milk and blood is the staple, and meat roasted on the ends of skewers. Sometimes, nowadays, they trade hides for grain, and then the women pound and cook it like their harder-working sisters of the uplands. But only now and then: for them no delving, no hoes, no *pangas*. The pastoral life they know to be the best because it does not turn women into slaves of the hoe. They have no envy for their sisters who bend their backs in the hot sun to dig, weed and harvest.

IV

Back in the village, at a new brick office built for the chief, eight members of the local grazing committee filed in silently to sit on two benches: oldish men who wore their hair matted with mud into a close-fitting cap painted with red and white designs, a white ostrich feather sticking up at the back. All had the Suk plug in the lower lip, and most wore ear-rings the size of new potatoes that looked like huge pearls. For the rest they were in ragged shirts and trousers: one wore split gum-boots, another sandals made of zebra hide. They spoke in Suk which a young schoolmaster translated.

'The story of this scheme goes back to olden times when we controlled our own grazing. At certain times the elders would decide to drive away all the cattle so as to let the grass grow. But then, as soon as the cattle returned, the grass was eaten up and it did not recover, because there were too many cattle. So our beasts grew thin and when the rains failed they died. We fed them with leaves and branches cut from trees, but this was not enough.

'Then came the Government and told us: you must divide your country by cutting lines through the bush. Then you must put all the cattle together, goats too, everything, between two lines. They must stay there until they have eaten the grass. Then we will open another block for them. And they must move and not return for one year.

'So we decided to try this. But many people were not satisfied. "This is a trick," they said, "to take our land; when the grass has grown, Europeans will come and seize it." Some hesitated, others crossed the Suam and fled into Uganda.

'But some of us stayed behind. After a while, we saw that this idea was successful. The grass grew higher than ever before, and people found that when the cattle moved away, the grass had not been killed. So our cattle got fatter, and no longer starved.

'Now the people who fled into Uganda have recrossed the Suam, and we no longer cut branches from thorn-trees for our cattle. We are getting more milk, the children are healthier. If anyone drives his cattle into closed pastures, we of the committee exact a fine—a beast for each offence. We should like to see the whole of Suk country made into a scheme.'

The root of all the trouble is the increase of stock, because vets have controlled the epidemics, mainly rinderpest, that used to keep animals and pastures in balance.

Once a year, all the beasts are rounded up at one of forty crushes, inoculated for rinderpest, and new stock branded. Now, in a grazing scheme, there is a ten per cent annual cut. Each owner receives his quota: this man must get rid of ten beasts, that man of seven, that of two. He sends them to a sale-yard, where regular monthly auctions are conducted by two

Suk auctioneers, called Achome Lotulianguio and Kipkopus, who have all the patter at the tip of their tongues. The highest price at the last auction was £24—these little scraggy beasts are no larger than donkeys and weigh five or six hundred-weight; an old man was so staggered at this fabulous wealth that he danced himself into a coma and then went off and bought a bicycle that he keeps wrapped up in brown paper and treats like some priceless Old Master.

These grazing schemes are the first successful attempt made in East Africa to tackle on a massive scale the restoration of deserts created in the last thirty years by continued over-stocking. These new deserts lie, broadly speaking, in a great arc along the lower reaches of the highlands, between them and the older deserts of the Northern Frontier which cannot be reclaimed because the rainfall is too low. They were, and still are, advancing year by year into the marginal pastures. All over Africa this happens, east, west and centre: wherever there are deserts, fringed by marginal pastures, the deserts advance because man overstocks and abuses his habitat.

Far from being checked, in most places the process is accelerating. That is why this work in Kenya has importance for the whole continent. It shows that you *can* stop deserts, if you really try—even put them into reverse. In these two districts alone, West Suk and Baringo, nearly 400,000 acres have been brought under grazing control.

The essence of the system is the practice every British farmer follows when he moves his cattle from one field to another: only here there are no fields, just endless bush that you must first divide into enormous blocks by cutting traces through the undergrowth. The art lies in knowing when to move the herds, how long to rest each block and when to let beasts back again.

Kenya follows a system evolved in Texas. You divide an area into four blocks and put the cattle into each in turn for four months. It then falls out that every block in turn rests during the four months' growing season during and after the rains. By the banks of the Suam we saw the result: grass literally waist-high, like a hayfield ready to mow—thick, nutritious star-grass, something unseen here for thirty years.

1 Young married women, old and new styles: from West Suk and North Nyanza

2 Man-made deserts in Baringo: arap Moi, M.L.C., and tree-roots exposed by erosion; and goats who live on twigs

Across the trace, outside the scheme, the baked dusty ground was literally bare as a table-top. Where does the grass come from? It seems a miracle. Seeds must lie dormant for years and years in this oven, only waiting a bare chance to germinate.

v

As in all successful enterprises, two essentials have been fulfilled here in West Suk. (The better to administer them, the Suk are divided into three: West, East and Kara.) The Europeans in charge have been left here for a reasonable period, not shunted about like trains; and they have worked together as a team. Both David Shireff, the district commissioner, and Hugh York, the agricultural officer, have been at Kapenguria, their headquarters, for over five years, and Ian Bond, the livestock officer, almost as long.

Mr. Shireff showed me some of the trees he is planting, block by block, on the precipitous, goat-ravaged mountain slopes down which storm-water now cascades unimpeded, tearing great gashes deep in the bones of the hills. These trees, if they survive, will re-create rivers murdered by men and their beasts. The saplings grow on a Gothic pinnacle high above a blue, speckled distance which stretches northwards apparently for ever; in that vast trough, enormous mountains lie like dice thrown by a god on the table of the universe, rivers like hairs fallen from his beard.

Mr. Shireff, used to the view, gazed lovingly at his little pine-trees poking up among the rocks and thought of cool, life-giving forests nurturing springs. To get them planted, to get all these revolutionary ideas across, he has had to be tough and patient with the Suk. Africans in the tribal state never, so far as I know, plant the seeds of trees. For trees are something put there by God; they are His business, not ours; if they vanish, that is His affair; there is plenty of bush for shade and firewood, and of what other use is a tree? As to the notion that in twenty years' time trees can be sold for money, that is all too remote and problematical. In twenty years we shall be old, perhaps fire will have destroyed the trees, and

17

B

why should we work to help a future generation? Rather it is their task to help us when we are old.

Persuasion, talks, *barazas*, lorry-loads of elders taken to see other schemes—slowly and steadily Mr. Shireff and his team have plugged away. Reluctantly, and with Government help, the District Council has allocated small sums towards the trees that one day will keep water flowing to the Suk cattle far away and down below on the plains. And there are two camps of detainees who have done the actual planting. These are left-overs from the *Dini ya Msambwa*, a semi-religious, semi-political and wholly fanatical movement that spread into these parts from the Lake Victoria basin a few years ago under the stimulus of a wild-eyed prophet who called himself Elijah, and led a band of adherents who roamed the country burning down schools and chiefs' offices to prepare for the second coming of Christ. They speared to death three young European officers in the Kerio valley, below these hills. The Suk, whose greased, plumed and ornamented young men, deprived of spear-blooding, have no occupation, can be explosive as well as obstinate. They are not easy to handle and the Kapenguria team has done the job well.

VI

The Tugen people who live round Lake Baringo, farther east, and just across the Kerio river, seem like poor relations of the Suk. Craggy, precipitous, furrowed hills rise jaggedly to right and left of you, all blue and misty in the heat-haze; you never see a flat horizon. And the acacias are always green, providing a sharp contrast to the raw-meat red of the bare earth under their branches. The trunks of one species (about the size of bush apples, called acacia *seyal*) have the most extraordinary twisted, tortured, Rackham shapes, as if a cosmic hand had kneaded them into freaks. They are clustered all over with grey knobs, like brussels sprouts. This is the after-effect, apparently, of losing all their bark in dry seasons to keep skinny little cattle alive. Such treatment would defeat anything but an acacia. But in these regions life is so tough as to be almost indestructible.

Sometimes you see the whole root system of an acacia—about eighty species grow in Kenya—exposed like a botanical specimen. The soil around them has been stripped away by rushing torrents of rain. Gullies fifteen or twenty feet deep yawn at their feet. Here is some of the worst erosion I have ever seen, not just in isolated patches but everywhere you look. In places, the landscape seems as dead as the moon's.

At one point we encountered arap Moi, the elected member of the Legislative Council for this region. He posed for a photograph in a gully, dead tree-roots about his head, in the harsh blinding heat of full day. He is an intelligent schoolmaster and, as a member of ALDEV helping to put over grazing management in South Baringo, seemed in no doubt himself as to the value of these efforts to reclaim his people's land.

Thirty years ago Europeans who came down to these Baringo plains—and not many did, it had no roads then—came back with hair-raising stories of over-stocking, denudation and the destruction of pastures. Colin Maher, then a young man angry about soil erosion, 'called attention' to it all in a series of reports which won him little more than a reputation for being a nuisance to everyone, and rather a bore. Once he tackled a visiting knight of the Colonial Office with so little tact, and at a cocktail party, that the knight called him 'an idiotic young puppy'.

There was no money then and most of the Tugen tribesmen, wild and aloof, took to the hills whenever they heard of the approach of an official. Eventually a farmer from Sussex known as Old Man Saltbush was sent down the valley where he lived for several years, experimenting with drought-resistant plants. A few of the seeds he planted in the minds of the Tugen lay dormant, like those of grass, for many years, to germinate when conditions were right.

It was not until after World War II and the formation of ALDEV—the African Land Development Board*—that experiments, started in 1937, on a block of 30,000 acres

---

*Started in 1945 as the African Settlement Board to resettle landless Africans, its emphasis gradually shifted to the reconditioning and reclamation of existing African areas and their development by more intensive farming. In 1957 its name was changed to African Land Development Board. One of its functions is to make loans to progressive farmers.

at Esageri under the Baringo Rules showed success. On all sides is bush, bush, bush, quite impenetrable where it has not been cleared. The rainfall here is reasonably high, about 35 inches (60 in 1958), and if the land were left alone it would in due course, by ecological stages, cover itself with forest. Bush is a half-way stage and presents by far the greatest challenge to the improvers.

VII

Ecology concerns the balance nature holds between all living things and that man so often, blindly and selfishly, destroys. In these bush-clad parts of Africa, for instance, the vegetation used to be kept in balance not by cattle but by game. The natural fauna, evolved over centuries into a miraculous complex of different species, never injured the vegetation nor let the harmony between the species go awry. Game did not erode the soil, destroy the grass, ruin the forest, reduce the rainfall, desiccate the climate, dry up rivers and create deserts. Man and his herds do all these things.

Many species of game, for instance, browse rather than graze, and so keep down the bush. Elephants do this in bull-dozer fashion, giraffe arch their necks to feed upon taller acacias, many other species like impala nibble smaller kinds of bush. Then there are grazers who keep the grasses balanced without treading them to death. Beasts of prey in turn prevent the increase of grazers and browsers beyond the capacity of the land to support them. Man the hunter keeps down beasts of prey. In the last fifty years, all this has gone because game has given way to goats and cattle, man has multiplied beyond his natural level and the balance of nature has been destroyed.

It can be restored—at a cost. First, by keeping out men and cattle altogether until nature has healed her own sores; then by regulating their demands upon her—for ever; this is no temporary measure that can be relaxed when vegetation has recovered. That is the rub. It involves permanent control over the actions of human beings, a sacrifice of freedom. And (whatever their race) permanent controllers?

It involves also a drastic reduction of livestock. The Tugen must get rid of three-quarters of their beasts within the next five years. Naturally they dislike this intensely, and it has taken thirty years to get them to agree. But once their stock has been reduced and—this is the vital point—its numbers permanently regulated, then their rejuvenated pastures will be able to carry *more* livestock than ever they could before.

But first the bush must be controlled, and here intrudes a terrible economic obstacle. The cost of controlling bush can be so high that any return you may hope for from the cleared land cannot possibly pay the interest on the capital you spend. How can you invest, say, forty shillings an acre on clearing land that is worth, in terms of what it will produce, half a crown?

I saw experiments with a heavy caterpillar tractor and a clever machine, a sort of roller with spikes, that pulverises bush and soil and allows grass to regenerate. In other places, two tractors drag a heavy chain between them like a trawl; it mows down trees and bush and everything it encounters—a tremendous shaving of the earth's beard. Bush can be cleared, but at a cost. Not only that, you have to go on doing it or, with that indestructible tropical vigour, it will be back again within a few years, tougher than ever.

Why not bring back some of the bush-controlling game? On the Uasin Gishu plateau Mr. Douglas, owner of a ranch near Soy, for years maintained a herd of giraffe for this purpose. Bush on his land became sparse, and then receded. You did not need to travel far to encounter black, all-but-impenetrable thickets on his neighbours' giraffe-free land. And Mr. Shireff attempted, with about thirty horsemen, to drive a small unwanted herd from the foothills of Mt. Elgon down to the bush-clad plains below Kapenguria. The giraffe were edged over the escarpment's rim, but the precipices terrified them and they broke back through an arc of horsemen; two broke legs and had to be shot. A second drive did get some giraffe to the bottom, but they climbed back during the night. Yet giraffes are captured at great expense, to be transported in great discomfort, to life imprisonment in zoos. It seems a pity this effort cannot be diverted to transferring the creatures to places where they would be useful, and enjoy their freedom as well.

And so we come back to the Africans' own traditional method of bush control: burning. But in order to have an effective fire, you need a thick grass cover to sustain the fire: it will not live on bush alone. Where cattle have destroyed the grass, fires cannot play their part because they never get under way. And so the bush, free from molestation, sprawls and spurts and thickens until it possesses the land.

VIII

At Esageri we stood knee-deep in star-grass while the ALDEV officer in charge and Sandy Storrar, director of all these projects in the Rift Valley, laid plans to demolish it.

Sandy Storrar is a forceful Scots farmer with a mop of prematurely grey hair, an eye for a sheep, a quick mind and tongue, some impatience, native shrewdness, and a formidable store of enthusiasm for anything to do with land and the craft of farming. We halted by the trackside while he explained the stages by which nature makes good what man has wasted.

When you 'close' an area, he said—a raw red area of murram and rock without a trace of green—the first plant to show itself, quite spontaneously, is the little pale, feathery-headed annual *aristida keniensis*: the pioneer. The main function of this intrepid plant is to break the force of raindrops and turn them into a fine spray so that they can penetrate the pores of the hard, compacted earth. Without this mechanical aid, water splashes off as if it had encountered cement, and runs away. Then bolder biennials like *eragrostis* appear; then the oat-grass *Themeda*, and a tall, wiry, common grass called *hyparrhenia* which is not very nutritious but an improvement on the annuals. Finally, as the climax, comes the highly-thought-of star-grass *Cynodon dactylon*, rich in minerals and devoured eagerly by stock. Land that was lucky if it could support one beast to thirty acres will then manage one beast to eight or nine.

As we walked along a yawning gully Sandy Storrar pulled aside a fallen thorn branch to point out beneath it a wisp of green, an incipient plant. A single seed had found protection from hungry beasts under the branch and bided its time; now it had germinated. The urge and resolution to survive and then to multiply is incredibly strong. On the grazing schemes this urge is being fostered instead of thwarted by man.

Esageri now has eight fenced paddocks, each of about 4,000 acres. On it graze 2,600 of those planners' abstractions, stock units. (Five sheep or goats equal one head of cattle.) These belong to just under two hundred Tugen families who live on the ranch and profit from its superior management. (There are about 80,000 Tugen in all.) Each owner pays a fee of 12 shillings a year per stock unit to help pay for the scheme, including the small dams, or *haifas*, that have been put in to provide water. One ALDEV field officer is in charge.

The Tugen are not impressive physically, being rather scrawny and with no distinctive cast of feature. The Masai pushed them into poorer regions because they lacked spirit and cunning to stand up to the aggressors, and they have not done much since. To start with they feared and opposed all grazing schemes. Many of them took to the hills.

'Now we can see the benefits,' said the chairman of the Tugen grazing committee. 'We are satisfied except for one thing: we are tired of moving from place to place. Sometimes we have a long way to walk to our huts, and the women complain.

'What do we want? To have our own holdings, each his piece of land. Then we can plant crops; perhaps we shall be able to buy a separator and sell cream; and our wives ask us to build better houses. We need a health centre, too.'

The bug has bitten, Progress has come, wants are poking forth like grass beneath the thorn: even among the Tugen, an unambitious tribe. Land enclosure has already started. I saw it in action in the Emening triangle, farther down the valley towards the northern deserts where rainfall drops to fifteen or twenty inches. Here the land is like a skeleton, each gulley a cavern between ribs of bare earth. Yet an area of 25,000 acres is being marked out in smallholdings of from 50 to 150 acres each—far too small a size, on this land and in this climate, for good husbandry.

Why? Because the people want it and the land is, after all, their own. The Government can show them how to get a bit of flesh back on its bones and how to nourish it, but in the long run cannot force its owners to treat it in this or in that way.

And the Government itself has a divided view. Agriculturalists are technicians who care deeply for land as such and mind about the way it is treated, whether it belongs to peasant or rancher, white or black, rogue or saint. They have found out how to reclaim this land from desert, shown the people how they can begin to raise their rock-bottom living standards, and now they do not want to see the whole thing thrown away. As for smallholdings, although in theory, with a high standard of management, you could do the same thing in miniature on 70 acres as on 30,000, in practice no one believes it will be done. The lack of water, the temptation to build up a larger herd than the land can carry in a poor season, and the obligations of family life, will be too strong for all but a few exceptional individuals. That is the view of agricultural officers—agricolas for short, a handy abbreviation I shall use in these pages.

Administrators are guardians. They are there to help and guide the people, to introduce better ways of doing things if they can, but not to bully or compel. They have used pressure to get the Tugen to embark on these grazing schemes. The people can see for themselves that the scheme works but now they want to try something else—individual tenure, a piece of land of one's own. The wish is a spontaneous one. Can the guardians say no? Isn't it their job to let the Tugen do as they desire while at the same time showing them the best way to do it? That is their view. And because the administration *is* the Government, and agricolas only technical advisers, it prevails. With money from ALDEV, the Emening triangle has been mapped and planned, roads laid out, a township site selected, provision made for schools, sale-yards, shops, a showground, a farm institute, a church, a social hall.

IX

We drove through Emening. Goats were standing on their

hind legs to nibble leaves from acacia bushes whose lower branches had been gnawed away. Huge gullies gaped. Here and there a line of thorn branches laid across bare earth marked the boundaries of a holding. Can anything be done with this? The answer is yes, even with this, if you follow the rules.

Of course, the visitor is taken to the show-places: but they are worth seeing. We called on an ex-*askari* of the King's African Rifles who retired after the war with a wound pension, has listened to advice, and prospered. His holding is more than twice the average size, about 180 acres. The Soil Conservation Service (which Colin Maher started, after years of struggle, together with an engineer-farmer called Robert Barnes) has surveyed it and, at no cost to the farmer, put in broad-based terraces to hold the rainfall and make it possible to grow things. We saw a crop of Rhodes grass, waist-high and lush, grown from seed given by a farmer from the settled area, Mr. Turner. But the smallholder's cattle, sleek enough in appearance, were in the throes of disaster. In the last fortnight eight had died—nearly half his herd—from some disease.

A quick inspection of the surviving cattle revealed bevies of ticks. So that was it: East Coast fever. Both voices of the Government, Sandy Storrar's and that of Mr. Butler the D.C., united in a homily. Hadn't he been spraying his animals every week? Had he checked the strength of the gammexane? Got into all the danger-spots—ears, bellies; under the tail?

The ex-soldier, already crushed by his losses, looked downcast, but cheered up a little when we admired his fine crop of maize, his half-built house and a water-tank filled from the pipeline which he and his neighbours share with European farmers farther up the valley. His wife, in a red spotted headkerchief and a cotton dress scrubbed colourless, enjoys the fabulous luxury of drawing water whenever she wants it within a few paces of her hut; everyone else must walk for miles, sometimes five or six miles, to one of the few permanent streams.

There is another settlement on the borders of Tugen country and the European farms. This is the most sophisticated part of Tugenland and has a township, Mogotio, with a few shops kept by Indians and Somalis. The mere existence of this dusty little dorp provides that vital missing factor in the whole economy: a market. Another prize Tugen farmer whom we visited has taken advantage of this to sell fresh milk in Mogotio, and to grow crops like green grams which Indians buy.

For ten years he worked for an auctioneer in Nakuru, Mr. Chettle, learnt how to judge cattle, and saved money. He started this miniature ranch before the movement to enclose became fashionable, and fenced it all at a cost, he assured us, of at least £1,000. To found his herd, Mr. Chettle gave him a good Red Poll bull. Now he employs eight or ten regular workers whom he houses, feeds and pays a wage of 35 shillings monthly, makes a good steady income—perhaps £500 or £600 a year—has a smart new house with a veranda, and a lorry of his own.

So it *can* be done: but only, at the moment, by exceptional men who have seen the outside world and its ways and then applied its lessons to their own lives. Most Tugen have not. By way of keeping a sense of proportion, we stopped to talk to a youth more typical than either the ex-soldier or the ex-auctioneer. Holding a light spear, clad in a brown *shuka*—a length of calico knotted over one shoulder—he told us that he was circumcised, but had never been to school. His father was away working for tax-money, so he was in charge of five skinny little cattle browsing on some bare earth and stones, and a herd of goats fat as butter on nothing at all, as is the habit of goats. A line of cut thorns laid on the ground enclosed the small family holding, a great gully ran past two skimpy mud-and-wattle thatched huts of which their home was comprised. Perhaps an acre of red subsoil had been scratched with a hoe to make a *shamba*, or field. They would be lucky if the maize crop yielded four or five bags.

To break the rigid and profound grip of poverty on these regions seems almost impossible. And yet, although this country could never grow rich, cattle can be made to thrive on it. They like these heat-shimmering plains. The Tugen and the Suk could turn out a regular supply of fat steers—if they could find a market to make it worth while.

The problem is not a technical one, it is social and political.

If you could forget about the people and treat the whole region as it should be treated, ranching it in great blocks, the people, like their beasts, would benefit and thrive. The Russians would do this, and the Chinese. But if you believe in the rights of individuals you cannot do that. Individuals, here as elsewhere, very seldom want to do what technicians know they should. It is true that they want to be richer, but they do not want to take the necessary steps. They want their bun and their penny, in fact, like all humans everywhere.

CHAPTER 2

In the Kerio Valley

I

'WE have been given meat to eat before milk,' said the cripple, a hunchback with withered legs, under a tree beside a village where Tugen tenants of the Perkerra irrigation scheme live. All is not well with the scheme, which so far has cost about £300,000. There has been no return beyond a pitifully small output of maize, hardly a paying crop to grow on land that cost £100 an acre to prepare before the first seed was sown.

The Perkerra river runs into Lake Baringo, carrying with it an estimated two million tons of silt a year, all topsoil wrenched from the hills surrounding its basin. Baringo is one of a chain of lakes lying on the hot floor of the Rift—Natron, Naivasha, Elmenteita, Nakuru, Hannington, Baringo and, far to the north, the deep and inaccessible Lake Rudolf among parched lava rock. Years ago, a small sub-tride called Njemps, irrigated this flat scrubland to such good purpose that they supplied grain to many caravans marching from the coast to Uganda. The discoverers of Lake Rudolf, Count Teleki and Lieutenant von Hohnel, visited their settlement in 1887 and called them the Wakwafi; they led a wretched life, von Hohnel remarked, cultivating millet and gourds, and 'quite spoiled by the constant and long visits they receive from caravans.' He commented on the cement-like nature of their soil, the strong dust-whirling winds and the depredations of birds, all headaches for today's experts as well as for yesterday's Njemps.

In 1917, their main irrigation river, the Molo, suddenly changed its course, leaving their furrows high and dry. The Njemps were too much discouraged by this to start again. Besides, caravans of porters no longer demanded grain. They took to fishing, hunting and herding the cattle they had managed to accumulate, and there was no more irrigation until 1956.

Then it arose as a by-product of Mau Mau. Oath-takers crowded camps everywhere, posing for authority the question: what were they to do? How be kept occupied? Almost every scheme ever drawn up by hopeful individuals for draining swamps, irrigating deserts, cutting canals, afforesting mountains, was dug out of its pigeon-hole, pored over and reported on. Many went back to their pigeon-holes but this one did not. If the Njemps had irrigated with hand-made hoes, obviously engineers with bulldozers and pumps could do better.

So lorry-loads of oath-takers were transported to a camp called Marigat on the Perkerra, near its entry into Lake Baringo, and long channels were dug by hand with picks and shovels across the sandy, acacia-speckled plain. Experts arrived from the Sudan to organize the irrigation. Nothing is wrong with the two main tenets of the scheme: water is there and the soil, once irrigated, will grow almost anything—at the start.

Normally, you begin an irrigation project with an experimental farm to find out what will grow best, the right treatment, and many other technical answers about rates of flow, times to plant, salinity, pests, diseases and so forth. That this stage was omitted at Perkerra was, in a sense, no one's fault, because the scheme sprouted from the Emergency. But it meant that everyone was working in the dark, and this made costly mistakes inevitable. For example, the first tomatoes to be planted grew with immense vigour and generosity, but after one or two crops had been taken they succumbed disastrously to eel-worm and sun-scorch, and had to be abandoned. A factory built to can them has since had to close down.

Then there is the 'flash flooding' of the Perkerra. From a platform above the barrage I looked down on a sorry sight of smashed concrete and displaced boulders where the river, coming down in spate, had carried away much of the engineers' handiwork. This arose again from ignorance: no accurate measurements had ever been made of the river's flow, which falls to three cusecs in dry weather and rises to

55,000 cusecs* during heavy rains. This fantastic variation is mainly due to overstocking and erosion, and here we return to the basic strategy of the Baringo grazing schemes: to protect the catchment area of the Perkerra from source to finish so as to allow the rainfall to penetrate the soil, as God meant it to, instead of roaring away down hillsides in chocolate torrents to transform this meandering river into a savage monster ripping up everything in its path.

II

Despite these and other difficulties, Mau Mau oath-takers dug channels and bunds and prepared for irrigation some 3,000 acres, of which about 1,200 were under cultivation at the time of my visit. But the last oath-taker left over a year ago and the tenants I talked to under the trees, whose spokesman complained of getting meat before milk, were Tugen.

All the oath-takers were Kikuyu and the Kikuyu are natural cultivators, the most intelligent and hardest-working of all Kenya tribes. Given good land and a bit of instruction, they know what to do, and they (or their women) will get up early in the morning and get it done. They grew good crops at Marigat and many wanted to stay on as settlers after their release. If Marigat were to be opened to any citizen of Kenya, the Kikuyu would be there in droves within twenty-four hours.

But Marigat is in the country of the Tugen—basically herdsmen, who cultivate only a little, badly and spasmodically. Like every other people, they do not want aliens in their country, least of all Kikuyu, who are universally mistrusted for the same reasons that have earned the Jews unpopularity from time to time, because their wits are sharper, their superior energies better harnessed to the business of success and they are clannish by nature.

Technically, the scheme should have been opened to the best tenants regardless of tribe. Politically, this would have broken pledges, imperilled the peace and infringed the country's land policy. Once more it was a question of adminis-

*A cusec = one cubic foot per second, the equivalent of 500,000 gallons in 24 hours.

tration versus efficiency, and once more administration won. The scheme was, and is, confined to Tugen settlers. Politically this was a right decision, technically it was wrong. With a few exceptions, the Tugen have failed abysmally to make the best of this costly and potentially productive land.

All the maize looked poor and weedy. As we approached, enormous flocks of birds rose like inky steam, spiralled round and settled back to feast upon half-ripened cobs a little farther on. This crop should have been already in the crib. No persuasion, apparently, will make the Tugen plant their seed at the right time. The scheme's whole economy is based upon two crops a year, but they get only one crop, and a poor one at that, and so have fallen far behind with their water-rate of £7 an acre. An assistant manager, out for an afternoon's bird-shooting, found loads of maize hidden under trees and in bushes all along the main canal.

'On its way up to the hills to be flogged,' he said. 'Then they take us to their granaries and say: Look, we have no crop. And what remains gets made into beer. A drunk and idle lot!'

'You hurry them too much,' said the district officer. 'Give them a chance, they'll come to it in time.' This was the cripple's point: they wanted time to get used to all these new ideas. The technicians remained sceptical. 'Hard work,' said one, 'isn't exactly a difficult idea to grasp. They were always a defeated people, pushed out of all the decent grazing by the Masai.'

Nowhere is the gulf between expert and guardian wider and clearer. Yet probably another 15,000 acres await development if money, markets and energetic tenants could be found.

The most hopeful place is the experimental farm where all sorts of crops are growing, apparently with strength and health: hibiscus, ginger, fennel, citrus, beans, even coffee and tea. There are cattle, too, in little quarter-acre paddocks that are flooded once a week and grow star-grass thick as velvet pile. It might be possible to make a go of fattening steers intensively. Once again, technical difficulties can be overcome: it is the human ones that baffle. All the tenants who had come to talk under the tree agreed. 'The fees are too high. We want more land, but we do not want to pay so much money. The work is hard. The birds are many. It is hot down here on the plain. We need more people to tell us what to do. Let in Kikuyu tenants? No! no!'

III

North of Baringo lies the country of the East Suk and beyond that of the Turkana, all desert and camels. (Sometimes the camels come down to the abattoir at Marigat, which buys up old screws too poor for auction and puts them bodily, insides and bones and all, through a machine called a digestor, to make fertilizer.) To the west, beyond a range of mountains, spreads the great Kerio valley and across that river are two closely intermingled peoples called Elgeyo and Marakwet.

Like the Njemps, the Marakwet practised irrigation before Europeans came. Theirs, however, was of a very different, and a much more complicated, kind. The Njemps merely cut ditches from the river across level land. But the system of the Marakwet was an engineering feat of a high order.

To reach it you must descend by Land-Rover down into the Kerio valley, about a 4,000-foot drop, and then along a rough track through thick bush between the Kerio river and the northern face of the Cherangani range. It is very hot and arid, and if you went on far enough you would get to Lake Rudolf. Jagged volcanic mountains loom up in the distance, craggy ranges overshadow you near at hand, the bush hems you in, and every hundred yards or so your Land-Rover lurches and scrabbles its way across a steep-faced gully which, in the rains, carries a brown foaming torrent ten or fifteen feet deep off the hills. Never have I seen worse erosion; the land is gashed as if by some cosmic cleaver, scraped bare, pounded into dust by the hoofs of little cattle and greedy goats.

All the villages, if one can call them that—little clusters of thatched huts made of withies, primitive-looking but well-built—are perched on crags jutting out of precipices on the hills, the thorn-scrub valley far below at their feet. Every morning down must come men and boys to herd livestock, women and girls to cultivate; every evening back they must clamber in the cool of the day, men and boys unencumbered,

3 On the Esageri grazing scheme: pastures before and after treatment

4 A view down the Kerio Valley

women bearing on their backs either heavy gourds of water or even heavier loads of grain in bags woven from bush fibre. They may have two thousand feet to climb every evening, at the end of a day's work. The women's muscles must be hard as steel springs.

They live up there like sentinels on crags, partly by tradition to avoid Suk warriors, partly to escape malaria, which is bad below.

In the valley termite castles, red as lung tissue, rise in phallic pinnacles through scrub thorn to match the crags of the hills. Now and again we came on a boy herding goats or a woman bending over her short-handled hoe in a rough clearing in the bush where a crop was sprouting. The women wore skin aprons or short ochre-stained cloth *shukas* and many beads and bracelets.

We came once to a sheet of water trickling across the track and two men going ahead of it with hoes making little paths for it to follow. Only the undergrowth had been cleared; trees and stumps had been left and the water probed and gushed round them, spread out, and soaked in. Then came the women with handfuls of millet which they cast about them and scratched in with hoes. This valley is like a hot-house, and on its scarred, abused surface is trapped the fertility of the hills carried there by centuries of erosion.

Within a week the millet will germinate, within four months the crop will be off: and then the Marakwet will enjoy a three months' holiday devoted mainly to drinking mead made from wild honey. They get two crops a year with ease and, unless victims of some unforeseen disaster, never go short of food, beer or leisure. They have their own customs, interests, remedies, government. 'Theirs is an African paradise,' said one of the local officers. There is a tax, it is true, which obliges some of the younger men to leave home; but now they have no tribal warfare (their greatest loss, perhaps?) it is natural for young men to go in search of the world. The older men have little need for money beyond the tax.

We stopped for lunch beside the Arror river where a school has started. Blue-shirted boys gazed at us in surprised little clusters. After a while they tired of this and began to cavort and prance about the dusty clearing with odd leaps and gestures, as if taking part in some queer ballet with more force than symmetry. They were catching flying ants and eating them, wings and all.

Beyond the Arror we traversed a red sandstone bank under the acacias as full of holes as Gruyère cheese. In and out were darting birds whose wings flashed in the dappled sunshine like handfuls of emeralds tossed above an Aladdin's cave. They were slim and graceful, built to hover and swoop, and had suggestions of red and of white about their brilliant green plumage. There must have been several hundred birds in the colony. They were white-fronted bee-eaters, *Melittophagus bullockoides*, among the most splendid of birds.

To the Marakwet, all birds are robbers. We passed a number of bird-scarers' huts perched on the summits of rocks, each with a rough roof of sticks for shade and each occupied by two or three children, whose duty was now and then to rattle gourds with pebbles in them, shout and throw stones. Others were herding goats under the trees. Both these occupations have died out in most parts, and will do so here when more schools come in. The initial by-products of education can be lighter crops and even more soil erosion, the one because of birds, the other because goats have to stay near the villages.

IV

We started early from our camp on the Embolot river to reach the source of several irrigation furrows up among the crags and precipices. My companions were Sandy Storrar, a great enthusiast for this forgotten country and its high potential, and the agricola in charge of an area stretching from the 10,000 feet high moorlands and forests of the Cheranganis down to the 3,000 feet bush-and-elephant Kerio banks. Mr. Bill Spencer, who spent his earlier years selling materials in a famous London department store, has foot-slogged over a good deal of it and scrambled in Land-Rovers over the rest, and is known—and well liked—by the most inaccessible crag-dwelling tribesmen. There are very few

roads in his domain and the nearest approach to a department
store is a little one-roomed mud-floored store near the camp
where we bought orange drinks. It also stocks flour, cigarettes,
tea, sugar, matches, paraffin, cotton cloth, aspirin and
Andrews' liver salts—popular for hangovers while the millet-
beer season lasts.

The mornings are tremendous, because the scale is so vast.
The sky before sunrise is an immense cauldron of crimson;
bands of pink stretch like mighty pennants from one horizon
to the other. Like a series of gigantic monsters, the mountains
crouch in every shade of blue and indigo. All is spread out as
if fresh from creation, and yet immemorially old. Man has no
part in it at all, he is invisible, nothing shows of him or his
works. So it was, you feel, a million years ago and so it will
be after another million. This scale, reducing man to insignificance, frightens some people and stimulates others: it is of
Africa's essence, at once comforting, because folly and mis-
fortune cannot matter, and crushing, because no human
effort can amount to more than a leaf floating in a stream.

The sun came up in a great golden flood in reverse, at first
illuminating the mountain-sides above a dark plain and then
surging downwards into the valley, starting into sudden life
every tree and bush and boulder. You could even watch it
creeping down a termite castle from tip to base. We climbed
a spur which grew steeper and steeper until we had to pull
ourselves up by hand, grasping tree-roots and tough-tendrilled
plants. On a bluff we met a party of Marakwet coming down
with springy, goat-sure strides: women mostly, clasping hoes
with crooked handles not more than two feet long, dressed in
shukas and beads. The boys would spend all day in warm,
aromatic bush under the shade of acacias: no school, no effort,
no worries, air and sunshine all about them. It seemed a good
life, and the boys gay and happy, running like antelopes
among the rocks with sticks in their hands. There was a strong
smell of sage and now and then a whiff of strongly-scented
jasmine. We searched without result for the originating
creeper, treading sometimes on a little plant with a blue
flower like a speedwell. Our guide pointed to a smallish tree
and told us that its leaves, when boiled, made an excellent

medicine for kidney trouble. The desert rose, with its pink flowers that spring from bare grey branches, was in bloom.

From a bluff we halted on for rest we could see, far below in the bush, green patches of irregular shape and considerable size (perhaps between eight hundred and a thousand acres) which were maize and millet, mixed, under irrigation. The custom is to take two crops only and then let the land revert to bush. As the bush has merely been lopped off at ground level, it grows up so quickly that in two or three years no one can tell where the cultivation has been.

We were climbing up the course of the Embolot river, a tributary of the Kerio, which comes down in a series of water-falls and cascades. Sandy Storrar, who has made a study of this irrigation, said that no rivers could be more difficult than these to tap for furrows, because they run deep in gorges and are hemmed in by sheer cliffs. A modern engineer would find the task of taking levels exceedingly difficult. (One can imagine, too, the high cost.) The men who built these furrows had, presumably, no devices for taking levels; it was all done by eye, and cost nothing. That it could be done so successfully without any equipment or technical knowledge was, he thought, in its smaller way, almost as great a feat as the building of the pyramids.

Thirteen furrows spring from the Embolot river, at varying heights above the valley they serve. The water is conducted down, in some cases, for 3,000 feet. Three or four rivers are tapped, all tributaries of the Kerio; in all there are between 25 and 30 furrows. At present they irrigate only about 3,000 acres but the potential is much higher, even with existing furrows: up to perhaps 10,000 acres. Each furrow carries about 5–6 cusecs and one cusec should irrigate 40 acres. Our particular furrow, which has been measured, irrigates about 200 acres on which 86 families live.

v

At last, panting like bellows, we reached a furrow. It was about three feet wide and made of mud and plaited withies. We climbed to its source half-way up a waterfall in thick bush.

The water rushing down was clear as crystal. An elder opens the furrow by removing a small barricade of stones and twigs. When he wants to close it, he jams the twigs, mud and stones back again as a plug. It is as simple as that.

We followed our furrow down. The builders had made magnificently clever use of the natural waterways of the mountains; one can imagine them watching the run-off during a storm. In places the water disappears into a crevasse between two huge boulders, to reappear fifty feet lower down, a miniature waterfall that must be collected in a basin of mud and withies reinforced by stones.

In places, the builders took the water straight across (not down) a cliff-face. This is the most remarkable feat of all. Their only materials were the clay and sticks I have mentioned, and strong poles made from brown olive trees. They wedged these poles into the rock below and used them as struts to support the furrow, which they made from plaited branches, like an outsize thrush's nest, and knitted into the rock. And so there was water flowing quietly right across the sheer face of the cliff with a drop of several hundred feet below it. Then on it went, tumbling about among rocks, sometimes conducted down a slope by an old tree-trunk, doing unexpected things but keeping to its hand-made channel for five, six or even up to ten miles before reaching the valley.

Of course the furrow sometimes breaks. Tradition lays down the response to every contingency. The *kokwet* is responsible. It is hard exactly to define a *kokwet*; really it is a parish council drawn from a geographical unit, the territory of a collection of families, whose boundary is never marked but never in doubt either. It is a unit common to all those semi-Hamitic, light-skinned, cattle-owning tribes loosely linked into the Kalenjin language group, which includes the Nandi, Kipsigis, Tugen and Suk. The *kokwet* was probably borrowed from the Suk by the Marakwet and Elgeyo.

Every day, one or two elders from each *kokwet* fill their snuff-horns, perhaps take a little food in a leather pouch and clamber up the rocks to the particular furrow in their charge. They open or shut it, as the case may be, and mend any small faults they find. We met an elder on our furrow weaving withies into a sort of hurdle to fill in time, as women take their knitting; it was to be the door of a hut. His day as water-bailiff, he said, came round every ten days or so, but there is no rota, and no pay; everyone takes his turn, and all seems to run smoothly. If anyone opens a furrow clandestinely, the *kokwet* elders fine him an ox or a cow.

Sometimes repairs beyond the elders' capacity have to be done. From time to time, for instance, the poles propping up the furrow need renewal. Then a party of young men goes up to the forest on the crest of the mountains to fell the brown olives, trim them and carry them down. They return carrying the tree-trunks on their shoulders with laughter and song.

Then companions tie ropes of bark-twine round their waists and lower them over the edge of the furrow. Suspended from on top, with a precarious foothold on the slippery rock, they drive the poles into position and cut away the old ones that have decayed. Meanwhile up come the girls and women with big gourds of beer, an ox is killed, fires are lit, there is a great smell of roasting. After the operation comes the feast, and then a dance for the young that lasts all night, while the elders sozzle over their warm, ripe beer and boast of their own prowess when they were young.

It still goes on, this traditional upkeep of the furrows, but it will not last much longer. We came to a breach where the withies had broken and a minor landslide occurred. Our guide, a *kokwet* elder, pointed at it and said: 'We are waiting for the Government to come and mend it.'

'Why the Government? Won't the young men do it as they have always done?'

'They say that they are tired, and the Government has lorries and cement and can do it better.'

And farther on a smaller breach had been healed by a sheet of corrugated iron.

The young men are no longer isolated; they go up the hill to work on farms, they take service with the police and K.A.R., they have seen railways and cities. They know that Europeans have machines to do hard work for you, and they know also that in other places dams and pipelines, irrigation schemes and

38

boreholes arc being made by the Government. If it can be done for the Nandi and the Tugen, why not for the Marakwet? Also they have been told that they must not cut down brown olive trees from the hilltops, which are in the forest reserve.

So the end has begun; and with that old, traditional way of mending furrows will go the songs and laughter, the roasted oxen and all-night dance, the tests of skill and courage for the young men. Progress will make them into clerks and store-keepers, messengers and teachers, contractors and pimps, houseboys and politicians, instead of masters of the rivers high above the plain on their splendid mountains; and perhaps one day the furrows will be all steel and concrete.

VI

That evening the local chief, a plump, youngish man in a khaki uniform, and the local teacher, a leaner type in love with Progress, sat with us in our camp beside the Embolot, drank beer and talked first of the history of the furrows, later of the future of their land.

They told us that the furrows had not been made by Marakwet people, but by an alien race of tall men from the north, perhaps from Abyssinia, who spoke a different language. Some called them the Sirikwa. One day a great sickness swept over the land; many died; the survivors went away, back to the north; but where then, who knows?

'There are Sirikwa today living amongst us,' the chief said. 'They built the furrows, but they did not teach us how to build them. We only know how to keep them as they are.'

And when the water reaches the plain, Sandy Storrar pointed out, the method of using it is as primitive and unskilled as the method of getting it off the hills is technically accomplished. He thought this fact supported the legend that others built these irrigation works.

Who were the Sirikwa? A legendary people, said to have come down long ago from the north. Up towards the Ethiopian border are wells sunk deep into limestone rock which the Boran say were made by a very tall people who retreated to the south and west. In various places in the Trans Nzoia region, near Mt. Elgon, are the remains of round stone houses, of a fairly high level of masonry, said to have belonged to the Sirikwa. And there is an island in Lake Victoria, terraced and in places irrigated, where descendants of the tribe are said still to dwell. But nothing is known of their origins and history.

'Perhaps they were the builders of Zimbabwe,' Mr. Spencer suggested.

'There are people amongst us who know words of the Sirikwa tongue,' said the chief, 'and stories of them too.' But he could not repeat them. 'Ask the women,' he added. 'They keep alive these tales. But I, a grown man, have forgotten the stories that my mother told.'

As to the future, the school-teacher has been elected a District Councillor; he wanted many new things quickly, like schools, health centres, roads. 'We are neglected by the Government,' he cried. 'We have no lawyers, doctors, rich men. We must advance. I try to persuade the elders to do away with female circumcision, but they will not agree.' He was a trader in his spare time, and after some haggling bought a sack of potatoes from the agricolas.

VII

Under the care of a young Marakwet instructor, various new cash crops are being tried at a small experimental station on the valley's floor. One such crop, a new thing altogether, was sesame. It looked healthy and decorative, with mauve flowers. A good market seems assured: an extract is wanted for a synergin to be used in the extraction of pyrethrin. So far as I could understand it, a synergin is a kind of catalyst. Anyway, there is said to be enough demand to use 40,000 acres of sesame. Hibiscus was growing also, a tall, thin plant whose fibres make a substitute for jute (which is all imported) and can be turned into bags. And chillies, and citrus fruit. But the transport question is hard. One could not call the track we came along a road, and there are at least fifty miles of it before you even reach the foot of the escarpment. To make a proper road would be appallingly expensive, because of all the streams and eroded gullies that come off the hill every few hundred yards and would sweep away all but the stoutest bridges in the rains. There is indeed a legend that the whole Kerio valley once was flooded so deep that everyone drowned or fled, and it was left unoccupied, to be recolonized gradually by the people who are there now.

We said good-bye reluctantly next morning to our camp on the Embolot, under the spreading thorn-trees, and drank our last orange pop in the village of Tot, consisting of three or four little stores beside the dusty track. A young married woman in the shop gazed at us so intently, as still as a startled gazelle, her eyes wide, her neck above its bead and brass coils quite stiff and erect, that Sandy Storrar asked if anything was wrong. The plump chief inquired in her own tongue, and then translated.

'There is nothing wrong. It is just that she has never seen a European.'

Yet we were within ten hours' drive of Nairobi and its hot-house politics, its drive-in cinemas and glittering car-parks and multi-storied banks, its one-man-one-vote. She bought ten cents' worth of sugar and I asked if I could take her photograph.

'No,' she said, through the chief. 'That was not done when I was born, so why should it be done now?' The question seemed hard to answer. Outside, two young men in pigtails matted with sheep's fat and red ochre leant indolently on their herding spears, their slim bodies beneath *shukas* brilliant with beads and brasswire, in the effeminate attitudes of Hamitic warriors, pretending to be Suk, who in turn pretend to be Masai.

We left the progressive teacher-councillor looking disconsolate; but he may well take heart, for Progress is on the way. A tractor, with a European to control it, is coming shortly to experiment in ridge-and-furrow cultivation which will make better use of water and so improve the irrigation. On the Arror river a health centre built of cut stone is going up, financed by the District Council. On the way home we met two lorries loaded with cement and timber, bringing down supplies. Elephants have retreated to the bush by the river,

41

tractors approach, we passed a borehole in the valley and a woman in a faded cotton dress. A single rock-hyrax was all the wild life we saw.

All floods start with a tiny trickle; soon the Kerio valley will be inundated for a second time and the Marakwet and Elgeyo as they have been, and are now, will go. A new race is taking over: indeed we saw them in their blue shirts, dancing by the Arror river in pursuit of flying ants, but with their primers open under the trees.

CHAPTER 3

The Transformation of Elgeyo

I

THE word settler, in the last few years, has changed its meaning: or, rather, changed its race. Now only the more conservative left-wing British journals apply the word to the company executives, salesmen, accountants, technicians, and second- or third-generation farmers who make up most of the European population. The settlers of today are Africans, who in the last ten or fifteen years have surged over the empty spaces of their lands to colonize new areas.

The Cherangani range, forming the western wall of the Kerio valley, is such a region. On the one side its feet stand in the dry country of the Suk, Elgeyo and Marakwet; on the other they taper out into the European-owned Uasin Gishu plateau. The mass of the mountain range itself lies in African possession; only a few spurs running down on to the plateau have been occupied by Europeans.

Until a few years ago it was one of the last of the empty, wild and unknown parts of eastern Africa. The rare, elusive bongo left his footprints by salt-licks in the forests, elephant and rhino thickly inhabited the slopes, you could walk or ride for days along the high, misty moorlands without sight of a human being. Now the settlers are in.

At the Kapenguria end they are Suk. The Suk of tradition is a nomad following his herds on the hot plain by the Suam river. But in late years Suk have come up into the hills, put away their spears and turned themselves, or at any rate their wives, into cultivators. For this the school at Kapenguria is mainly responsible, and the activities of a most enthusiastic headmaster, Mr. George Chaundy, who taught them how to grow crops as well as how to compose essays. He also taught them how to prepare and eat the crops they had grown, and how better food improved health, and added to the pleasures

43

of living. This sort of information is seldom given in schools, but some of the Suk absorbed it, and among Mr. Chaundy's pupils are the pioneer farmers in the uplands, the first to plant seeds instead of watering flocks, the first to eat meal instead of milk and blood, the first to clear bush and forest from these splendid mountains and flay them with the plough.

There are parts of Kenya that must have been created when the gods were in a furious temper, spewing rocks and lava and blasting everything with burning breath; and parts that were created in the mellowest of moods when they decided to give all they had with both hands: fertility, depth of good soil, a rainfall exactly balanced to the needs of cultivation, high forests for timber, a healthy climate, sunshine by day and coolness at night, water in abundance, pure running streams, magnificent beauty. Nothing was left out. It was in this frame of mind that the Cherangani ranges were formed. These are the inheritance of the Suk, the Elgeyo and Marakwet.

II

The pioneer settlers of these hills took the land they fancied from no one; it was not only unoccupied, it was unclaimed. No elders had to be consulted, no goats given to heads of clans, no boundaries demarcated, no payments made. Land was there for the taking and the amount taken depended on the settler's view of his own capacities and on the number of his wives.

Mr. Matayo, for instance, took a plot which turned out to be 45 acres when it was measured later on. From the first he was receptive to advice, which appears to have been sound; at any rate, Mr. Matayo now prospers and has all his land laid out on the contour in seven-acre fields. For cash-crops he has sunflowers and pyrethrum, whose white daisy-flowers his wife and children gather and dry in the sun for him to take on his bicycle to the agricola in Kapenguria, who in turn takes them by car to Kitale where they enter into the stream of world trade.

'I will never leave pyrethrum,' Mr. Matayo said, 'it has been good to me; but now I am also planting a hundred coffee trees.' His maize, grown for food, looked excellent; so did his millet grown for beer; and best of all were his pastures of Rhodes grass which he cultivates for seed.

Around him clustered his nine children and a single wife by no means worn out by toil or reproduction, evidently with many years of both ahead. All looked well-fed, cheerful, gay. Mr. Matayo was building a new house of timber and materials off his land, but like a good farmer he had first put up his sheds for storing crops and housing the pride of his heart, a Guernsey heifer presented to him by a local farmer, Mr. Pudsey, after he had won a shield for the best smallholding at the Kapenguria agricultural show. All the admiration this heifer received had gone to her head—either that, or she was imbued with a most deplorable colour bar; she kept herself aloof from the rest of the herd, the humped small Zebus, disdainfully cropping clover-rich pastures in her own corner of the paddock. Mr. Matayo beamed on her, and seemed to approve.

What a place he has here, what a prospect! Forty-five acres of some of the best land on earth, 6,800 feet above sea-level in a sparkling sunshine robbed of all viciousness by altitude; a rainfall that will keep grass green and nurture two crops a year; no bitter cold, no scalding heat, but temperance and clemency; timber for shade and building, streams for watering stock, deep rich soil for fertility, a view fit for kings—this seemed as near as anyone could get to a new Garden of Eden. All without the payment of a cent, with no more struggle than was needed to mark the bounds and lop the bush with a *panga*.

Did Mr. Matayo relish his good fortune? No one does; we all take our benefits for granted and concentrate on the short-comings life must always offer; the hungry, toiling, landless millions of India, the peasants eking out a living on fractions of an acre throughout the East, the bored and discontented workers in mean-streeted industrial cities; all these were beyond Mr. Matayo's range of thought. An English farmer would seem to him rich beyond all dreaming: yet no English farmer has the same opportunities open to him as a man without capital.

45

His nine children grouped themselves round their parents to wave good-bye, the podgy baby on its mother's back, its head lolling like a drooping flower, the eldest boy, in his blue school shirt, alert as a squirrel. Two neighbours had strolled over and their families were just about as large. There was the menace, though they did not know it, to this happy realm: the snake in Eden. When those children grow up, where will they go, what will they do? They will want land. There will be none left unoccupied. All of it has been claimed and pegged out by settlers like Mr. Matayo. It can be had only by purchase, or by dividing these farms into smaller holdings. In a few cases they are large enough to stand this, but not in most. Sub-divisions will be too small to offer to the sons a fair prospect of a good living. They will be too small to allow those acts of husbandry by which the soil's fertility is maintained. They will start off the old, sad, one-way progression of over-cultivation, over-stocking, soil deterioration, loss of fertility, poverty and discontent.

Even could sub-divisions be prevented, what is to become of all these children? What work will they do, where is their future? In the cities, with their squalid crowded houses, their dull fruitless jobs, their lack of jobs because there are always too many people? Where are the industries, and the raw materials of industry? These are the true problems of Africa, not politics, votes, and constitutions. This is the change that must be mastered if Progress, not poverty, is to possess the future.

Back in Kapenguria, I listened to a meeting which was trying to solve a lot of smaller problems in a sensible way. Each district now has a mixed committee of administrators, vets and agricolas, foresters and African and European farmers to direct operations in their sector of the better farming drive. Local Europeans provide the experience; having been farming in the district for years—one at least on this team had succeeded his father—they alone can say: 'If you do that, then this will happen', and they have saved enthusiastic teams from a good many miniature groundnut schemes.

Moreover, it is a way of training local Africans to take responsibility, to think for themselves, rather than to follow the simple prescription of accepting a proposal without question in backward areas because the Government says so, and rejecting it because the Government says so in the more progressive ones. The great difficulty in places like Kapenguria is to find Africans who understand English well enough. As a rule only the schoolmaster qualifies, and he is seldom a farmer.

III

Whoever invented the Land-Rover, or perhaps its father the jeep, did more than anyone since the inventor of the high-velocity rifle to change the face of Africa. The high-velocity rifle enabled men to wipe out the wild animals, the Land-Rover enables them to destroy the last of the wilderness, to bring the last captive back in chains. That stocky, snub-nosed, undefeated little olive-green object, the mechanized pack-mule, has carried administrators, policemen, soldiers, doctors and technicians into the heart of darkness to obliterate the most secret haunts of civilization-shunners, human and animal. It has brought blackboards to nomads, vaccines to mountain-tops, law courts to fishermen, police posts to the depth of the desert. With the Land-Rover there is nowhere that white men cannot go, and nowhere they have not been, and are not penetrating like a stain of oil, wiping out for ever the majesty, the antiquity, the mystery of Africa. The death of the elephant and the coming of the pylon; the end of the warrior and the beginning of the clerk.

On our jeep-track, which followed the spine of the Cherangani mountains over tufted downland and through tongues of dark forest, we met a few Suk women, their skins greased and coppery, their eyes glittering and deep as ironstone pools, their necks encased in wide ruffs of copper wire and beads, their heads shaved, their bodies clad in tanned goatskins. In a few years they will probably be waitresses in roadside cafés hoping for tips. A few will be left in their traditional finery to pose for photographs, the money to be paid in advance—rushing greedily at tourists like the once-proud, turbaned, swarthy dhow-captains of Zanzibar, with crooked silver

47

daggers at their waists, who shake their fists and threaten until money has been paid over before the camera clicks.

On our left, the hills tumbled away into an immeasurable basin of blue: everything was blue, the distant ranges, the jagged volcanic eruptions, the sky, the shimmering bush, the melting horizon. And of the blues there were a hundred subtle shades and gradations. The wind blew hard as from a tunnel. Merely to stand on these peaks imparts a strangely mingled sensation of godlikeness (one looks down as if from heaven) and of grublike insignificance. Amid such immensity, what is one human being, one individual—or indeed what are a thousand, a whole tribe? 'As flies to wanton boys . . .' One thinks of midges hatched, swarmed, crushed and forgotten in an hour while the universe rolls on through the millennia.

Here nature is by no means motherly, but immeasurably vast, implacably indifferent, latently hostile. One thinks also of the impermanence of such thoughts. Surrey was once a deep forest full of wolves and mastodons. The Northern Frontier District we looked across to, the far-distant hidden cup of Lake Rudolf, the mighty valleys already stripped of their native elephants and rhino, the camel-cropped dry plains, the lava deserts, all these might become, one feels, at any minute, a nuclear testing ground, an oil-field gaunt with derricks, a playground of armies, a site of tourist camps where necking couples with iced drinks and chilled face-creams raucously pursue a lost secret. This jeep-track ends one Africa and ushers in another; the trip-line of splendour, a thread leading to the death of the bull.

Down in the great trough lies the cone of a sacred mountain called Metalla, but no one could tell us in what its sacredness consisted. The Suk make pilgrimages there at certain times and no one may climb it except priests who carry out the sacrifices. Somewhere down there, too, is a hill sacred to puff-adders. A friend of mine came on eight or nine adders in an hour's climb, more than he had seen in several years of trekking about the area; they never attacked anyone, his guide said, and must on no account be molested themselves, for they were spirits, and the people left them food at the foot of the hill.

5 In the
Kerio Valley:
a Marakwet
village

6 Kiter arap Tiren of Elgeyo with part of his family, and Senior Chief arap
Tengetcha of Kipsigis, with his son arap Sang

IV

Our track wound and twisted up to over 9,000 feet. Here on the heights are belts of forest and glades once deep in grass but now cruelly overgrazed, scabrously barren. Raw earth shows through like hunks of meat on a butcher's slab. Here and there a tall scarlet flower, *Econopsis*, flares boldly from the khaki glades. We came to bracken, and herds of skinny cattle browsing in the forest in defiance of the law. Mr. Shireff, a lean, quiet gimlet of a man, looked at these cattle without rancour or surprise.

'They are sent up from below to escape branding—refugees from the grazing schemes. We shall catch up with them in time.'

We saw no human habitations, only views and trees and glades. And then suddenly we came upon a neat little tin-roofed house and a thatched mud-and-wattle shed: the chief's headquarters, and a school. And—sure enough—a grazing committee: six Suk elders with aluminium ear-rings, ivory bracelets and mud caps. They knew their lesson. 'Cattle should be kept out of the forest to protect the trees, which bring rain. Now we control the grazing in three blocks and the grass is coming back. Things are better since we began control; cattle are fatter and give more milk, people are glad . . .'

It was all a bit slick. 'They don't like being kept out of the forest at all,' I was told; 'in fact they hate it. The moment we relax the pressure they're back again. They've masses of cattle—perhaps forty apiece on average, plus about two hundred sheep and goats. They don't want to get rid of a single one. And they're denuding the forest. For the moment we've checked it, more or less; left to themselves, they'd have all the forest off the Cheranganis in a few years—off the watershed. And then? Dried-up springs: no streams: no rivers down below: death to the herds: enforced emigration. Do they understand it? Not really: God gave us rivers, they say, and God will look after them; if they dry up, that is God's affair.' Just as the Trobriand Islanders had not per-

49   D

ceived the link between sexual union and the birth of babies, so have the Suk failed to grasp the less obvious cause-and-effect relationship between grass or forest cover and the birth of streams.

Under a tree sat a gathering of ladies who were members of a Maendeleo club, a sort of Women's Institute. Sometimes people come to talk to them about child care, sewing, cookery. Sometimes they just talk to each other. We like it very much, they said. They looked impassive and had fine, almost almond-shaped, oriental eyes, and carried with them the faintest possible suggestion of Egyptian blood.

Beyond, we came to giant groundsels, those queer cabbages on stilts that show you are high up on the mountains, around 10,000 feet. The air had a frosty bite to it, the sharpness of diamonds. Streams were born in the spongy moss of forest glades. We came suddenly to an orchard of *protea* trees which shed their foliage in tints of autumn; red and russet leaves glowed on the ground. Here all the grass was cropped to nothing, eroded gullies appeared, and in their sides were holes like those of sand-martins where green bee-eaters darted out and in.

Here is a land for hunters: one looks for the square-snouted rhino standing like a bulldog, for broken branches marking the passage of elephants, for the whistle and the leap of reed-buck, the bovine tang of buffalo, the crash of forest-pig in bongo-haunted undergrowth. We saw, smelt or heard none of these things. The game has gone, and we saw even denser herds of cattle, even poorer beasts—for Zebu do not thrive on cold pastures, they like the heat-soaked plains. But here they are safe from branding, culling, taxes, and general attention. So long as the grazing lasts.

v

An invisible line across these mountains marks the boundary between the Suk and the Elgeyo people. Soon after crossing it, you notice cultivation on the bare downs that lie between belts of forest. It is so cold up here, the soil so swampy, the wind so keen, you wonder who can have had the hardihood

50

to settle, what crops they grow. No roads, no markets, schools, contacts with the world outside, yet here they are—straggling brushwood fences, round thatched huts, a woman bent over a hoe.

Elgeyo settlers have made their way up from the valley they share with the Marakwet to find land. Down below, it is all worn out and eroded. Here it is fresh, pure, untouched. Not only do they get fresh land for nothing here, they escape the discipline of elders, the obligations of society, the tax-collector.

Now government is coming after them—but with gifts as well as dues. An agricola (the same Bill Spencer of Marakwet) has fenced off a thousand acres which has been divided into forty-acre plots. He has brought them splits (as it were cuttings) of pyrethrum and a handful of Corriedale sheep, and started an experimental station. Sandy Storrar surveyed this open, windswept country with a prophet's rapture. 'The potential is magnificent, tremendous, immense!' he cried. 'Sheep and pyrethrum, a perfect combination! A ewe to the acre—they have a hundred thousand acres here that can produce a million pounds' worth of lambs and wool a year, plus half a million pounds' worth of pyrethrum. And all off forty-acre holdings. The potential is here.'

The need is for capital. Fencing costs are high. Ewes are too expensive for smallholders. Roads need to be put in. Above all, people need to be trained and then to work steadily. A revolution in outlook, in behaviour.

But this enclosure of land, entirely spontaneous, is in itself a revolution and the elders disapprove. They know that fences are killing something within the tribe—its unity, its solidarity, the spirit that governs groups of people, just as it governs flocks of birds that turn and wheel together without a visible leader. All this must die, in order that an annual million pounds' worth of lamb and wool should be born.

Right on top of these cold, bleak uplands with their scattered pioneer settlers we met another Land-Rover bumping along. It contained an African health inspector, engaged on a campaign to make everyone dig latrines.

The track began to fall. We were descending the western

flank of the mountains that flatten out eventually into the Uasin Gishu plateau. Great views opened up before us: at first deep, gashed valleys, rounded hills, cultivation; below, the plateau's rolling expanses with Sergoit rock rearing up like the horned head of a snake. Shadows of clouds lay like bruises on the vast quivering flesh of the plains. The Land-Rover bucked and writhed over steep hillsides, into deep gullies, and everywhere on these precipitous slopes was cultivation, fences and erosion so profound that, in places, nothing remained but rocks and scree. Everywhere herds of small cattle and flocks of sheep and goats jostled and hungrily browsed—about four times as many beasts as the land can possibly carry. And no grazing schemes.

But down below, near the boundary with the Uasin Gishu plateau, one may see by contrast some of the best African farming on this side of the continent. The Elgeyo appear to like extremes—of climate and terrain, from ovens at 3,000 feet to chilly blasts at 10,000, and extremes of behaviour, from primitive tribal soil-scratching and goat-herding to advanced Westernized husbandry. After the moorland crests and the eroded slopes I saw the fat foothills and the prize farmers of Elgeyo.

First Samonge, a dark and stocky man who spent the first half of his life as a carpenter on European farms, saved money, and came here ten years ago to pick out and fence forty acres of good land. His pride and joy was not a heifer but a tap. The pipe to which it is attached runs from a dam put in by the Government to serve a group of such farms.

'My daughter has a suitor,' Samonge said: 'two suitors, in fact, rivals; both have cattle, both can pay the bride-price; I told her she must choose. When the first man came she asked him: Have you a tap on your *shamba*? No, he said, I have no tap. When the second suitor came, she asked the same question. Yes, he said, I am getting a tap on my *shamba* from the Government. So my daughter has chosen the man with the tap.'

These taps are part of what is called skeletal planning, an idea imported from America after a visit there by Sandy Storrar in 1952. The first move must come from the people.

52

They must want to be skeletally planned, although perhaps they do not call it that, but just say they would like taps and terraces, and are ready to pay. Then surveyors map the whole area and caterpillar tractors with scoops make terraces and cut-off drains, and dams if possible, and lay out roads. The people pay for all this themselves at the rate of ten to fifteen shillings an acre. After skeletal planning, and after all sorts of adjustments have been made and disputes settled, the land is registered in the name of each owner, who gets the title-deeds.

Samonge said that he had spent £600 in ready cash on wire and cedar posts alone, to fence his forty acres. I could hardly believe it, and had the figures checked, but it seemed to be true. Nor did he borrow any of this sum. What will he get back? Last year he sold nearly 300 bags of wheat, worth in cash perhaps £700, and got £50 from a single acre of pyrethrum. But he is an exception. The agricolas are worried because a lot of disappointments lie in wait for smallholders whose enthusiasm outruns their skill and luck. Some, they fear, will spend all their money, fail to reap the return they expect—and they are optimistic by nature—and then feel that they have been cheated by the Government.

VI

Arap Tiren is a Samuel Smiles hero, African style. He was kind enough to ask me to tea, and it turned out to be a garden party: sandwiches and sugar-coated cakes on trestle tables under trees on his lawn, twenty or thirty people in his neat garden (which is tended by two full-time gardeners) among its weeded flower-beds and brick-edged paths. His stone bungalow with its veranda, its flight of steps, the marigolds clustering at their foot, was trim as a newly refitted vessel, arap Tiren himself immaculate with shooting-stick, his wife, in her gay printed silks, a smiling and assiduous hostess, and the presence of several District Councillors imparted the flavour of a mayoral garden party in some English country town.

After tea he took me round his 150-acre farm, and actually scratched the back of a pig with his shooting-stick, just like

Lord Emsworth. Every one of arap Tiren's paddocks is neatly fenced and watered and he is building himself a stone dairy and cowshed, and grading up his herd with Red Poll bulls. Around a yard are grouped the farm buildings of which the most important is a store holding, at the time of my visit, 700 bags of wheat worth about £1,700. Arap Tiren has his own combine, but one is not enough and he also employs an Afrikaner contractor. He has, besides, a tractor and various implements, and for himself a shooting brake as well as one or two lorries, and employs about sixteen whole-time men as well as casual labour.

None of this would be remarkable outside Africa, although by any standards arap Tiren is a successful and efficient farmer. But it is remarkable almost anywhere on this continent, for although many Africans are doing well out of trade and contracting, and from professions such as medicine, politics and the law, only a few do so out of farming. As a rule the ambitious, up-and-coming man leaves the land for the cities.

Like many successful British farmers of an earlier generation, arap Tiren is illiterate. He was born on a European farm on the Uasin Gishu plateau and became a chicken-boy to his employer, Mr. Wright, whose own son Alec was about the same age. When, as a boy, Alec went shooting—there was abundant game then—young arap Tiren sometimes accompanied him, and they roamed on foot over the tall-grassed plain that now grows eight bags of wheat to the acre.

In due course Alec Wright inherited the farm and arap Tiren, with saved money, decided to start on his own. Like so many others, he just took what land he wanted, it belonged to no one. Alec Wright lent him a plough and gave him seed and good advice. As a side-line, arap Tiren started a beer-shop; this did well, and in time financed his developments.

Now he is something of an entrepreneur. He has several beer-shops, little stores dotted about in most of the townships in Elgeyo (I encountered one even in Tot), a petrol station in the nearby village, and a mail contract between Tambach, the administrative capital, and various local chiefs and trading centres. Two sons help him, one as his garage manager and the other as accountant and clerk. Yet arap Tirens has not been spoiled by success, there is nothing arrogant about him. He is polite, quiet and dignified, like a Scots church elder, or an old-fashioned country solicitor. Alec Wright is still among his closest friends, and still his farming adviser. He has never played any part, or seemed to take any interest, in politics.

VII

Next day we were stopped on the road by a bearded Afrikaner who waved a letter at Mr. Spencer and handed him a bill. 'I hope you will get them to pay something on account,' he said politely. This debt had been contracted by the Elgeyo wheat-growers co-operative, which has about 250 members and employs as contractor one of the European farmers on their borders; all their wheat is marketed through the Kenya Farmers' Association; here is partnership in action, with no fuss or publicity. And partnership largely with the Afrikaners, too, who in their homeland are so uncompromising. They do not seem to mind collaboration here, even working for Africans, as in effect this farmer was doing. His bill was for £1,200, which perhaps had something to do with it.

There does not seem to be any friction to speak of; Elgeyo and Afrikaner get along well and both use Eldoret for a shopping centre. It is here, on the Uasin Gishu, that Afrikaner influence is strongest, and you can drive for miles seeing only Dutch names on the plough-discs used as markers for the farms. On one of these farms I was shown a wagon that had come up from the Transvaal in the historic trek—historic because it was the last trek of the Boers—led by van Rensburg in 1908. The few survivors of this trek will tell you how they carved out farms for themselves from the empty veld, just as the Elgeyo are doing fifty years later, and fashioned harrows out of branches and thorns bound with thongs, and burnt bricks for houses, and made *veldshoen* from giraffe hide, and soap from the fat of elands. Now it is the turn of the Elgeyo, but they have an easier time; their District Council, helped by the Government, makes dams and sells them taps and advises them what to grow, and how; combines come to harvest their wheat; there are loans to help them build dips, sheds and houses; and there are roads.

We went on to the home of Chief Willi arap Chirchir, a large, loose-limbed, paunchy man with an air of confident prosperity who would be quite at home dining at the Institute of Directors. Chief Willi has a thriving farm with a flock of English sheep, a herd of cows, pyrethrum and potato crops, a labour force of fifteen men. When young, however, he was a politician and an 'agitator', and must have been an altogether more prickly character, for it was he who started the whole enclosure movement in 1949, when it was a heresy among the elders. One can see why the behaviour of the enclosers was considered anti-social. They wanted to help themselves to common property.

> The law locks up the man or woman
> Who steals the goose from off the common,
> But leaves the greater villain loose
> Who steals the common from the goose.

Read 'goats' for 'goose', and that is what they did. They started a landslide. Everyone enclosed, and by 1952 scarcely any land was left in communal ownership. At this stage, the movement was not officially inspired. It was spontaneous. Then in came agricolas with their skeletal planning. This involved the tearing down of every single fence that had been erected, and the refencing, on the contour, of thousands of acres. All this the Elgeyo did, without protest and without pay, in six months. (About 30,000 acres was planned in this district alone, at an average price of 10s. an acre which the people paid in cash without a murmur—£15,000 out of a district ostensibly backward and poor.) Years of propaganda had left little mark when the land belonged to the whole clan or tribe, but as soon as individuals took possession of their own segments, they saw the point at once of securing its fertility and limiting their stock.

Chief Willi is a District Councillor, which is generally a more important post than that of chief or Legislative Councillor. The local District Council (a small one) disposes of a budget of £90,000 and controls a lot of patronage. We had tea with another member under a tree and there was a distinct feeling of sitting in with members of the Establishment. Women poured the tea and handed round cakes while our host's high-grade Guernsey cattle chewed the cud contentedly nearby. Their plump, well-cared-for calves are his particular pride, for they are the product of artificial insemination. One would think A.I. almost impossible in a land of no telephones and great distances, but thrice a week an inseminator on his motor cycle checks in at certain specified points to which an owner brings his cow, and the rate of pregnancy, while not as high as in Britain, is encouraging: 1 pregnancy to 2.7 inseminations.

Chief Willi and his neighbours do not in the least question the mechanics of the system nor feel, as English farmers did when A.I. started, that 'it's going against nature'. The progeny are known as 'calves of the rubber', and gladly accepted as creatures of much greater value than calves of the bull.

VIII

Chepkorio is a lovely station on a flank of the mountains, set amid rolling, generously watered country and offering glimpses of tremendous views down over the sunlit plateau. A few years ago there was nothing here except a single store on a rough track climbing to the edge of a great escarpment, where you can drop a stone three thousand feet into the Kerio valley, and where an up-thrusting wind will carry a hat back to your feet if you hurl it into the abyss. Now there are half a dozen Europeans, each with his neat villa, his lawn and garden and his family, bringing Progress to the Elgeyo. Each one is in charge of some aspect of it: agriculture, health, community development, co-operative societies, administration.

One of the experts has been to Scandinavia and thinks their system better. It is applied especially by the Swedes in taking Progress to the Lapps. If you have six specialist inseminators, as it were, of Progress, instead of collecting them all together in a clutch, you partially train each of them in all six subjects and scatter them separately over the district, each in charge of a sub-division. The influence of each Progress-inseminator upon the people is thus closer, wider and more sustained. The British system gives free rein to the natural tendency for people of one race to congregate together; the Scandinavian thwarts it.

'We live too much among ourselves,' this expert commented. But the British, we agreed, would not accept the Scandinavian system; we are too gregarious, and anyway the wives would object. Most volunteers for jobs overseas expect all the comforts and conveniences they would find in Europe plus the advantages of Africa as well. It is a question of attitude: of whether you sell your time, so many hours of it, finish at four o'clock and then are free to enjoy your leisure, or whether, like a parson or a communist, you have a mission from which you can never escape. There is no reason why civil servants running co-operative societies, health centres or veterinary services in Africa should display the ardour of missionaries, but a liberal dash of it is needed if they are to succeed at their tasks. Bachelors are best, as a rule, but nowadays they have become almost extinct.

In Chepkorio I started on an early morning walk along a winding, narrow footpath, typical of paths all over Africa that lead through bush, tall grass and plots of cultivation to a group of huts, and then on to the next homestead, and the next, indefinitely. But this path ended at the first homestead; farther on, the way was barred by a fence of split bamboos. I scrambled over it, only to find another fence a little way on. The whole hillside was divided like a honeycomb into walled cells: there was no path, no bush, nothing but fences and paddocks, mostly under cultivation. Only when, after a lot of scrambling, I reached a road, was it possible to walk rather than scale or crawl. By the roadside a man was chopping branches off an olive tree for firewood, so bare is the country now of anything but crops and pastures.

It was a shock to realize what the fulfilment of a progressive land policy is doing to Africa. Ten or fifteen years ago, everything was wild and African, open and free as nature made it;

now it is all stout fences, measured plots, crops and rotations, roads of access, and a lorry on its rounds collecting for the co-operative. Schools, inseminators on motor cycles, compulsory latrines, taps and taxes, ambulances and radios, a health centre equipped by the Americans with Japanese sewing-machines.

A wonderful achievement, all in so short a time, and by a tribe previously considered backward and rather spiritless and dull. As to the causes of this extraordinary change, many of them working for years under the surface have converged and fused; the greatest single one, perhaps, was the war and the return of the travelled *askaris*—and the presence of one agricola in the same place for ten years.

This progress is new and exciting and still has wonder in it, like the scent of jasmine. When the newness fades the scent will die and boredom will stain the petals; that will be the trying time. Man needs excitement as the desert needs water. Without it he is sterile. Farewell to the elephant, the dance, the spear, the cattle-raid; welcome to the fence, the compost heap, the better calves, the co-operative dividend. No one can take a stroll to look at the morning. At present, there is an air of purpose and enjoyment; people are so proud of their A.I. calves, their seed potatoes, their home-built pyrethrum driers, the little carts they have made from a few planks and bicycle wheels, the water pipes, the new houses with tin roofs to catch water, the cattle sprays, the cattle themselves. When time has turned these from adventure into drudgery, will something break under the strain?

It would create a false impression to suggest that the whole of Elgeyo has been enclosed, that everyone has access to water, or belongs to a co-operative. Most of it is now enclosed, but only a fragment has as yet been skeletally planned and contoured, only a handful of settlers have piped water or use A.I., and the co-operatives deal with only a small proportion of the crops. The great majority of Elgeyo still draw water from rivers in drums and keep scruffy, useless cattle; only about a thousand acres of wheat is dealt with by co-operatives, the pyrethrum co-op has about two hundred members. I saw here a series of beginnings, most of them round Chepkorio, which for various reasons is a growing-point. But the important fact is that nothing short of some revolution or disaster can halt the movement. Within a few years all Elgeyo will follow Chepkorio's lead. It is very hard to get a movement started but, once it does start, it becomes a landslide.

There is perhaps one factor which could deflect, halt, or even reverse this movement, and that is politics. Elgeyo has gone ahead faster than almost any comparably backward region largely because, in the absence of local politicians of influence, its people have accepted technical advice. While this has now and then proved faulty, on the whole it has been sound, and so far there has been no lack of reasonable markets. So Progress has found an open road, an amenable following. He has revolutionized the countryside, and the casualties that cannot help but go down before him have not yet been counted. Perhaps it is only sentimental to refer to them at all.

CHAPTER 4

Laibons versus Vets

I

THE first Europeans to make any sustained contact with the Elgeyo were three Afrikaner brothers called van Breda who took up land, in 1905 or thereabouts, on what is now the borders of the Uasin Gishu plateau. One of the brothers was speared to death by Nandi warriors and so was an American called Wendt. Apart from these two murders, it is astonishing how little border trouble arose, in those early unpoliced days, between tribesman and newcomer. These plains had been the grazing-grounds of the Uasin Gishu Masai who had been virtually exterminated by another Masai clan, the Purko, in a great battle thirty or forty years before, and survived only in scattered remnants living more or less as refugees. Eventually these surviving settlements were moved by the Government to join their fellow-tribesmen south of the railway line.

The Elgeyo were never a warlike tribe but the Nandi, the Afrikaners' neighbours on their western flank, fought the British on and off for ten years until their final defeat in 1906. No Nandi warrior walked abroad without his spear, nor Afrikaner without his rifle. The Nandi were in the hills and the Afrikaners on the plain, but the two peoples traded for cattle and tobacco and joined together in lion hunts. An old Afrikaner farmer to whom I once talked, who had come up with the wagons in van Rensburg's trek, had himself shot over three hundred lions on and near the land he took up beyond the Eldore river.

The Nandi were a tough, arrogant race in those days. Holding an impregnable escarpment high above the lake, they would descend in sudden savage raids upon the fat Bantu and Nilotic people of Nyanza. 'The Nandi considers himself the equal of any man, and superior to all who are not Nandi,'

Mr. Huntingford has written.* 'He respects no chief, for he has none to respect, and gives in to old age only; he fears the *orkoiyot* (the ritual priest) because his powers include witch-craft, but the *orkoiyot* is not a chief and never has been.' In war, however, their obedience to their leader was complete.

The *orkoiyot* is the equivalent of the Masai *laibon* and this latter word, because more familiar, is often applied to the ritual priests of all Kalenjin peoples, who share this system of chieflessness and government partly by the parish council (as it were), the *kokwet*, and partly by the witch-doctor priest. There is no word for chief in Nandi and, as with many other East African tribes, the institution is a foreign one introduced by the British. That is not to say it has not caught on, together with much else alien and Western.

The institution of the *orkoiyot* was borrowed from the Masai only about a century ago, and its inheritors are still descendants of the original Masai *laibon* who took refuge from his own folk among the Nandi. The institution was handed on to the Kipsigis (another tribe of the Kalenjin group) by a Nandi ritual priest called Kipchumber, who had quarrelled with his colleagues. Although it is a position of power and wealth, the path of the *orkoiyot*, *laibon* or witch-doctor can be dangerous; one Kimnyole was clubbed to death, about 1890, after his failure to avert an outbreak of disease and a military defeat. He is said to have prophesied, as he died, the coming of foreigners and the subjection of his people, and so while losing his life he strengthened his office, for when his prophecies came true so soon after his death it was on the murder of his sacred person, and on the vengeance of his spirit, that all the troubles of the tribe were blamed.

II

The Nandi were the only tribe in Kenya to put up a stiff and sustained resistance to the British incursion, which consequently became a conquest rather than a peaceful take-over bid for control of government. Between 1896 and 1906 five

* *The Nandi of Kenya.* G. W. B. Huntingford. Routledge and Kegan Paul. 1953.

military expeditions had to be sent against their warriors. These young men were not only inclined to run a spear through anyone who came near them, but persisted in their habit of raiding cattle and removing railway lines and tele-graph wire to make ornaments and weapons.

During the last of these operations, which has been well described by Colonel Meinertzhagen, one of the participants, in his *Kenya Diary 1902–1906*, the *orkoiyot* Koitalel was killed and the tribe subdued. 'The only people I am sorry for are his wives,' Colonel Meinertzhagen wrote after the death of Koitalel, whom he had shot. 'They most certainly will be buried with him as is the custom.' In this he was wrong. Koitalel's chief widow, far from dying, brought up her sons to hate the white men who had destroyed their father, and to plan a deep revenge.

In due course Koitalel's son Parserion became *orkoiyot*, and in 1923 there fell due the ceremony of the handing over of power from one generation to another, which involved a gathering of the clans. Parserion laid his plans to concentrate all able-bodied Nandi men at the rendezvous and then to destroy Kapsabet, the administrative capital, kill its white inhabitants and attack Kisumu, on the plains below, and all European farms within striking distance. Every Nandi work-ing on the farms left his post, beer was brewed and Parserion prepared his medicine to make warriors invincible.

Although these movements had an apparently innocent purpose, official suspicion was aroused and the Government's intelligence system did its work. The country as a whole was then in the throes of a political crisis, and very short of troops and police; an open revolt, had it broken out, could not have been controlled without reinforcements from outside the Colony. By a handful of police, and in the presence of several thousand Nandi warriors, Parserion was arrested a few days before the ceremony was due to take place.

The plot collapsed, and Parserion was deported to Meru 'for life', which proved to be until 1930, when he was allowed to return and resume his position as *orkoiyot*. He was not reconciled, and started again to plan a rising. Two years later another gathering of the age-sets took place and once again the mood was ugly; this time Parserion was left alone, but an aircraft appeared overhead and dropped on the meeting 'bombs' which caused a panic, but were made of flour. Once again, the rising was stillborn. Even so, Parserion did not lose heart. He moved, after some years, to a European farm in the Laikipia district and established a sort of government-in-exile, with an armoury of arrows made to his order. This was discovered in 1957; Parserion was once again arrested and banished to an island on Lake Victoria where he still lives—and is still recognized as *orkoiyot* by the older Nandi.

The basic fact about the Nandi is that they were, and still are, primarily a cattle people. But, unlike the Masai, they dug the ground before the European came, mainly to grow millet for brewing beer; the idea of cultivation was familiar. The love of cattle lies at their heart and all that goes with such love—pride, self-reliance, a contempt for others, conservatism of thought and habit. Cultivation was always the woman's affair, cattle the man's. Yet the breach in the wall was there, and Europeans have been able to exploit it in order to turn young Nandi men from warriors into farmers, from cattle raiders into policemen and auctioneers.

III

The country by tradition is divided into parishes, the *koret*; and the *kokwet* is the parish council, which meets always under a tree. (Every *koret* has a name, generally derived from some plant or tree or animal, such as the river of nettles, the hill of wild banana trees, or the place of a woman's under-garment.) Each *koret* embraces a certain number of homesteads and the elders of every homestead form the *kokwet*. There is also a larger territorial unit called a *pororiet*.

Each *kokwet* has a leader of discussion to whom the others defer. The process by which he emerges is essentially African. No formal vote records his election; to canvass for support, like a Western politician, would be a solecism carried to un-imaginable lengths. No one can tell you exactly why this elder or that has been chosen, or how the choice was made, or when one man ceased to lead and another arose. Mr. Huntingford

7 Among the Marakwet: a bird-scarer's platform, and an indigenous irrigation furrow in the hills

8 Skeletal planning: a landscape after treatment

has listed the following qualifications for a *kokwet* leader:
he must be old, but not too old, for his life is active; generally
he belongs to the age-set just below the oldest. He must have
intelligence, a knowledge of tribal lore and some personality;
he must be one to whom people naturally listen. A sense of
humour is necessary and a reputation for honesty and common
sense. Finally, he must have a certain amount of property,
and for preference two wives or more, to enable him to provide
food and beer for the honourable entertainment of visitors.
He becomes the *poiyot* and his word, though not law, is always
respected. It is seldom expressed as an order or decision. 'We,
the elders, say that arap Kipoilel should pay five goats to
the complainant; we have agreed that this is just . . .'
'It would be a good thing if arap Cheptum were to settle his
debt so as to end the bad feeling, and for this we think he
should pay a heifer, a bull calf and five gourds of beer.'

There is no police force, no jail, no compulsion, yet the
word of the *poiyot* and his elders is always obeyed, though
seldom immediately. No tribesman dares to defy public
opinion; the pressure of his family, his clan, his age-set, is too
strong. The immediate sanction is disapproval, a stronger one
a sense of guilt, and the ultimate one banishment or death.
So the elders are obeyed, and the whole system of jails and
policemen unnecessary. When the historian reckons up the
size and equipment and constant activity of a modern police
force, the expense, paraphernalia and element of luck in courts
of law, the cost and squalor of prisons, and sets them against
the *kokwet*, the *poiyot* and the *orkoiyot*, it will be interesting to
know whether he reckons the game worth the candle and
whether future generations of Nandi would not settle for a
lost simplicity.

Before the European advent, most African tribes had so
organized their lives that married men and elders had probably
more leisure than any other people on earth. Wives looked
after crops; sons herded cattle and fought wars; elders sat
under trees, drank beer and either talked of local matters or
dispensed judgement. Every man was a councillor and a
magistrate, but attended to his duties more or less when he
felt inclined, having to observe no hours or rotas.

A tree for shade, a gourd for beer, a horn for snuff; obedient wives, respectful sons, hard-working daughters; sun for warmth, milk, meat and millet for nourishment; a fertile soil, a perfect climate; the protection of magicians against the spite of spirits and the schemes of evil-doers; it would be hard to imagine a life nearer than theirs to fulfilment of the hopes and dreams of the elderly male of any race or nation.

No life on earth is perfect, and it had its set-backs from time to time, but for everything there was a remedy, and if the remedy failed there was a reason; for everything there was a purpose, for every man security within his tribe, his age-set, his clan and his family; and from this soil grew and thrived the blooms of dignity and contentment. Women did not come off nearly so well, but even so their work gave them pride, and no woman, whatever her looks, age or nature, was ever unwanted, lonely or without the matrix of a family.

It becomes continually more difficult to sustain a conviction that the introduction of money, literacy, taxes, votes, the doctrine of work and the religion of materialism; that the suppression of cattle-raids, magic, dancing, sacrifices and indigenous justice; that the end of contentment and the beginning of *angst*; that all these aspects of civilization have made life happier and fuller for the tribesmen. When they have turned their arrows into duodenal ulcers, their *kokwet* councils into political parties, their cattle-raids into football matches, their virgins into strip-tease artistes, will they be better off? But such questions now are academic; the Nandi have joined the rat-race, sometimes with enthusiasm, and must do the best they can.

IV

Kapsabet means 'the place of porcupines'. Civil servants have replaced the porcupines; on a small scale Kapsabet is a boom-town expanding not on commerce or industry but simply on the spread of government. One may wonder where the money comes from but, in one way and another, come it has; even if it were to dry up, it would leave behind many houses and offices of modern design, if flimsy construction, which the Nandi may perhaps regard as a useful legacy.

Today the district commissioner, here as elsewhere, is in part a chairman of committees. Of these the key one in the regeneration of the country is the district team, consisting of the heads of various departments which are turning the Nandi hills from over-stocked, dusty, denuded, brown, abused stretches of gullied pasture into a garden of green fields as generous as those of Somerset or Normandy.

These hills of Nandi, between 5,000 and 7,000 feet, full of streams and with a 50- to 70-inch rainfall, were once thickly forested; in the last forty years nearly all the trees have been destroyed, and matters reached such a pitch that in parts of the country, which is about the size of Hertfordshire, firewood was exhausted and people were burning dung.

The enclosure of the land got into its stride after the *askaris* returned from the war. As in Elgeyo, they pegged out claims in the bush, cleared vegetation and grew crops without asking leave of anyone. There was plenty of bush and forest, and each man took as much as he thought he could manage; fifteen to thirty acres was the average amount. The *kokwet* elders disapproved—land in Nandi had never belonged to individuals—but they did not overtly try to stop the movement. They perhaps knew that they could not restrain men who had for so long been away from homes and families and had seen foreign countries and learnt foreign ways. Possibly they hoped that in time the *askaris* would revert to the sanctioned customs of the tribe. So, uneasily, they watched fences go up, and square houses; saw common pastures divided into paddocks and cattle confined in them instead of grazing with the family herds; felt matters of importance slipping out of their control.

How did the shade of Koitalel view these things, or the living Parserion? Perhaps it was Koitalel who sent a plague of jackals to gnaw the maize-stalks, and so steal the succulent cobs. Never before had such a plague been known, nor had maize been eaten by jackals. The Government issued poison, the jackals perished and the shade of Koitalel was defeated, if not appeased.

Enclosure reduced the area of communal grazing, while cattle continued to multiply. The unmanaged commons went

67

from bad to worse until ALDEV started a betterment scheme which banned cultivation from river-banks and steep hillsides, limited livestock and built dips to protect the cattle from East Coast fever which, when allowed to have its way, kills off at least half the calves. Of course this could have made the situation even worse, but it was linked to a scheme of stock control enforced by rules passed by the District Council. The Nandi are intelligent, many of them work for European farmers and I was assured that the limitation of livestock, dipping, sales by auction and grazing control were now so well accepted that pressure no longer had to be exercised from above, although constant vigilance would always be needed. The difference was that most of the invigilators were now Nandi, not European, officials.

Nandi cattle belong to the usual Zebu race of Africa whose capacities to yield milk and put on flesh, judged by European standards, are lamentable. Few cows give more than a gallon of milk a day and few bullocks weigh more than 500 lb. when, after six or seven years, they reach their long-delayed maturity. A good British bullock should weigh 1,300 or 1,400 lb. when he is two years old. But the exceptional Zebu animal will give up to three gallons of milk, and will put on weight much more quickly than the majority.

Selecting these exceptional animals and breeding from them—the basis of all livestock improvement everywhere— was started many years ago, mainly by European ranchers who selected from a larger breed of cattle in the semi-arid north, called Boran. But this was overshadowed by a much quicker and more spectacular method, the crossing of Zebu with British breeds. Instead of waiting three or four generations for your higher yield you got it, by this crossing, in a single generation. No wonder most people went for the quicker, simpler method—indeed, they had no economic alternative.

The snag about crossing proved to be that, while yields improved in a sensational manner, the Zebu's capacity to resist disease and to thrive on poor, dry, indeed almost non-existent pastures was impaired. In the long run, an improved Zebu may give better results, especially in unfavourable conditions, than a crossbred animal, which can fulfil its possibilities only when it has plenty to eat.

At Baraton, a station in the Nandi uplands, a livestock officer called Warwick Guy began to breed from a few selected local animals twenty-eight years ago. He crossed fathers with daughters, brothers with sisters, mothers with sons. All this bovine incest evolved certain lines of high-yielding, quicker-maturing animals. At first the Nandi were suspicious but now they will pay large sums for a Baraton bull, and even more for a heifer; demand far outstrips the supply. Baraton blood is spreading out gradually and Warwick Guy, who refused promotion in order to stay at Baraton for over a quarter of a century, will be remembered by the Nandi long after his bones have dissolved. Now the Veterinary department has fifteen such centres in different parts of Kenya and uses bulls of the Sahiwal breed—a much improved Zebu—imported from India and Pakistan to speed up the process, without loss of disease-resistance and tolerance of heat.

v

We stood beside a circular concrete tank on a hill-top with a view of bare, green, rounded ridges tumbling away towards the hazy margins of a horizon blue as jacaranda flowers, with clouds patterning the down-like hillsides. (Absolutely no trees.) Water was gushing into the tank from a large dam we could see beneath us like a huge, unwinking eye.

'This is a *mama* scheme,' said Mr. Gain, the water engineer. 'Down there, that dam, that's the *baba*.' (*Baba* means father.) ALDEV puts in the *baba* schemes with money from the Swynnerton plan.*

*This plan, compiled by Kenya's Director of Agriculture, Mr. Roger Swynnerton, and published in 1954, outlined a scheme to accelerate the development of agriculture in African areas, based on the individual tenure of land, on the growth of cash crops, on the improvement of livestock and, in semi-arid pastoral regions, on the development of water supplies and grazing management, protective afforestation, and the control of tsetse fly. The general aim was that every family should provide its own subsistence plus a cash income of at least £100 a year. The money was drawn partly from general revenues, which allocate about £2¼ million a year to agricultural and veterinary services, partly from African

'That's the Government contribution. *Mama* schemes are financed by loans on which the people themselves pay interest through the District Council. These *mama* schemes pump from dams into reservoirs which serve a group of families. Then come the *toto* schemes.' (*Toto* means child.) 'These are up to the individual. He can tap a *mama* pipe to water his own holding, and that he has to pay for himself.'

Perhaps it is because Nandi women are by nature rather more independent than those of most tribes that the idea of tapping water instead of carrying it on the head for miles has proved so popular. Tall, upright, graceful, with handsome eyes, they display a free, self-reliant attitude in strong contrast to that of most Bantu women, and have the reputation of making the best prostitutes. Those who stayed at home have urged their men to accept the father, mother and child pipes of the water scheme, to work hard to install them, and to contribute both labour and cash to other improvements such as digging new wells.

Now the Nandi have even become sanitation-minded, thanks largely to a health officer left in Kapsabet to pursue his task for ten years. Once again, staying put and getting results are two sides of one coin: it might even be that the degree of progress in Africa has depended largely upon over-sights in the postings department, which appears to exist in order to move as many people about as quickly as possible. Mr. A. T. Matson is not only a tremendous enthusiast for better health through cleaner living, he has become an amateur historian with a great wealth of knowledge at his fingers' ends about the early development of Kenya. Not only has he got the Nandi to accept latrines and to protect from fouling over 2,000 springs, but he has seen epidemic malaria virtually eliminated in three years by a hut-spraying campaign

District Councils and partly from an initial grant of £5½ million from the U.K. The plan was put into operation at the end of 1954 and up to 1959 had cost, in round figures, about £8 million. As it nears completion, most of the enterprises to which it gave birth have either become self-supporting, or are being absorbed into the general structure of the country. The plan was a stimulant which quickened the tempo of development and re-vitalized the rural economy. Much of what is described in this book is a result of its application by local teams of administrators, agricolas, vets, water engineers and foresters.

sponsored by the World Health Authority, and the conquest of typhoid. Now he pursues a campaign against tapeworm and in favour of growing European vegetables—and of getting women to cook them, which is much harder.

VI

Arap Sambai, tall and lanky, his ear-lobes looped up over their tops, split his long face (which reminded me of Fernandel's) in two with a tremendous smile and introduced me to his gaily be-cottoned wife with her four small children at her knee, all plump as partridges. It was an idyllic scene. The wife had tamed a pigeon and kept it on the roof for her children to talk to, and it came and pecked maize at our feet. Arap Sambai had been a sergeant in the K.A.R. and you could tell this from his manner, at once authoritative and civil; and from the slouch hat he still wore.

We drank tea under a tree while a sleek tethered Guernsey calf cropped the short grass beside us and its mild-eyed mother browsed beyond one of the neat, dark hedges of Mauritius thorn which have chequered the hills of Nandi. Arap Sambai told us how he had taken his land from the bush as soon as he was released after the war, cleaned it, planted hedges and bought seed, cattle and a plough with his gratuity; how he drew water from taps in the fields; how Mr. King the livestock officer (himself a Kenya farmer's son) got for him two in-calf Guernsey heifers which he loves like his sons, and how much rich milk they give; how he has planted a third of an acre of the new crop, tea, which needs care and patience but will bring great wealth one day; how he and his wife, who shares all his work, grow onions, potatoes, beans and other vegetables to sell in Kapsabet, so that his income is already beginning to swell.

Then conversation drifted back to the war and the distant places he had visited: Madagascar, Burma, India, Ceylon. He and Mr. King had served together then as now; and Mason the interpreter had his own story. He had been in the *City of Paris* which was sunk by Japanese bombs off Colombo, when very few survived. 'Eighty-six European sisters were drowned,' Mason said. 'Not one escaped. I should have been drowned too, but when we were waiting to embark at Mombasa my European officer taught me to swim. So when the ship sank I swam until I was picked up. The officer? He was drowned, too.'

Once a year there is a reunion at Kapsabet of hundreds of Nandi ex-soldiers who come with their uniforms, their slouch hats, their medals, to parade and drill as if they were again at the victory march in Nairobi; the band puts its soul into the marches; a senior officer takes the salute; then there is a feast and many stories. Every Nandi is at heart a warrior and, when the K.A.R. goes round recruiting, the young men still come in droves to give their names, and depart to seek adventure.

Perhaps they will do so less often now that there is an alternative at home to drink and idleness. But the curious thing about this revolution—not just in Nandi, one finds the same everywhere—is that it is not a revolution of the young men, but of the middle-aged. No man can start to farm till he is married and few can afford the bride-price, which like other things has risen, before he is in his late twenties at the earliest, and then he needs cash to equip his farm. So first, as a general rule, he must go forth to join the K.A.R. or government service, to work on farms or in the towns, and find some way to make a bit of capital.

But soon there will begin a second generation of farmers with enclosed land, and what will then be done about inheritance? If a man has five sons, what is he to do? Primogeniture is unknown, and would be thought most unjust. If you select one son out of five—or even two sons and split the farm in two, which might be feasible—are the others to go without an inheritance?

VII

This is the big, the overshadowing, question of the future; on it the whole success or failure of the experiment will hinge. Wherever I went, it was being discussed alike by African farmers and by European planners. I sat under another tree and drank more tea with a neighbour of arap Sambai's. Tea is everywhere most generously supplied, and has its own flavour: leaf, milk and masses of sugar are all stewed together in a kettle and treated like French soups, being added to from time to time to strengthen the brew. The neighbour was an oldish man who worked for many years on European farms, has four growing sons, over an acre of tea ready for its first plucking, a herd of seventeen cattle—his main income, until the tea gets going, comes from the sale of four fat beasts a year, which brings in about £100—and a labour force of three men. He is a Christian, with one wife only, but the four sons may well increase to six or seven.

'When my sons marry, they will need cattle and land,' he said. 'I took this land from the bush, but now there is no longer any bush left without an owner. This farm cannot be divided, for there would be nowhere to graze the cattle. I do not know what will happen.'

He shook his head and looked melancholy; it is a matter that weighs on many of his generation and one for which neither *kokwet* nor *orkoiyot*, who between them once solved everything, can settle. What is the European solution? 'Decide which of your sons will make the best farmer and leave the land to him. Then educate the others in different skills—one may become a teacher, one a mechanic, one a policeman, and perhaps there will be one very bright son who will go to the university and become a doctor or a district officer. In Europe, only a few people own land; there would not be room for everyone. Besides, many people do not wish to be farmers. You will be the same.'

The old Nandi shook his head and patted the dog by his side, while his wife poured more liquid from her enamel kettle. 'Perhaps. But what is a man without land and cattle?'

Yet some are coming to it. There are, for instance, several syndicates of young men who between them have bought a tractor and plough, and work on contract for improved farmers. Mortality among tractors is distressingly high, but gradually their owners are beginning to see that they are like cattle, and must be fed and tended, not merely hit with a spanner when they go wrong. There are traders with lorries, schoolmasters and building contractors, clerks and auctioneers.

Yet as soon as a man makes a bit of money, he invests it in land and cattle. A state of landlessness will be as hard for Africans to acquire as a state of grace amongst all of us. Yet it will have to be done. Doctors and surgeons, teachers and community developers, nurses and welfare workers and Red Cross, all these have achieved a brilliant, a spectacular success in reducing infant mortality and defeating disease. And birth control still remains virtually unknown among the tribesmen. Nor is an industrial revolution comparable to the agrarian and social one in sight.

Unless those two checks and outlets can be established, all these upward-climbing people will find themselves once more on the downward slope. They need only look as far as India to see a grisly example. The more food is grown, the more mouths appear to eat it, and all efforts to raise living standards are brought to nothing. Stabilization and re-deployment of population is the key to all.

A rising population has already brought the Nandi to a situation where it is no longer possible for every male to inherit or acquire land. Of their own accord they have allocated thirty plots on which to build villages for the landless —including women of independent means, often retired prostitutes, who wish to return to their homeland to bring up their children. Virtually the only employment open to landless men is to work for their fellows on progressive farms, but few Nandi like to do that. Most of their hired labour is drawn from other tribes.

Such questions trouble people like this old Nandi sitting under a tree, his cattle browsing beside his deck-chair, while several charming half-Sahiwal calves—and Sahiwals, with their big sad eyes, have more charm than any other cattle— frisked about like playful lambs and children stared with round eyes at the visitors.

'God will help us,' said the elder. One can only hope that He will.

We drove north from Kapsabet over rolling, treeless ridges and came to a strange, bumpy stretch of country where the earth was puckered like gooseflesh on a human skin. Each bump, six or eight feet in diameter, almost touched the next, and all were grassed over; nothing else grew. These bumps are the remains of old termite castles. What has become of the termites? No one seems to know. The only theory I heard advanced was that all this country had been forest, the forest had been destroyed by fire, then termites had colonized the dead stumps and eaten them away. Each bump was an old root; when the stumps were finished, the termites moved on.

VIII

Sarora is a successful settlement scheme. An officer left in charge without disturbance? The name is Hans Middleboe, a Dane with all his people's energy and thoroughness. Now he has left Sarora, but left his mark upon it too.

The main object of the scheme was to provide a future for Nandi families who had been squatting on European farms, and had to leave to make way for more intensive development. Some returned to their old *korets*, but others had lost touch, and had nowhere to go. An exodus took place to Tanganyika, Masai and even to Uganda—many of these Nandi had no taste for life under the authority of chiefs and elders—but others were given holdings at Sarora, an area of about 7,000 acres of originally Nandi land that had been bought back from European farmers and taken over by ALDEV, who put in contour terraces and roads. Now two hundred families are settled there.

Sarora is a region ruined first by flogging under maize, and then by over-grazing by Nandi cattle. Stripped of all its trees, grey rocks jut like bones out of a thin, scrubby soil. Vermillion *erythrinas* flare from the hillsides, and in places groves of Londiani thorn, which has deep red seed-pods, grow among the boulders. From Governor's Rock, that towers high above the ridges like a seat of kings, you can see, as if from an aeroplane, the bare gullies with their trickling streams, the contoured cultivation in long swaths like ropes of hair streaming from the scalp of an earth-giantess, the dry eroded pastures with their specks of cattle, the red thorns, the rocks, the heat-shimmer, the sense of age and timelessness. This is the raw, run-down material on which the land-improvers have to work.

The first step was to remove by forced sales about three-quarters of the livestock. Today, no settler may keep more than ten head of cattle; tomorrow, he will get from his ten as much milk and meat as from twenty or thirty in the past. There is a bull camp where any settler may bring his cows to be served by a Sahiwal of superior looks and inheritance. The best of the settlers may, if they wish, buy a Guernsey or a Red Poll bull to use on their cows.

It has been, and is, difficult to keep these settlers up to the mark, for they are not a hand-picked lot, and some had grown accustomed to a life of idleness. The inborn Nandi notion of the good life is to watch his cattle graze at will and multiply, not to confine them in fences, dig the soil and make compost. The settlement is run by a committee of six Nandi and the European manager; they decide policy, and have power to evict disobedient tenants. The settlers help each other with major tasks like fencing and terracing, and have built their schools with voluntary labour: old traditions of group working have been revived. Altogether the picture at Sarora is a hopeful one, but it is also expensive; each family has cost about £200 to settle on the land.

IX

Paulo arap Boit is a large, strong, bullet-headed, light-skinned, self-reliant man, with a slightly Oriental caste of feature—Arab blood perhaps, from caravan days? He has made a success of, and probably a small fortune from, the trade of auctioneering, and lives in a European kind of house. His farming methods would be well thought of in any European area and his income is probably higher—and his taxes certainly much lower—than those of some Europeans. He farms at present about seventy acres but seems certain to expand. His farm is fully paddocked with cedar posts and wire, every paddock has its trough fed by *toto* pipes, he has a brick dairy with a separator, a sleek silage-fed herd of cross-

bred Sahiwals grazing Rhodes grass leys, a fine young
Guernsey bull bought from a European breeder, and a red
tractor, belonging to a Nandi company, which ploughs for all
the members and has a paid manager. There is a Luo labour
force. Probably the capital value of his improvements runs
into at least £2,000 and his income to £600 or £700 a
year.

On his veranda I met the local land registration committee,
something so deeply alien to the spirit and tradition of the
people that no one who knew them of old would credit its
existence. (Mr. Matson told me of an old man who all his
life had refused to cross a road near his home because he would
not touch anything made by Europeans.) The committee
comprised eight oldish men, each the land elder of a *kokwet*.
There are eight *kokwets* involved in this particular scheme,
which covers about 400 landowners. Its object is to enclose and
then to register each holding as an individual's property.
Before long, the whole of Nandi will be so registered.

What has been the mainspring (I asked) of such a complete
reversal of the traditions of centuries? Such a *volte-face* in
outlook?

'People were tired of land disputes,' one elder said, his
ear-lobes dangling, his hair grizzled with age. 'When we were
young, we took our cattle where the grass was green. But now
that everyone is cultivating, the cattle must stay in one place.
And so there are many disputes. The D.C. has told us: if you
wish to end these quarrels, you must mark out your land as
Europeans do. And without this you will not grow heavy crops,
for you are spoiling your land. And you must plant trees.'

'We want our boys to go to school,' another said. 'In the
old days, after they were circumcised, they herded cattle;
now they are away at school. There is no one to herd the
cattle, so they must remain in one place.'

'Our people want certificates,' a third elder added. 'If a
man has this certificate, nobody can take his land. It is all
written down in a book kept by the Government.'

Already, in this area, the people have temporary title-deeds
which they will be able to convert into permanent ones after
a second survey has been made. A junior district officer in a

caravan is touring the area giving out title-deeds. Before that, the elders walked over every foot of the country, settling disputes and persuading people to exchange land so as to straighten out wiggling boundary-lines. If anyone rejected the elders' judgement, he could appeal to the district officer and, beyond him, to the African Court, but in every case—there were very few—the Court supported the *kokwet* elders.

Now that land enclosure is working smoothly it all looks easy and one tends to forget how big an obstacle has been surmounted—the conservatism of this highly conservative, independent, warlike and superstitious people. One of the pioneers, a chief called Willie arap Boit (no relation to Paulo) who ploughed a large *shamba* in the early thirties, so outraged tribal opinion that the *laibons*, after a long campaign of intimidation, placed cow dung, blood and magic in his furrows to blast his crops and destroy their sacrilegious owner. Another rocklike character, senior chief Elijah, similarly defied public opinion by ploughing up a *shamba* and by fencing off a badly eroded piece of communal grazing. These were test cases: public opinion ran high against both chiefs and, had they weakened, the cause of land improvement would have been lost for many years. Their crops, watched anxiously by local officials, luckily thrived, and so did their families.

This was the first real challenge to the *laibons*' authority. They rallied, however, and soon after World War II whipped up a resistance campaign against cattle dips. Once more they were defeated, and some left to join their principal, Parserion, on European farms and carry on a sort of *émigré* resistance movement.

Chief Willie flourished, and his family: one son, a District Council cashier, captained the Kenya team at the Empire Games at Vancouver; another, a junior district officer, is also an Olympic runner; and one daughter is a fully-qualified teacher. Chief Elijah received the M.B.E.

Behind these and other stalwarts lay the patient and persistent work of Mr. Sholto Douglas, the first whole-time agricola to be posted to Nandi—and that was not until 1948. His was the initiative, and his also the tricky task of competing

with the *laibons* for the people's confidence. The buoyant state
of Nandi twelve years later is the measure of his success.

X

However good its field officers, no army would get far,
as everyone knows, without staunch and efficient N.C.O.s: in
this case the African instructors whose job it is to carry all
these theories, ideas and modern practices to the individual
farmer and his wife on the *shamba*. He is the one who gets the
kicks and grouses, as well as the rewards of prestige and respect
when things go well. The training of instructors is obviously
a key factor in the whole campaign.

At Kaimosi, on the borders of Nandi, I saw a fine new
training college for future instructors of the Kalenjin language
group built with the help of £30,000 provided by the International Co-operation Administration of the United States.
Here a mixed European and African staff trains about a
hundred young men at a time, each for two years. One or
two pupils from the distant, still unsophisticated Suk were
sitting at their desks learning simple soil chemistry, or peering
at microbes in the laboratory. The school was not full, for it is
hard to find boys of a high enough educational standard.

A market was in progress at Kaimosi, filled with colour by
the Nandi women's bead ear-rings which dangled to their
shoulders and by their wide, intricately patterned bead
necklaces, and the copper wire coiled round their ankles.
They strode along carrying sugar-cane and bags of millet on
their heads. In the cattle-ring Nandi dealers, for all the world
like their British counterparts, leant on the rails and gave
terse bids to the auctioneer who was knocking them down for
between two and three hundred shillings apiece—a good price,
considering their quality and the fact that by-laws enforce
de-stocking all over Nandi, limiting the general level to one
and a half acres to a beast. This pushes out a regular flow of
animals to feed the meat-craving millions of the Lake Victoria
basin and Uganda.

It was surprising to see at this market a lively group of three
sombrero'd Europeans, two of them women, playing on

trumpets and trombones rousing tunes which had attracted a cluster of women nursing babies, children chewing cane-sticks and young men looking on in dark sun-glasses, fly-switches in hand. The Salvation Army, perhaps saving souls.

By contrast, on a road nearby we passed a girl swathed from head to foot in soft leather aprons fringed with beads, which hooded her head completely except for slits made for her eyes. She wore beads and bells on her ankles and ornaments on her wrists, and looked as queer and antediluvian—lorries rattling by and a tea factory within sight on a ridge—as one of Boadicea's chariots would look rolling down Piccadilly. She was a girl undergoing her period of purdah after circumcision, when she lives in the bush with her fellow-initiates under the care of old women whose task is to hand on the secrets of tribal customs, and impart a code of correct behaviour for wives and mothers.

Mr. Cyril Barwell, an agricola who lived for ten years among the Kipsigis, told me that one day he stumbled upon an enclosed compound in the forest and walked through a narrow entrance before he realized that it was a girls' circumcision camp. Inside the fence he saw a circle of round thatched huts in miniature, each one complete, like dolls' houses. He was hustled out, concluding that these were demonstration models used by the old women as part of a course in domestic economy.

Virgins are entitled to wear bells on their waists, and are known as Girls of the Bells—an honoured title, which improves their marriageable value. In the old days, both girls and boys remained for six months in their bush camps undergoing instruction. This period has now been reduced by a District Council by-law to one month, in order to coincide with, but not exceed, the school holidays.

9 Nandi cattle going through the dip

Chief Kipto arap
Chirchir of Elegyo
with a Corriedale

10 Enclosure completed: part of a countryside that was all bush and forest twelve years ago

CHAPTER 5

Somerset Without the Trees

I

NANDI and Kipsigis regard themselves more or less as two branches of one tree. Only about forty miles separate their homelands, but what in Nandi is just beginning has been virtually completed in Kipsigis. Almost every inch is now enclosed within neat hedges of Mauritius thorn.

Kipsigis looks like Somerset without the trees. It rolls away, green and smiling as on a summer's day, white clover in the pastures, clear streams in the valleys, beauty everywhere. It would be hard to find a land more favoured, more clement; rainfall is generous, days are balmy, everything sprouts and blooms and grows. In the rare patches of bush are yellow cassias and the big-bloomed, mauve, bee-loved shrub called *Vernonia*; wildflowers shelter in the pastures, everything is bright and clean.

I arrived from Sotik, a small enclave of European farms occupying land that once formed a buffer state between the Kipsigis and their neighbours the Kisii. In contrast to the fertility on either hand, that of the Kisii to the west and the Kipsigis to the east, much of Sotik is what is called impeded drainage land: there is a thin coat of black soil on top of murram, and nothing much will grow; the natural vegetation is a coarse, tufted grass with clumps of bush and creeper-swathed trees. These clumps grow on the sites of old termite castles. The termites dig down deep to make a nest for their fat white queen, who lays an egg a minute for several years on end; in doing so they punch a hole, as it were, in the murram, and make a sort of drainage pipe. Here, and here only, deep-rooted plants will grow. But most of this land is virtually unploughable.

As our Land-Rover sped out of the European area into

Kipsigis we saw an immediate change, the deep chocolate soil and green grass and tall occasional tree, and the Mauritius thorn hedges. The cup between every hill and its neighbour held a swamp or stream. So to Bomet, a new station, with a magnificent view down across hills towards the Chepalungu forest and the boundary of Masai. This was once among the best game country in the world, alive with elephants, rhino, buffalo, a score of lesser breeds. There is not a single one left now. Only humans.

Even ten years ago, all this country round Bomet was under native forest and empty of men. After the war a great land rush took place* and now trees are as extinct as game, except for a narrow strip along the banks of rivers under the theoretical protection of by-laws. So black, charred and devastated was this landscape, at one stage of its clearance, that local Europeans called it Passchendaele.

Probably members of the present generation are luckier than any Kipsigis has ever been in the past, or can be again. They are the first generation of landowners. With no one to contest their right, they took as much land as they wanted. Their holdings are relatively large, between twenty and fifty acres, more than one family can handle on productive soil. These will be divided as the population grows, for there is no more empty land. Soon, inevitably, in ten years perhaps, land pressure will begin.

II

'Everything here is tied to the cow's tail,' the local experts said. 'Crops don't really interest the Kips.† We have plenty of beautiful neat thorn hedges with nothing inside them.'

To clear bush and plant hedges does not take very long.

---

*The first enclosure actually started in the mid-thirties round an African Inland Mission at Litein. During the war years enclosure was pressed by two agricolas, Mr. G. Gamble, M.B.E, and Mr. C. Barwell, M.B.E. The seed fell on fertile ground, and sprouted vigorously from 1948 onwards.

†Maize was not introduced until 1919. Before that there was only millet, grown almost entirely for beer.

Then comes grass, succulent and sweet. But grass by itself is useless, you cannot run a combine-harvester over it, you must first convert it into something you can sell, like meat or milk. Native cows, here as everywhere, do little more, if anything, than bring up their calves. The Kipsigis could not afford to scrap them, even if they would, and buy a complete new outfit of Guernseys or Jerseys. Nor would it as yet be safe to do so, for there are still disease-carrying ticks in the pastures and, until the land is cleaned by several years of dipping or spraying with tick-destroying chemicals, to introduce exotic cattle on a large scale would be to court disaster.

So there is a hiatus: some of the finest pasture-land in the world and nothing coming off it except a few third-rate little beef animals and a handful of ghee. The Kipsigis even import milk. They pay collectively about £14,000 a year to a European creamery for milk delivered from a Land-Rover at certain points along the main road, and produced at higher cost from greatly inferior pastures. Nothing could be more absurd.

'Our trouble is complacency,' I was told. 'The Kips have very few ambitions. Once a man has paid his taxes and his children's school fees, bought a bicycle perhaps, and a new dress for his wife, what more does he want? It's our job to make them discontented.'

'That seems absurd, too. Why not leave them alone?'

'Yes, but then events will catch up with them. The population's going up by leaps and bounds. What happens when the land runs out? Besides, they all want more schools. They think the Government should build them and pay for everything, but if they put their backs into it they could do all these things themselves.' And then:

'They won't look ahead.' Much as I dislike generalizations, I think it is true that Africans come nearer than most other peoples to obeying the commands of Jesus to take no thought for the morrow, to say not: What shall we eat? What shall we drink? Wherewithal shall we be clothed? These attitudes are surely climatic in their origins. Those who have to face a long, hard winter learn to think ahead; to salt down beef in September to eat in March, to fell timber before the mud arrests haulage, to saw logs before the frosts come, to plough in fall for spring sowing. It becomes a habit. Africans have never had to acquire habits like that, and not until the Christians arrived has anyone tried to wean them away from these particular teachings of Christ.

'Here's an example,' said a young man who was helping to build a new farmers' training centre. 'We've got a cement mixer. The other day I found the Kips mixing the cement, shovelling it into a barrow and wheeling it thirty yards to the building. Why don't you move the mixer, I asked them, to the place where the cement is needed? And save yourselves wheeling it all thirty yards? They grew confused, upset and sullen. They liked doing it that way, they said—yet they were on piecework, and it took them much longer. The point was, they had to make an *initial* effort to move the mixer. This would have saved them a lot of work later on; but, at the time, the effort required to move the mixer was greater than that required to wheel a barrow. So they went on wheeling barrows. They just don't think even ten minutes ahead.'

Little wonder, then, that few Kipsigis will brave the extra exertion needed to produce a surplus of crops, or maybe of milk or ghee, which they don't need themselves, to make money they don't immediately want. It is nicer to sit in the sun and drink beer. They are tremendous beer-drinkers. Older men will sit round a huge clay pot, clasping long pipes made from a tree with large floppy leaves which grows in the valleys, through which they suck the warm beer. They suck and suck and talk and talk. When a man gets fighting drunk, a master of ceremonies calls for two stalwarts who tie him up in a hut kept for goats and sheep until he is sober, when he rejoins the party. Beer-drinks are apt to go on and on until the women tire of it, and fill the beer-pot with hot water. Fumes rush to the men's heads and make them fuddled; they grow comatose, and soon the party is over. This happens so often that it is not surprising very little strenuous farming gets done.

Of course there are exceptions. Every district has its prize farmer—arap Tiren, Paulo arap Boit, and here Elijah: a tall, grave man of perhaps forty-five or fifty, dressed in a slouch hat, shorts, a check shirt and large boots, who lives in a semi-modern house : that is, it has a thatched roof and not a tin one, it is made of mud and not of bricks, the floor is earthen not cement, but it is rectangular not round, and has several rooms and a narrow veranda. His wife, in a print dress and head-scarf, gave us tea and two wrapped European loaves of bread, and butter from her own dairy.

'I come here to learn, not to teach,' the agricola said. 'What Elijah does today, the rest of the Kips will be doing tomorrow.' Yet Elijah is not an educated man, nor a young one. Most of his life he has spent on European farms, observing things; ten years ago he returned to take land from the bush. He has today fifty or sixty acres, a tractor, a tank holding 10,000 gallons fed from the corrugated iron roof of his maize store, a lorry and a pick-up van, a herd of seventeen cattle with a pure-bred Sahiwal bull, and four permanent workmen, to whom he pays a monthly wage of 40 shillings plus a house, but no food. His yields of maize would be the envy of many Euro-peans : last harvest they were as high as twenty-three bags to the acre. (The colony average is eight.) But then he plants early, a practice which experts strive and strive to inculcate, generally with no success at all. Elijah speaks no English, but can read a little in Swahili; the new *arriviste*, he will no doubt found a dynasty and the brightest of his sons will find their way to Makerere, to Oxford, to London University, and become barristers, doctors, civil servants, politicians.

III

There are two main roads to wealth the Kipsigis can follow, if they want to. One is through cattle, the other through tea.

Just across their boundary with the Europeans lie tea estates which, together with the coffee round Nairobi, form the most productive single piece of land in Kenya, probably in eastern Africa. Here are tea barons driving in their long, sleek motor-cars; here are factories that stand on hill-tops like cathedrals and cost a quarter of a million pounds; here are hillsides green and glossy with the level-topped camellia that can bring a higher profit than gold. This is the country of the companies, of big business, dominated by two giants, Brooke Bonds and the African Highlands (James Finlay and Company).

If tea will thrive on one side of the boundary, so it will upon the other; soil and climate are the same. Probably at least one-third of the Kipsigis' 630,000 acres would grow the shrub, if asked; the Kipsigis, about 160,000 in number, could become a race of tea-planters and relative millionaires. That is a dream of the agricolas, who have the same sort of itch to see rich land put to fruitful use as a painter has to cover a canvas with shapes and colours.

Tea is normally the prerogative of large companies. The main reasons for this are the very high costs of bringing it into bearing and the equally high costs of processing the leaf and maintaining the plantation. Such figures vary; in Kenya, at the present time, it costs, with the factory, up to £500 to bring an acre of tea into bearing. There are not many individuals, black or white, who can afford this.

Moreover it is no good having one acre, you must have enough to justify a factory, 200 acres at least, and you must put up a factory, which will cost perhaps £100,000. Nor is tea an easy crop to handle. The leaf must be plucked regularly, at a certain stage of growth, and treated in the factory within a few hours; the bush must be skilfully pruned to a certain shape; the land must be kept clean and in good heart.

Once in the factory, the processes involved in turning out a well-made tea are highly technical and complicated, and make all the difference between profit and loss. Altogether, you could hardly find a crop less suitable, in modern times, for peasant farmers without experience of growing such exacting plants and with a traditional aversion for any regular and meticulous work.

Yet this is now an aim of the Kenya Government: to create from nothing a major tea-growing industry entirely in the hands of African peasants. All its officers I met are imbued with a profound enthusiasm. The very difficulties of the project stimulate them. It is a project that emanates entirely from Europeans. So far as I know, there has been no tea-wish on the African side; it has been a question of whipping up interest, not of canalizing demand. But now the agricultural service is full of tea missionaries. There are two main areas ripe for conversion, in their view. One, the largest, is the great belt of superb soil and high rainfall surrounding Mt. Kenya, and along the eastern flanks of the Aberdare mountains, occupied by Kikuyu and allied tribes; the other is this comparatively small, but equally suitable, belt of high, fruitful land occupied by the Kipsigis, Kisii and Nandi.

The difficulties are formidable. To begin with, the tea, instead of growing in large blocks several hundred acres in extent, must be planted in little plots, as small as a quarter of an acre, dotted about all over the place and not subject to any central control. Each peasant must be taught all the processes, cultural acts like pruning and plucking which are generally controlled by highly-trained, well-paid experts who take up planting as a life's profession. If anything serious goes wrong at any stage the quality of the leaf falls off, the price drops and the whole thing becomes uneconomic.

How, for instance, is the leaf to be got to the factory? It must be hurried there, not kept waiting for several hours. This involves not only prompt action by the smallholder, but a high degree of organization; there must be lorries, collecting-points and schedules, not to mention reasonable roads in a country of steep hills and heavy rains. Then there is the siting of the factories themselves. They cannot be placed very far apart, or the leaf will take too long to reach them; yet tea grown in quarter-acre plots must be thinly scattered over the ground, compared with that concentrated in plantations. Here again there is a heavy risk of high costs and poor quality.

IV

This whole tea project, one of the boldest and most ambitious ever taken on in Africa, is a tremendous gamble. It is a gamble primarily with human nature. Can you turn an indolent, cattle-loving, illiterate, easygoing and suspicious tribesman into an industrious, steady-going, intelligent and meticulous tea-planter, all in a few years? Tea will grow, undoubtedly: but can you ensure that it shall be tea of good quality? Everyone agrees that if poor tea is grown, the experiment will fail; prices of low quality grades cannot stand the costs of production. It must be good tea or nothing: as good as the big companies grow on their estates, with all their experts, training, capital and experience. Is this possible?

The experts say it is—given certain conditions. The first of these must be prolonged and skilled supervision. Unless trained experts remain in charge, armed with powers to enforce certain rules, the scheme is bound to fail. Here is another enormous gamble, political this time. All African countries are proceeding at breakneck speed towards self-rule. When African nationalism triumphs, will European experts be left in charge and, above all, given powers and backing to enforce rules that must often be unpopular?

When you are a hundred miles from Nairobi, all these great political changes seem a world away. Between the turgid clichés of demagogic politics in the multi-storied capital, and the peasant in his hut with his couple of cows, his patch of maize, his aspirations for an iron roof or a wheelbarrow, stretches an enormous gulf. Yet ours is a society in which theories sweep like tornadoes across the world, engulfing the little men and women who cannot understand their origin nor influence their course.

There is one major asset, without which the tea project could not have been launched. That is the existence of an established industry which has already found out how to grow the tea bush, where to grow it, and how much all this costs; which can, and will, provide the necessary seed or young plants; and which will treat the first African-grown leaf in its own factories, so that expensive machinery need not be erected until the crop is proved as a peasant industry. Fortunately, the European companies have done all the pioneer work.

The first steps along this path of practical partnership—that much-abused word—in Kipsigis country have been taken at a place called Kimulot. Here is another settlement scheme, only this time the land (just under 8,000 acres, with a 70-inch rainfall) came from one of the few surviving stretches of native forest. It is a dual-purpose scheme: to absorb landless Kipsigis, and to start peasant tea-growing. The area has been chopped into twenty-acre smallholdings, and on each the owner will plant, to begin with, up to one acre of tea.

Mr. Pickford, the officer in charge, came to Kericho when tea planting started there in 1925, and even before that he grew tea at Limuru, so he has a lifetime of experience to put at the disposal of Kipsigis smallholders. No settler depends wholly on tea. Each has his herd of cattle, each grows maize and beans to keep his family. Each plants up to one-third of an acre of tea at a time, for it is an expensive business. The cost of buying stumps alone—stumps are two-year-old seedlings cut back—works out at £55 an acre. The plan is for each settler to get his first thousand stumps well established, and to show that he can look after them properly, before starting on his second thousand. (There are 3,750 stumps to an acre.)

The first settler we called to see, a tall, thin, elderly ex-sergeant of the K.A.R., put on his jacket and came towards us with his *panga* in his hand.

'There's the fundamental change,' Mr. Pickford said. 'Before he came to Kimulot, he'd have thrown down his *panga* when he saw us; it's a woman's implement, to use it was *infra dig*, to be seen doing the work of a woman.'

Now he was himself working on the land, with his wife nearby—she went on hoeing while we talked to him. We inspected his patch of little stumps, kept scrupulously clean of weeds. The Kimulot settlers are growing tea on faith alone, because agricolas told them to; they do not know whether all the hard work it entails will reward them. All the ex-sergeant's tea, with that of half a dozen neighbours, was planted in a single day by *kokwet* labour, a turn-out of the whole neighbourhood—men, women and children—cheered on by beer brewed by the wives.

I sought out the ex-sergeant's wife and asked her views. It was cold here, she said, and misty, and maize didn't thrive; she had to give her children potatoes; perhaps that was all right, but she would prefer maize, and went on trying to grow it. As for tea, she had seen no profit yet; her husband said that one day it would pay the school fees for her children; well, perhaps. She bent down and went on working, the youngest baby bobbing on her back.

The first leaf was nearly ready for plucking. Both Brooke Bonds and the African Highlands Company have agreed to take all the leaf that can be grown until 1970. If, by that time, the experiment has succeeded, a tea-growers' co-operative should be able to borrow the capital for enough factories to handle a steadily rising output of leaf. At present, the companies pay for every pound of leaf delivered at the door a sum sufficient to provide the Kipsigis, on average, with an income of £85 an acre a year—an unheard-of sum for any normal peasant crop. If the risks are great, the stakes are high. And even greater possibilities lie ahead. The Tea Boards of Kenya, Tanganyika and Uganda jointly finance a research institute whose staff foresee the doubling of present yields, without extra cost, by growing tea bushes by vegetative methods instead of from seed.

All paths have dragons in then; this one is no exception—the dragons stand in the shape of question marks. One is called Work: will the Kipsigis, and others like them, be able to keep it up? The hard, methodical, *sustained* work that must be done at just the right moment? The other is called Politics. If white officials go from Nairobi, will they be able to stay in Kimulot, Bomet, Kabianga, Kericho? If not, will there be Africans to replace them? Or who will give the orders that must be obeyed?

V

Like the Nandi, the Kipsigis had no chiefs, only witch-doctors and the parish council; but fifty years of British rule have pretty well built them into the structure. Chosen for their strength of personality in the first place, wealth has followed naturally; this in turn has enabled them to educate their sons. Chieftainship is not hereditary, but often chiefs' sons occupy superior jobs—less, probably, through influence and wealth than because of the start they got in education.

The senior chief of the Kipsigis, arap Tengetcha, has four wives and many sons: one is a junior chief, one a clerk of the African Court, one an interpreter, one a sub-inspector in the police, one a treasurer to the District Council. They are well dug in; arap Tengetcha himself is a forceful character and the lustre of his name imparts to his descendants a certain authority.

One of the sons, arap Sang, took me in his Land-Rover to see some of the up-and-coming farmers who, as in Nandi, took their land from the bush after the war, and took what they wanted. The first was a schoolmaster with forty acres, on this soil more than a single family can cope with, especially as it is almost all suitable for tea.

'Yes, I have four sons; when they marry they can live with me and have a share of the farm; but when I die . . . that will be difficult.' We looked at his pure-bred Sahiwal bull and several sleek little calves—little, but still about fifty per cent larger than a native calf at the same age. On these pastures, Channel Island cows would thrive and everyone wants them, but official policy is to build up first a population of crossbred Sahiwal females to mate with future Channel Island bulls. Undoubtedly this would result in better herds, but whether the Kipsigis will be content to wait all that time is another matter. Like others, they want short cuts.

Here you can see some of the best pastures in the world— better even than in Nandi, because less overstocked—and some of the worst cattle. I remember particularly a small-holding we reached by a very winding and precipitous track along a steep hillside, above a valley where a little of the indigenous forest survived. How splendid those forests must have been when they covered all the hillsides! Great variety, no two trees alike, some with enormous floppy leaves like those in old tapestries, some with tightly clustered leaves like beeches, nearly all tall and slender with silvery trunks. We emerged on to pastures of blinding green, hilly and rolling, the grass springy underfoot and starred with clover, and above it all a pure blue sky with white fluffy clouds, and the sparkling sunshine, never vicious but kindly: a farmer's paradise.

This farmer had learnt the value of trees for shade and in his paddocks, hedged by Mauritius thorn, he had left tall crotons standing, and under them his little herd stood half-asleep, dreamily swishing tails. A wildflower with a face like a violet's and a leaf like a pea's grew in the deep star-grass pastures, but I could not discover its name. With his wife, he was clearing a patch to plant tea. It had to be terraced first, so he had signed on a Luo labourer. It is a measure of Kipsigis prosperity that about forty per cent of the smallholders now employ paid labour, nearly all Luo, for they are said to be too proud to work for one another.

'This could be the main cream-producing area of East Africa,' the agricola said. 'One day perhaps it will be. But look at it now!' A few humped native cattle with a dash, here and there, of Sahiwal blood, nothing coming off the pastures, everything still revolving round the bride-price, not the creamery. Auctions, it is true, have caught on, but the quality of the beasts passing through the ring is still abysmal.

VI

Agricolas and vets want to sprinkle the countryside with separators and organize the transport of cream to processing centres, to be run by co-operatives linked with the Kenya Co-operative Creameries, the European organization that also handles African cream. The only thing that stops this going ahead at present is inertia.

Our smallholder with the violet-starred and croton-shaded pastures is one of those who is giving a lead. With a party of fellow-smallholders he went to see the separator at Itembe, a pilot scheme started by ALDEV, near Bomet, on 10,000 acres of land exchanged with Europeans for another area.

Because, like Sarora, it is not part of the Kipsigis land unit, the settlers can be obliged to follow certain rules. It has been divided into thirty-acre farms, now has about 320 settlers and operates smoothly: but it had a stormy start. Three *laibons* in Kericho, sons of *orkoiyots* who had been banished for wickedness twenty years before, directed their sorcery against the first officer in charge, who died there, within a few months of his arrival, from stomach ulcers. The second was moved away after a short spell of duty; and the *laibons* claimed both these events as victories. Then a third came who was young and tough and half Italian, and spoke Kipsigis; he stayed.

Gradually the settlers began to show an interest in new ideas, especially in a scheme to separate milk at a central dairy, send the cream to Sotik and divide up the proceeds, sometimes as much as 150 shillings a month per man. This leaves them the skim, which they drink in the form of a mastic mixed with various additions like cows' urine and charcoal made from roots of the cassia shrub. The agricolas want to see beef calves reared on the surplus skim milk, and an output of cream rising year by year to bring as much wealth to Kipsigis farmers as to Danes or New Zealanders.

So impressed with Itembe was the party of visiting small-holders that afterwards they formed a group of forty-nine members resolved to buy a separator of their own. Already they have built a house for it by voluntary communal labour. Senior Chief Tengetcha has promised to lend them a separator to start them off until a small cess on milk brings in enough to buy a permanent one. The cream will have to travel on the back of a bicycle to a collecting point on the main road, whence a trader's lorry will take it to the European creamery at Sotik.

The fact is, the Kipsigis could all be rich if they tried, but is it worth while to be rich at the cost of incessant toil? But then, the Kipsigis want schools and health centres and possibly roads; the Government wants money; so agricolas and vets, like conscientious nannies, push and prod—bring your cow to a Sahiwal bull for three shillings, mind you spray once a week, you'd enjoy a nice co-operative with your own separator, why don't you put a corrugated iron roof on your new house, a lot of people nowadays are going in for tea, it's the coming thing, you don't want to be left out—there, you've forgotten that contour terracing *again*! The times I've told you; never mind; yes, I know you're tired, but look at arap Soyet over there, *he's* not complaining, and he's built ever such a smart night *boma* for his cows . . .

Meanwhile, politicians in distant Nairobi apply their sense of urgency to constitutions, votes, boycotts, strikes and meetings.

'It's creameries we want here, not self-government,' one of the young officials said. 'Why don't the politicians come down here and persuade the Kipsigis to do a bit more to help themselves, instead of whipping up all the Nairobi spivs at Makadara Hall every Sunday afternoon? I'll tell you why— people here would argue back, and no one's name would get into the papers! And there's no £3,500 a year ministerial job going here—only hard slogging up and down hills in the mud arguing with people lazy as tortoises and as obstinate as the backside of a camel!'

VII

Senior Chief arap Tengetcha is an old man now, well over seventy. A picture of the royal family hangs on the wall of his European-style bungalow. A large clock stands on the central table, flowers are bunched in vases on the mantelpiece, a darts board on a stone wall invites relaxation; there are loose chair covers, ashtrays, a cement floor. We lunched well off onion soup, grilled steak with sauté potatoes, green peas and cauliflowers, and tinned pears and cream. Arap Tengetcha and his wife have little or no English but several sons speak fluently, and one is generally around to translate. The chief has been to England, and returned deeply impressed with the English capacity for work. 'Those who work hard are happy,' he remarked, having formed a somewhat idealistic picture. 'Only the idle are discontented. Britain has been built up by co-operation among the people. That is what we must do. We shall not advance by quarrelling amongst ourselves, nor by quarrelling with Europeans. I am old, and I think that we shall advance only if we co-operate and love each other, white and black together. I tell my people: what has the Government taken away from us? It has brought us civilization. It teaches us. Can you learn civilization without the Government?' He spoke with a conviction that official spokesmen, when European, generally lack.

To what extent, I asked him, are Kipsigis customs dying out? 'The boys will still be circumcised,' he said: 'even educated boys. There was one whose father, a mission member, sent his son to a doctor; but the son wanted to join the circumcision of his people, so he took a brand and burnt down his father's maize store. It is not as it used to be, because of schools, but it will go on.' He was less certain about the survival of girls' circumcision.

The Chief can remember a time before any European had settled in his country: before a post was set up at Kericho, or at Sotik. He has served the Government loyally; he believes in it, and spoke of the end of famines and witchcraft and tribal war, and of the breaking of the power of *laibons* who, as in Nandi, were rounded up and deported to an isolated place in Nyanza, after they had stirred up one cattle raid too many against their neighbours the Kisii. It all sounded, like his idea of Britain, rather idyllic.

He showed me round his well-kept house, and in his bedroom was a *cache* of weapons—bow and arrows by the bed, a long-bladed warrior's spear leaning against the wall, a sword in its scabbard. 'You are not going to be caught unawares,' I remarked. With a grin that made his wrinkled face look years younger he whipped aside his pillow to reveal a *panga*. He took it up lovingly, then put it down and handled the spear. 'You see how the blade is twisted? That came when it killed a Masai warrior. The blade stuck fast, right through his ribs; I had to twist and turn to get it out, I was so powerful then that even this hard iron bent . . .' He ran his fingers over the grooves with pride and delight in his eye. 'Yes, I was a warrior then, a strong warrior, and when we crossed the river in the night to raid the herds of Masai we travelled silently but at daylight, when we returned, the elders greeted us, and all the girls welcomed us home . . .'

He had not spoken quite in the same way about civilization, this grizzled, monkey-faced old man with so much character, so much pride, a sense of humour underneath. Old men forget—but not the glories of their youth. His sons can recollect no such glories, only success or failure in examinations. By comparison, they wear a worried, harassed, an unmoulded look. Not so the grandsons, bright-eyed in the schools, with blue shirts and exercise books and curiosity. When the old chief dies, perhaps his weapons may be buried with him. Perhaps his grandsons will play the Masai at football; and perhaps they will be satisfied.

11 'Like Somerset without the trees': part of Kipsigis country now enclosed. But (*right*) old customs remain: a girl after circumcision in her traditional skin robes

12 Kipsigis elders enjoy a beer-party, while their educated sons receive instruction at the Siriba training centre

CHAPTER 6

The Reluctant Luo

I

THE Luo are the second largest tribe in Kenya, coming next to the Kikuyu, and at the moment the most influential politically. This is because most Kikuyu politicians went into detention camps at the time of Mau Mau. While Kikuyu cats were away, Luo mice played vigorously, and grabbed the best political cheese. Speaking generally, the Luo are hefty, black-skinned, somewhat ox-like people with prominent teeth, a reputation for making good labourers and a rather slow-witted approach to life.

Needless to say, there are plenty of exceptions. Mr. Tom Mboya is a Luo and, while he has been called many things, 'slow-witted' has never been among them. Their natural food is fish and they are not by nature a cattle people. Their sturdy women smoke pipes with long clay stems. The Luo are not Bantu but Nilotic and their affinities, lingual and tribal, lie more with people in Uganda, such as the Acholi, than with any other Kenya tribes. They are surrounded, however, by Bantu peoples, with whom they share the wide, fertile, steamy and mainly flat basin that surrounds Lake Victoria. Around this basin lie hills from which warrior tribes look down on them, formerly as an eagle looked upon its prey. Far to the south lie the plains of Masai.

People who have dealt with other tribes find the Luo difficult. Their obstinacy is legendary, they are inclined to be sullen and suspicious. The Kikuyu can be all these things, but they are nimble-minded, subtle and, for those they like, have charm. Luo people can be brave and loyal but charm is rarely among their attributes. They are faintly Teutonic, in an African fashion.

So it is not surprising that of all the major Kenya peoples, leaving aside the Masai, the Luo have put up the stiffest

97   G

resistance to the forward march of Progress in the agricultural field. No spontaneous wish for any branch of Progress except the political seems to have gripped the collective Luo mind. Here, on these hot and apathetic lakeland flats, all the impetus has come from Europeans.

It might be argued that the Government has no call to make people change their ways against their will. This indeed is an argument much used by Luo politicians. It is an old story: should nanny sit by and watch Master Robert break up his toys—in this case, ruin the soil, create acute erosion, turn the whole of Nyanza province, which contains one-third of Kenya's population, into a great rural slum?

Beyond question, that was going on. In Nyanza province there are over two million cattle, about one to every two acres. It would be a job to support this rate of stocking on the finest pastures under skilled management; here it is utterly impossible. The cattle have become so small and shrivelled that they are really not much larger than Great Danes, but their sharp hoofs can still make and deepen gullies as they track a way to springs. During the last three years, the output of crops in the province has halved, because yields have dropped so sharply. Yet there are more and more mouths to feed.

All the evils of land abuse were here displayed in concentrated form. No manure, no rotations, no resting land under grass; maize or cotton again and again, planted too late and in the wrong manner; no trees, communal grazing destroyed by useless skinny little beasts. It was not for want of trying by the technical staff. For years they had been urging, persuading, bullying, demonstrating, and they had scarcely dented Luo indifference and complacency. Famine was beginning to threaten these overcrowded areas—for the one thing the people continued to produce more and more of was their own kind.

II

And so the Government decided that the only salvation for the Luo lay in dividing their communally owned land into individual holdings. Land consolidation—the first stage towards enclosure—was proclaimed as the official policy and, in 1958, an area called Nyabondo picked out for an experiment. The edict went forth that everyone must define his holdings, mark them out and do, in fact, as the Kikuyu were doing with such success, not to mention the Nandi and Kipsigis and many others.

On the heels of the agricolas with propaganda, local politicians moved in to tell the people it was all a trick to steal their land. Whether or no everyone believed this, no one dared to quarrel openly with the politicians, and not a single land-holder obeyed the Government.

'On 30th December, I called a meeting and closed the whole thing down,' Mr. Peter MacEntee, the D.C., told me. 'All right, I said, if you don't like it you needn't have it; ruin your land if you want to, as much as you like; what do we care? It's your funeral. Go ahead, and good luck to you. The agricolas will leave you alone from now on, the instructors are pulling out to places where people want them; we understand now that this sort of thing is *far* too advanced for you. Keep up the bad work, and good-bye.'

Mr. MacEntee had evidently enjoyed this. In time the Luo, when in their mule-like frame of mind, subdue the greatest enthusiasts. But there was a sequel.

'Three weeks later, half a dozen men from Nyabondo turned up in my office. They had a little plan, with some *shamba* boundaries marked on it. "We have decided to consolidate," they said. "Here are the boundaries of the first *shambas* we've completed. We've marked out each man's fragments and exchanged them as you said. Now we want to lay them out on proper lines. Please send us an instructor and a European."

'This was the first deputation. Others followed. Now the whole of Nyabondo is completed—the first in central Nyanza. We know what to do now. Use the couldn't-care-less technique.'

Another example: on the Kano plains, where rice grows under irrigation, until this year the agricultural department has looked after the bunds. They had endless trouble—arguments, sullen silences, even sabotage. They got the output up to 30,000 bags and there it stuck. Then they withdrew, telling the rice-growers they must make and maintain their own bunds. Last season the output jumped to 50,000 bags.

III

We drove to Nyabondo across the Kano plains. No one loves these plains. They are not only flat, they are absolutely treeless, dry, cracked, windswept, overcrowded, dusty and mean. The soil is 'black cotton', an especially viscous clay in which any vehicle bogs down irrevocably in wet weather— very fertile potentially, but soul-destroying to work. 'The people are like their soil,' I was told. 'They break your heart and yet you go on trying, something's there.'

Everywhere are circles of a particular euphorbia, a dark-green, harsh, ugly plant that grows about eight feet tall and surrounds every group of huts. When a family head dies, his homestead is evacuated, his huts are left to rot away and only the euphorbia hedge remains, so the plains are covered with old circles as well as those in use. People have tried planting eucalyptus trees, but white ants eat them before they are man-high.

No individual cultivates his land in one piece. He digs or ploughs a patch here, a patch there, another bit over there, two more bits down the hill and a piece two miles off across the valley that belonged to his mother's uncle. This is known as fragmentation; it is almost universal among Bantu people, exists also among others such as the Luo, and is like a net spread for the feet of Progress in which he becomes enmeshed and stultified.

The first stage of land enclosure must be for every cultivator to exchange fragments with his neighbours, so that all his land is gathered together in one piece. It is the first stage and also the hardest; land is life's blood to the people; it is like exhorting men to exchange their blood, or their children. Suspicions dart out of their holes like bee-eaters. Won't so-and-so, my neighbour, get an unfair share? The bit he wants to swap for my piece is smaller. Give up my fertile patch by the river where bananas flourish for that barren stretch of hillside? Never! Somewhere there is a trick in all this. . . .

Behind and beyond are old beliefs that are still alive. A man can lay upon a piece of land, when he is dying, an oath that binds his heirs to hold on to it for ever, and will destroy anyone who sells it out of the family—an entail with the sanction of magic. And then old homesteads on the Kano plains sheltering behind euphorbia hedges contain the bones of the deceased owner, who is buried under the floor of his hut. So consolidation may ask the son to exchange not merely a field of maize, but the bones of his father, the terrestrial anchor of his father's spirit. No wonder it is often too much to ask, and that politicians find these deep fires easy to fan.

To reach Nyabondo we climbed a small escarpment, the beginning of the Kipsigis hills, left the car beside a track and walked to the farm of a young, pleasant-mannered school supervisor called James Onyango, one of the leaders of the enclosure movement. We sat under a tree near his new tin-roofed modern bungalow, above a shallow valley with a stream. The country here is gently rolling and thickly dotted with roofs of homesteads. Many people had gathered in a circle; the women sat together in bright cottons and gay head-scarves, plump and glossy, most of them with grave-faced, round-eyed babies sleeping in their arms or crawling about the grass beside them. This question of land touches the women at the core. James Onyango told his story in English.

'The idea of exchanging gardens came to us two years ago; we had heard of it in other places; most of us were interested, and asked the Government to advise. We held a meeting and agreed unanimously to consolidate, all of us within the Kadianga clan, fifty-nine families. In our clan are three sub-clans; each appointed three men to form a committee. Each of these three was a *m'guru*—an elder whose task is to look after the land, and one of these was made the president.

'We started to exchange our gardens, and at first everything was fair. Then came elections for the Legislative Council and the District Council. The candidates thought they would gain popularity by speaking against the land schemes. They campaigned among the people, and some listened. They had clever ways. In each sub-location they had an agent who would write to the papers, or sign letters written for him, saying the people were against these schemes. And so some of us became confused. In this location we still wanted to exchange land, but some of our neighbours turned against it, and we had to stop.

'At the end of 1958 the opposition became very strong and the D.C. called a meeting to decide. The opposition staged another trick. They packed the meeting with supporters from other locations, even women who knew nothing about it at all. This was a noisy and a difficult *baraza*. Even with these methods, when it came to a vote the meeting was evenly divided. The casting vote was left to the D.C. He decided against it, and so the scheme was closed.

'We who had always been in favour were greatly harmed. We wanted the Government to bring water from the river, and surveying had already started for a piped scheme. Some of the elders went to the D.C. to ask him to change his mind, but he refused. In January, he agreed to send two people to Elgon Nyanza to see what was being done there. They saw it all, and when they returned we elected *liguru* after the pattern of the Elgon people. We called everyone together in groups, men, women and children, to plant hedges round the *shambas* that had been exchanged. I myself exchanged four pieces, and in some cases I paid money and cattle to get all my land in one piece. We managed to plant hedges round two or three *shambas* a day. Then we went to the D.C. and told him what we had done and asked him to send an officer to help us plan the use of our *shambas*. When he heard what we had done, he agreed.

'Now we have enclosed all the land of our clan and we want to have it registered. We asked the D.C., but there were still six men who refused, and the D.C. would not do it until everyone agreed. In the last few days two more have agreed, so now there are only four against it. When they agree we shall have titles to our land and then no one can upset the work we have done.'

IV

After Mr. Onyango had spoken, others said their piece, and I asked the opinions of some of the women, who will never speak unless they are directly asked. One replied, through an interpreter, in these words:

'I was against consolidation. My own land was fertile and I did not want to lose it and have other land not as good as mine. I tried to persuade my husband. We had many arguments, and the peace of our house was destroyed. At last I saw that I must give in if our home was to become peaceful again. We exchanged gardens, and then I saw that the new gardens were as fertile as my own. Now the men are helping women on the land and this is something that has never happened before. Men and women are working together. This is because the men see that there is money in growing crops and that bigger crops will make them rich.'

A second woman—both were middle-aged—spoke after her.

'I was not of that opinion. I wanted consolidation before it came here. If you have land near your home, you can work to improve it. If it is a long way off, you cannot put on manure. I understood the value of manure by seeing crops grown by the Better Farmers. Before, I had four *shambas* and one was over a mile away. Now they are all together and near my home. There is only one difficulty. Our custom is, when a son gets married, he leaves his father's *shamba* to start one of his own. I do not want to break this custom, but now I have a married son and there is nowhere for him to go.'

And a third woman, rather older, added her piece.

'I was in favour of consolidation too. The boundaries of land have caused many disputes and quarrels amongst us. When there are fixed boundaries, these quarrels fade away. So I wanted consolidation before it came, and my husband agreed. Now I can farm properly and put manure on the *shamba*; we have a shed for the cattle to stay in at night. Besides that, my husband employs two men. When he goes away I supervise them and the work is not so hard. Men and women never worked together before. Now they do, and this is a big thing. When we get some money, I shall ask my husband for a better house. We are in the way of progress now, but there is another thing: the Government must help us with our water, we need a scheme to bring it—that is the biggest thing.'

It is often said that women are the most conservative, and in some ways perhaps this may be so—especially in regard to marriage customs; but it struck me, almost everywhere I went, that it is the women who are most anxious to see these basic land reforms brought in, the men who oppose—not the old men so much as the younger, educated ones who have been to cities. Africa so often seems to reverse the expected order of things.

At any rate, there was no doubt of what these women thought about land reform. It is they, after all, the cultivators, the workers, who know where the shoe pinches, and no wonder they are out of patience with those young men of the towns who, while crying for political freedom, do their best to deny to their own women that measure of relief from hard, grinding toil which land consolidation and enclosure can afford.

Among the Luo, everything is done by clans—extended families would be a more correct term. This group is called the *jokokwaru* and consists of all the descendants of one grandfather. They hold their land in common and each individual, as he marries, is allocated a *shamba* by the *liguru*, the land elders. In time he probably inherits cultivation rights over other pieces from various mothers, uncles and cousins, and that is how fragmentation arises. All grazing land is held in common, as among all other tribes.

The *jokokwaru* system is at once a strength and a weakness, from a modern point of view. Livestock improvers regard it as an unmitigated curse.

'All the members of the group must agree to any sale of stock by any individual,' a vet told me. 'That makes destocking almost impossible, if only out of bloody-mindedness.' The livestock picture generally is a gloomy one. 'We are still trying to get across one or two of the most basic principles, such as dipping or spraying against ticks. Among the Kipsigis, over 5,000 people are spraying; here, with sixteen times the population, not 500 are. In the whole of Nyanza, with its 300,000 families, we have only sixty-seven Sahiwal bulls.

'On cattle, most of them won't budge. For instance, a man's prestige is somehow linked with that of his bulls, and they are most reluctant to castrate anything. Pioneers who try improved methods are unpopular and their neighbours are apt to gun for them; one man, for instance, had his pigs burnt alive. Still, we plug on. We have controlled rinderpest, if not East Coast fever—every year we give about 200,000 rinderpest inoculations. We export half a million hides and skins and are trying to improve their quality.'

It is perhaps worth noting that crops, whose improvement is considerable, are grown by women, but livestock is the exclusive concern of the men.

'In the years ahead,' this rather disillusioned vet concluded, 'we have only got to get across two basic principles: that a cow wants food all the year round, and that a calf needs milk. But it will take another twenty years before we make any real dent in Nyanza.'

On the other hand, some things unexpectedly catch on. A district officer who had seen fish-ponds in Malaya made half a dozen and stocked them with tilapia. Local people observed the ponds and, without any serious propaganda, dug others like them. Now there are over a thousand in Nyanza. They cost nothing, the Government provides free fingerlings and is full of plans for fish-ponds everywhere as the basis of a small industry.

V

Maseno is a dynamo of education. It was started by the Church Missionary Society. 'The general plan of campaign was based on the model of Iona,' wrote the Rev. John Willis, later Bishop of Uganda, who with Bishop Tucker chose the site in 1904. On 14th January, 1906, the first resident missionaries, Mr. and Mrs. Hugh Savile, moved in—there was not much to move into, merely a grass hut under a tree that housed both the Saviles and a primitive dispensary. Nearly fifty years later their son, Mr. Paddy Savile, after many years' service in Tanganyika, was to become Chief Agriculturalist to the Government and help to make a path for Progress through the land of his birth. Maseno mission was envisaged as 'a Christian base from which the Gospel might be carried far and wide into the surrounding country, with a school for the sons of Luo chiefs at which future leaders of the country would be trained in a Christian atmosphere.'

Four small boys called Onduso, Odindo, Owiti and Oroa were drafted from Kaimosi to form a nucleus and every 'chief' was asked to contribute two sons. 'Chief' was an arbitrary term, and the leading Luo objected strongly to the disappearance of their sons, probably regarding it as another form of slavery. In those days the Luo went stark naked, used beads or hoes for currency, and prized most highly the black ostrich feathers which warriors wore as head-dresses.

'In five years' time a hundred small boys from the school were sent out, two by two, for a fortnight at a time, to teach in Kisumu and in the villages. Then they came back to Maseno for a month for further teaching. In this way the original Iona idea began to be realized and Maseno became a base of Christian influence.' Bishop Willis developed this idea in a letter: 'It affords a shelter amid a sea of temptation; it makes Christian teaching applicable and Christian living a possibility.'*

So from four small and doubtless bewildered boys under a tree, Maseno developed until by the time of its golden jubilee it embraced primary, intermediate and secondary schools, a teacher-training college, a Jeanes school for adult education, a college for agricultural instructors and veterinary scouts. Even the girls had by this time been included, although their education for years lagged far behind that of their brothers.

At the time of my visit this part of Nyanza was a-buzz with rumour and diatribe, for the District Council in Kisumu had just been dissolved by Governor's decree. To balance the official line on this, I asked to meet a firebrand or two, and everyone agreed that Maseno was the place for a crackle of

*From *Fifty Years in Nyanza*, by Elizabeth Richards, M.A. Maseno Press. 1956.

firebrands. So in a small brick room put up by Bishop Tucker in 1911, and now the secondary school's common-room, I met a bunch of schoolmasters, all fluent in English, well-informed and politically-minded.

I put to them the question that most puzzled me; land reforms are unquestionably progressive and of benefit to Africans; by raising living standards they will advance the prospect of self-government; why, then, do so many educated Africans appear to oppose them?

The answer I got was unexpected. Mr. Samwell Ayan, a history teacher, a Makerere graduate, head of the Kenya Teachers' Union and an elected member of the District Council that was embroiled in trouble, spoke impressively—and with moderation and logic.

'People are not getting justice,' he said. 'Men are losing land they are entitled to because of bribery and corruption in the African Courts. Everyone is being bribed—land elders, chiefs, witnesses. Yes, from the African Courts a man can take his case before the D.C., but what can the D.C. do? He sees only the evidence in front of him; it is all rigged; the man loses his land. I know of many cases like that. The Courts are rotten—a washout.

'I know of a case where the president of the Court altered all the evidence after it had been given and sent it up to the superior Court. When the plaintiff heard the false evidence read out, he was hopelessly confused. Clerks take bribes to keep appeal cases beyond the date when the right to appeal lapses. This is being done even in Kisumu. All the land elders can be bribed. The hunger for land is so great.

'What should be done? First, hear land cases before everyone in the location who has, or is entitled to, land—a real people's court. Then, make tape-recordings of evidence in the lower courts; if the evidence is changed, everyone will know. And let the district officer take all land cases so that he hears everything.

'It is because of this corruption and unfairness that people oppose land consolidation. All the same, it has got to come. It is progressive. But do not let it be forced.'

Mr. Ayan spoke with sincerity and even passion. This

question of bribery and corruption crops up everywhere and all concerned on the official side recognize it as their deepest enemy. But when I put Mr. Ayan's points to them they were a little sceptical. 'Of course there is bribery,' they said, 'but it is not as bad as that. And it is not the people who oppose land reforms, it is the politicians.' Mr. Ayan had just sent a telegram to the Governor asking for the removal of the 'reactionary D.C.' in Kisumu, so relations were naturally a bit strained.

VI

On the way to Maseno we had passed the ostensible *casus belli* between District Council and Government: the Kisiani hills, a barren, rocky bluff entirely denuded of vegetation and a scene of the most gruesome erosion, given over to goats browsing on boulders and any indomitable weed that had managed to germinate. This place had been leased by the District Council to the Government for the purpose of afforestation and about 800 acres of trees had been planted at a cost of £13,000.

Afforestation is unpopular. Goats were allowed to destroy the Kisiani seedlings and, when the forest department put up fences, people came and tore them down in the night. Others started to cultivate in defiance not only of the terms of the lease, but of regulations which forbid cultivation on steep hillsides. All this, in the official view, was part of a deliberate political campaign to stir up anti-Government feeling.

The Kisiani quarrel brought to a head bad feeling between the Central Nyanza District Council and the Government. All the Councillors are African save for the chairman, who is the D.C. Most of its senior technical staff are European and, in particular, it employs (as do all District Councils with large revenues) a fully qualified accountant to manage its finances.

Those elected Councillors most anxious for unrestricted freedom objected strongly to this accountant. Africans, they said, should have the spending of African money without European interference. Officials retorted that in proper, honest accounting lies the only defence against wholesale bribery and corruption—against the sort of thing Mr. Ayan had complained about so powerfully.

In the midst of this controversy the Council, with its elected majority, repudiated the lease of the Kisiani afforestation area and refused to take steps to stop sabotage of the plantations. The Government retorted by demanding repayment of the £13,000 spent upon them. This would have meant raising the Council's annual rate from eighteen to twenty-one shillings on each adult male.

This demand to increase the rate was, of course, turned down flat by the elected Councillors, who in their anger sacked the accountant, appointed a totally unqualified African at £1,000 a year to succeed him, and threatened to dismiss other European staff on grounds of race. They also voted large increases in their own salaries and allowances.

Naturally I asked Mr. Ayan's views. The Kisiani trouble, in his account, boiled down to a number of misunderstandings. The individuals who owned cultivation rights in the hills had not, he said, ever fully understood the matter, it had not been properly explained. They thought the trees would be theirs, not common property. They had never given their permission on paper, with marks or signatures. The matter was explained to them by an unpopular chief who did not wait to hear all their objections. When they grazed their goats in the plantations they thought they were on their own property and were much aggrieved when they were fined. They had no land elsewhere. Land hunger was so acute as to be a more important matter even than marriage. 'If a man should lose his wife he can buy another; but once the land is gone you cannot buy any more.'

It looked like one more failure in public relations. But the officials denied this. 'We explained over and over again,' they said. '*Barazas*, news-sheets, radio . . . Everyone had a chance to put his case. No, behind it is the old story—politicians spreading rumours that it's all a trick to steal the land.'

CHAPTER 7

The Kingdom of Mumia

I

AT Siriba, the teacher-training college near Maseno, co-education has reached a point where men and women students are completely 'integrated', the Principal said. They work, eat, and take their leisure together, only parting at the dormitory door.

'They have more sense of decorum than most of their contemporaries at home,' the Principal remarked, 'not to mention America.' No vulgarity, no necking, no drunkenness, no rock 'n' roll. These students take their mission seriously; all future teachers know themselves to belong to an *élite*. Members of the senior classes have passed Cambridge school certificate, the equivalent of 'O level' in Britain and a passionately sought-after distinction, but at present others who have not reached school certificate level are trained to become teachers of a lower grade.

The Principal told me how impressed he was with his students' sense of responsibility. They elect their own house leaders and their judgement, he said, is mature and sound. Although the Luo and Abaluhya of Nyanza are in a strong majority, often they elect leaders from smaller tribes like Kisii and Kipsigis. 'They are afraid of the destructive effects of tribalism,' he said, 'and consciously avoid it.' They speak in English; it is not done to revert to tribal tongues. This year's choice of head student surprised him: they picked a man from the lower grades, not a school certificate holder, whom the Principal had scarcely noticed; on inquiry he proved to be a clerk who had taken course after course in his spare time to improve himself and passed the necessary examinations by correspondence. He was a married man with nine or ten children. 'Respect for age and experience is ingrained, even among these young men in a hurry,' said the Principal. 'Their powers of organization are considerable. Their troubles arise lower down the chain of command.'

'The troubles Mr. Ayan told us about?'

'Yes, and more than that. A failure to *care*.'

I was given an example. Every morning a lorry leaves at seven o'clock to take several batches of students to their schools, for practical training. Then it returns to get further batches, and the whole operation has to be carefully timed. So the management is firm: if anyone is even a few minutes late, he is left behind.

'If they ran it themselves the lorry would never be on time, not because they couldn't organize it, but because they wouldn't think it mattered very much, and they'd never leave one of their friends in the lurch. It's a question of values. The sense of time isn't there, and the sense of the importance of doing things properly. You can't have a curriculum without keeping rigidly to time.' Some people fear that the whole machine would slowly run down—unless the values shifted from an African to a Western scale. These, of course, are merely opinions. What appear to us as failings may be virtues in other eyes. Africans seem less severe than Europeans with one another, unless in the grip of some theory (like magic) or passion (like Mau Mau). They may not mind torturing to death an enemy but do not like to inconvenience a friend.

Almost every student is passionately political; they want, they mean to have, self-rule. Everything at Siriba, the teaching, the board and lodging, the clothes, the bedding, the books, the sport and games, is absolutely free. When an American Negro on a lecture tour told them how much all this would cost them in the United States, they did not believe him. 'We are slaves,' they cried. They wish above all to bite the hand that feeds them because it is an alien hand, and because they believe it to be faltering. They are part of a story much greater than themselves.

Next door the Jeanes school copes with their fathers and mothers. 'The strongest reason for the popularity of our courses,' one of the teachers told me, 'is that they help fathers to keep up with their sons.' About two dozen seniors chosen for their common sense and local influence, who may be farmers or shopkeepers, church elders or football referees, come here to sleep in barracks, sit at benches and be lectured to on everything from manuring to inheritance, and to travel forth on inspections of Better Farms, co-operatives and youth clubs. Probably the farmers' courses do more than any other single measure to spread abroad the gospel of land reform.

The course I looked in upon was for elders, who sat self-consciously at schoolboys' desks confronting a blackboard on which a model holding was depicted in chalk lines. They were deep in a discussion with their young teacher about a father's need to accumulate cattle for the bride-price of a son, balanced against a farmer's need not to overstock. 'The best plan,' one of them suggested, 'is to sell the surplus cattle, keep the cash, and use it to buy other cattle in the market when bride-price has to be paid.' They all agreed with this, and it sounded sensible, but one felt that somewhere there must be a snag.

II

'If you map land consolidation with Kisumu in the centre,' I was told, 'it comes out in zones. Within twenty miles of Kisumu, nothing; twenty to forty miles, a little starting up here and there; forty miles and over, going like a bomb.' In forty miles you are out of Luo country and into that of the Abaluhyia-speaking Bantu in the north and the Kisii, also Bantu, in the south.

North of Maseno, we paid a call on John Ogou, an elected member of the District Council which is in disgrace, and a brave one, for he alone stood out against the majority and sided with the unpopular Government. A massive bull of a man, six feet tall at least and weighing fifteen stone, a strong, jutting chin and a personality one can feel rippling like a tide over his human surroundings. No wonder that, when he decided to consolidate, others followed. But he could do nothing until all the members of his *jokokwaru* agreed, and he had a long struggle to persuade them. When the last elder gave a grumpy consent, he summoned a meeting of all heads of families in his clan under a tree on his land.

The first step was to bring together all the fragments

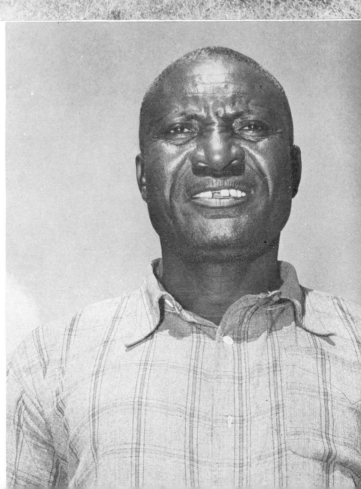

13 The meeting of
a Better Farmers'
Club in North
Nyanza, and
Mr. John Ogou,
leader of
land consolidation

14 Coffee planting in Kisii: an instructor at work and a planter's wife preparing to pick berries

belonging to each family by a process of exchange. 'This was done within one month,' John Ogou said. 'We planted hedges as we went along, directed by the elders. When they were completed, the elders asked the Government to send an officer to make a plan for each farm.'

An instructor came forward and showed me his book of farm lay-outs, kept with scrupulous neatness, each with a sketch of the *shamba* and its fields. Most farms are in the shape of a long, thin strip running down to a river. At the top is the house, with some fruit trees round it and the cattle shed nearby. Then come fields for cash crops, and permanent pasture on the steeper slopes below. Each farm has a spinney of trees for firewood and a patch set aside for 'famine crops', mainly cassava, which is dull but never fails. The average size in these parts is seven to ten acres, though *shambas* vary from a single acre to twenty-five or so.

'We have revived old customs for this new work,' said Mr. Ogou. A woman in a khaki uniform spoke up to endorse his words. 'In olden times, everyone worked together in groups. That custom is so old that even middle-aged people do not remember it. Now we have been doing this again to plant hedges, to make terraces, to sow grain. For three days a week men and women go out together and this they like, because they see with their eyes the work of their hands. My own work? I am an instructor for the women. Men only tell their wives; it is better to show the women in the fields when they are working, as I do.'

There is an air of confidence and purpose in these places where the people are themselves transforming their land, very different from the apathy of the plains. New, improved houses were springing up everywhere. With pride Mrs. Ogou showed us hers, tin-roofed and made of whitewashed mud blocks, and, with a charming short speech of welcome, gave me a present of eggs.

III

Next we called on Mr. Sakayo Opoundo, a youngish man, well-dressed in a neat suit, speaking good English in a soft voice, with a rather deprecating manner, mild eyes and a gentle smile; his complexion was light, his intelligence manifest. Under a tree he served us with tea at a long table piled high with sandwiches, helped by a tall, thin, grave-faced wife. The women always look older than the men—no doubt their toil brings this about, and the habit of shaving their heads which gives them a look of masculinity. Over the bare scalp they wear a brightly coloured handkerchief and on their feet, as a rule, plimsolls.

Mr. Sakayo Opoundo's father, Luka Omolo, was an old, white-haired, wrinkled man who wore a turban, perhaps the sole relic of a faith acquired when, as a boy, he was captured by Arab slavers and marched to the coast. Here he managed to escape, to hide for some years among a coastal tribe and then to attach himself to an up-country caravan and find his way home. We sat beneath some dark-leaved, clumpy mango trees—a sure sign that Arabs had camped here, for wherever they established posts they left mango trees.

The old man has several distinguished sons. One is a Makerere-trained doctor, another a headmaster, and Sakayo drove one of the Governor's cars and saved enough to retire to a farm of forty-five acres, which boasts a David Brown tractor and two men trained to look after it. Mr. Opoundo employs eight men in all and grows many crops, including pineapples, groundnuts, bananas, onions. But he handed his smart tin-roofed and veranda'd house over to his father and himself lives in a thatched rondavel masked by ebullient creepers.

'Our greatest need is for loans,' he said. 'How else can we improve our *shambas*? Loans for corrugated-iron roofs, for ploughs, for cattle sheds, for piped water. Why do politicians in Nairobi not press for this? How can they speak for the farmers of the country, when they do not know our difficulties?'

Then came Mrs. Sakayo's turn. 'Before we enclosed the land, I used to carry manure out to the *shamba* in a basin on my head, a little at a time. Later on, I managed to get a wheelbarrow. Then the instructor advised me to build a shed for the cattle at night. I did this, the manure made heavier crops, and from the profits of these crops I bought a cart. Now life is easier, because with the cart I can take out more manure and so grow more crops. From these profits, we are able to educate our sons. One of them went to Makerere and now he is studying in Britain to be a teacher. All this has been with money that has come from enclosing the land.'

Sometimes it seems as if these stories, told so often, with local variations, by the Better Farmers and their wives, must be some kind of lesson, they point the moral so forcibly and plainly. Yet they are told with such sincerity and conviction that one cannot, on the spot, for an instant sustain this idea. These are simple people and they speak with biblical directness of the things they have done and seen with their own eyes. They speak of life as they encounter it, a life in which a wheelbarrow is a great revolution, the school-fees of a son far more important than all the moon-rockets and nuclear fission in the world. It is impossible, when one sees and hears them, to doubt that they are speaking from the heart.

IV

My guide on this outing was Benjamin Osundwa, a junior district officer: the kind of man one instinctively trusts, solid, slow of speech, careful, strong, middle-aged. One feels that no crisis would ruffle him, that any emergency would find him prepared. His air of quiet authority perhaps springs from a consciousness of descent from fourteen chiefs. He is a nephew of Mumia, the most famous chief of all Nyanza—one of many nephews, for Mumia was reputed to have over five hundred children, though probably they were never counted, and about fifty wives.

Mumia was an important figure when the first caravans marched from the coast to Uganda in the 'eighties and 'nineties of the last century, and his village became a place of rest and replenishment. In 1902 a missionary called the Rev. W. A. Crabtree wrote: 'All the Kavirondo chiefs I have known hitherto have been clad in skins. Imagine, then, my intense surprise when a tall man greeted us, wearing a long white *kanzu* and over that a long black coat embroidered in silver; and on his head a Turkish cap, black velvet embroidered in blue and silver.' In 1909 he was gazetted paramount chief of the Bantu Kavirondo, and he died on April 24th, 1949, at the estimated age of ninety-two. In a single lifetime he spanned two ages, from the Arab slaver, the yoked children and the captor's lash to the car-borne Councillor, the aircraft and the nuclear bomb.

It was at Mumia's that the four survivors of the massacre of Bishop Hannington and his caravan of fifty, annihilated in 1885 at the orders of King Mwanga of Buganda, found sanctuary, and in his walled village that the Bishop's skull was buried, and later disinterred by Bishop Tucker for reburial at Kampala. It was here that the old Sclater's Road from Mombasa, which before the railway was the lifeline to Uganda, ended its adventurous course on the Nzoia river. And it was here that Chief Mumia raised in a few hours an army of a thousand spearmen to hold the station against the Sudanese mutineers who, in 1897, advanced from Eldama Ravine towards Uganda, driving before them cattle looted on their way.

Mumia was the Nabongo,* or senior chief, of a tribe called the Wanga, and inherited from his father Shiundu (in about 1875) a considerable empire over neighbouring tribes such as the Kabras, Kitosh and Teso. He held it with his warriors, in those days fierce and well-disciplined, and in alliance with a branch of the Uasin Gishu Masai whom they called the Abasebe. Raiding the Luo was a favourite occupation; both tribes lived, then, in fortified and moated villages. Mumia himself had homes in seventeen villages because his wives were so numerous that they could not all be concentrated in one spot. He combined the duties of judge and priest and had a hierarchy of courtiers and advisers, a pale reflection of the Kabaka's court in Buganda, which the Wanga may have been trying to imitate.

When Mumia died in 1949 the ceremonies of a Nabongo's death and succession were carried out for the last time. On

---

*For the following I am indebted to Dr. Paul Bohannan of Northwestern University, Illinois, who collected details of Mumia's life in 1955 and kindly let me see his unpublished material.

his death-bed he nominated one of his many sons, Shitawa, as his heir, and after he died certain of his elders pretended to strangle him—no doubt a relic of the ancient Nilotic priest-king custom by which no ruler could die a natural death lest his magical potency should be ended.

At the funeral Shitawa speared an ox which fell on his father's body; had he failed in this, the people would not have accepted him. Then he was acclaimed by spearmen on the veranda of his father's house, sitting on an ox-hide. Mumia was buried in such a way that his head was showing. The elders covered it with a cloth, cut slits for eyes and mouth, placed Mumia's own drinking-bowl, full of beer, beside him and ran a straw from the bowl into his mouth. Thus he was left for a year or so, until a ceremony of remembrance when meat and beer were sprinkled on his grave with prayers to his spirit.

The final ceremony was the burial of Mumia's bones, an occasion of feasting, dancing and high holiday for the whole Wanga people. All Mumia's sons killed oxen and brewed beer, everyone gathered at his village, even European officials were invited. After the sacrifice of a bull, the elders of a certain clan, the Abachero, washed Mumia's bones, smeared them with butter, sewed them into a specially prepared goatskin bag and, very early next morning, carried them over the Nzoia river. Everyone followed dressed in his finery; the spears and shields of past victories had been unearthed, polished and painted; drummers and musicians played; a whole concourse of men and women surrounded the new Nabongo, who was dressed in black monkey skins and preceded by an elder leading a bull. They marched to the burial place of the Nabongos on the banks of a small stream called the Matungu. The bull was sacrificed and his flesh shared between the spirits of dead Nabongos, by sprinkling bits over their graves, and the living elders, some from each clan.

A great feast and dance followed, lasting several days, and then Shitawa was officially installed by putting Mumia's bracelets on his arms, sacrificing a black sheep, taking him round in a sort of royal progress, and finally seating him on a ceremonial leopard skin. Then Shitawa ruled, but over a ghost kingdom, split now into locations under official chiefs and in truth managed by elected District Councils.

Mumia has become a legend of the past, but his family is helping to shape the future. Here was his nephew, one of many, a budding district officer trusted alike by his own people and by Europeans. 'One day you will be a D.C.,' I remarked. 'Never!' he exclaimed. 'The work is too hard, the responsibilities too heavy; it is worse for an African than for a European.'

'You must have a lot of cousins,' I suggested.

'Very, very many—all over Kenya, in every town, everywhere in Nyanza province.'

There can be scarcely an evening when, returning from the day's work, he does not find one of them waiting to greet him and probably to borrow money to help educate a child, acquire a wife or pay a debt. No relative may be refused. The more money a man makes, the more he must give; a refusal would not only go against all custom and morality but very likely provoke a family curse as well. These heavy obligations crush many Africans and, at the least, erode their will to succeed, rather as high taxation may erode European ambition when a man reaches the top. But in our own society, ambition is ingrained—less so in Africa; and, while one may live in hope of finding ways to wriggle out of some taxation, the African family can never be evaded.

By the people's manner one could see that everyone was glad to see Mr. Benjamin Osundwa. I asked one of the farmers why he had such influence: was it the prestige of his family, or the strength of his personality?

'It is because he is always working with the people,' was the reply. 'He passes in his car, he sees women planting a crop, or men putting in a boundary, and he stops, and takes off his coat, borrows a hoe and works beside them in the heat of the day. They are not used to this, so they respect him. And Benjamin does not think too much about himself. He is always working for others.'

V

An African who refuses bribes and accepts responsibility is generally trusted more than a European, partly on grounds of race and partly because Europeans move about so much that people have little chance to sum up their qualities. Why should one follow anyone, white or black, until one can form an opinion as to whether he is the sort of man likely to give good advice?

'It has got to be advice, not orders.' That is the view of the agricola in charge of this crowded, sweltering province with its two million people. Mr. Tom Hughes-Rice is a lean, wiry, indefatigable Welshman with an airman's moustache and a humorist's eye who came to Kisumu with a reputation for moving mountains of prejudice and suspicion, based on a regeneration of the exhausted lands and obstinate hearts of the Kamba people.

'Hitherto,' he said, 'we have tried to enforce a policy and we have failed. Now we issue no more edicts, we've stopped telling people what to do. We're ready to advise them, certainly, but they must seek our advice. What we have to do now is to stage a break-through to a personal relationship of trust that makes people ask us of their own accord. And pull their legs, that's half the battle; act a bit; be a clown. They like clowns. I find it very easy to be one myself. In our *barazas* we put on some fine clowning acts.'

With his Welsh gift of oratory, Mr. Hughes-Rice can also be as impressive as an Old Testament prophet foretelling earthquakes and disasters. He enjoys putting on an act. When his audience understands his excellent Swahili, they are moved either to laughter or to tears, often to both in a single *baraza*. It is more difficult with an interpreter, who is apt to lower the temperature. Addressing, once, a *baraza* of Masai, Mr. Hughes-Rice came to a tremendous peroration about the dangers of over-stocking. 'Deserts are forming hour by hour, your springs are drying up, soon your cattle will waste away as they search desperately for drops of moisture among the rocks. Are future generations to say—look, that was the country of the Masai, of that great warrior nation, the scourge of lesser breeds. Because they lacked the sense to preserve their own heritage, they have dwindled to a few poor families who beg a meal from the Kikuyu and Luo, now the rich and strong. There is not a day to lose, not an hour; warriors, awake; delay no longer!' Pointing dramatically to his watch, and tapping his left wrist with a forefinger for emphasis, he cried impressively: 'I say to you, time is against you, the sands of time are running out!' Well satisfied with the drama of this appeal, he paused for translation; amid a rapt silence the interpreter rose to render into Masai the momentous words. The message was short and blunt. 'The *bwana* says his watch has stopped.'

VI

With Mr. Hughes-Rice and his wife, who has adorned the drab town of Kisumu with many brilliant shrubs and flowers, I walked on the shores of the Kavirondo Gulf to look at birds: little stilts dabbling in the shallows, spoonbills fishing farther out, two large pelicans weightily flapping across the evening sky, black flights of whistling teal wheeling over the mirror-smooth water, a lily-trotter delicately poised upon the vegetation, a pair of Egyptian geese winging with speed and purpose towards the distant blue shape of the hills beyond Homa Bay—the bay of fever. Reeds grew sadly on the level mud-sand of the tide-lapped shore; in the silent waters floated clumps of papyrus laced together into floats for hidden fish-traps.

Along the lake-shore are fishing villages where dhows beach under trees on the papyrus edge and set off very early to seek the day's catch. They are gaily painted with simple geometrical designs and return with tilapia in their nets. But nowadays the nets no longer bulge and sometimes the fishermen's journeys are abortive. One reason is the use of small-meshed nylon nets instead of nets of tradition, hand-made from the wild sisal plant, and another is the near-extinction of crocodiles. No one has a good word to say for crocodiles, but now that they have paid the penalty of human disapproval it has been found that, after all, they have their uses to mankind. They devour mudfish that live on the lake bottom; these mudfish in turn eat tilapia eggs; all but freed from their predator, mudfish have multiplied and tilapia declined. Now there is even talk of restoring crocodiles in some areas, so as to reimpose a balance of nature upset by man.

As we walked, the sunset blazed across the water and lit the whole sky, the distant hills, the reeds and beach and papyrus, everything burned with a wild, dramatic evening glory. Cumulus cloud massed over the horizon was lit from below as if by crimson searchlights of unimaginable power that cast tremendous beams right across the lake to lie in long swathes of splendour over the shore and to invest the trees and huts and tired grasses with a sudden, strange glory. Only the birds wheeled and flighted in the stillness, black against this orgy of colour, their whistle piercing the suspended air. There was something about this excess of royal colour, the crimsons and purples and the gold, that disturbed the heart. To see a tropical sunset in a sky full of cumulus magnified by a lake the size of Ireland is almost too much for the human eye.

Silenced and reduced by the works of nature, we strolled back among the works of man, represented in this instance by railway sheds and sidings adorned with rusty oil-drums, old tin cans and bits of corrugated iron, and by scattered squalid bungalows, shapeless and unpainted and gardenless, where poorer Asians lived. Civilization has spewed itself right up to the edge of this tremendous lake in a vomit of rusty wire, cracked concrete and old iron; man the magnificent dwells here with less dignity than scorpion or spider.

A herd of semi-tame impala browses among the wiry grass and bush that straggles round the city. With their symmetry and beauty, their innocence and grace, they are the last of an Africa that is dying by the railway sidings and the squat bungalows and wastepaper and privies of the new order. Man, the paragon of animals, the beauty of the world, seems to have gone downhill a bit since the sixteenth century.

On the edge of the lake a small peninsula juts into its waters and commands a fine view of blue and purple hills across the bay, looking into the sunset. Here, where the Greeks might have placed a temple to the goddess of wisdom or the moon, a fun-fair is to arise. (An Asian concern has, at least, made an application to start one.) This proposal offends those who imagine without pleasure the canned, raucous music floating out over a silent lake where long war-canoes used to streak by and a deep war-chant provide the only music; and who can envisage the smeared ice-cream packets, empty pop bottles, torn cigarette packs, orange peel and scattered peanut shells next morning—the trail of modern man, like the slime of a snail.

As we strolled home in the gathering darkness, lithe young Asian boys passed us on bicycles or strolled by with aimless feet looking for distraction. Nowhere to go, nothing to do, they could not even paddle in the shallows of normal love as either white or black might do; the girls were safely at home under strict parental discipline. The long, deadly boredom of the evening was upon these young males, softly prowling like cats among the garbage cans on the outskirts of their native city. A fun-fair would at least give them something to do, something to look at, some illusion of joy and purpose and activity. And illusions of pleasure seem kinder than realities of boredom, than the pursuit of the neutral which so often appears to be civilization's aim.

VII

We looked down over Maragoli from a hill of boulders crowned by a grove of figs. The roots of the fig-trees were like knotted ropes among the crevasses and their neat, small-leaved foliage gave the only shade for miles around. Down below, between the distant blue glint of Lake Victoria and the far hills of Nandi, everything was bare of trees as the plains of Kansas, and pimpled all over with a gooseflesh of huts. Here the population rises in places to over 1,000 to the square mile, yet everyone is a cultivator, there are no towns or even villages. The average holding is only about two acres, the lowest in the country.

My guide was Chief Matthew, burly and solidly built as a heavyweight boxer, immaculate in khaki uniform and crested topee. He is one of the modern school of chiefs, a Makerere graduate. With us was a court elder of the old order and several women of the new: a community development officer and two presidents of Maendeleo clubs.

So closely settled is this land that people burn dung and have to import thatching grass. Maize is the crop everyone grows, but yields are falling: the District Council's tax of three shillings a bag brought in £127,000 four years ago but in 1958 only £24,000. People can no longer live wholly off the land and at times three out of every four of the able-bodied men are away, sending money home to their families. I asked:

'Why don't they take their families with them?'

Chief Matthew ticked off the reasons on his fingers. 'Houses are hard to find. They leave their wives to keep their hold on the land. When they are old, if they have no land, where will they go? And then, in the cities, their children go to schools where they will not be taught in our Maragoli language.' So Maragoli has become a sort of dormitory area for places as distant as Mombasa, and its commuters return for a month or two every year after harvest to drink millet-beer and procreate a new crop of babies.

Looking down over their country, the Chief and the old court elder outlined its history. 'Our ancestors came here from Bunyori in Uganda four or five generations ago. They crossed the lake in canoes bringing nothing with them, no cattle. Then they met the Luo who defeated them in a great battle, because our people did not know how to use spears. They moved eastwards until they met the Nandi, who defeated them again, because they did not know how to use arrows. So then they went north, and learnt to use both spears and arrows, and came back and drove away the Luo and the Nandi and settled where we now are.

'Four brothers led our people from Bunyori: each took an area for himself and started four clans. They captured cattle from the Nandi, and this was the origin of our herds. One of those clans understood the use of magic and was responsible for sacrifices which took place in a certain cave protected by snakes to the north. The last of the priests died about ten years ago and since then there have been no sacrifices.'

Have the Maragoli suffered from this? No, they did not think so; the people had increased; yet there was discontent. 'Our trouble today is that the young men who stay at home are bored, there is nothing for them to do. The women look after the *shambas*. There is no fighting, now there is no work. There is much frustration here. The land is overcrowded, some of the *shambas* are far too small and this makes land consolidation very difficult, indeed all forms of improvement meet with stalemate. There are too many cattle, yet not enough to provide manure for the fields.

'What will people do? Some are going north where they can buy land. Others go south into Tanganyika.'

This could only be a temporary palliative. Wasn't the only long-term answer, I suggested, to limit the size of families?

'No, people do not want smaller families,' my companions told me, and the women agreed. 'They say: the land here is full but there is plenty to be had in the white highlands. Why should we have fewer children when there is land there? Let us have all the children we can and then we can take the highlands from the Europeans.'

That is being said all over these thickly populated parts of Africa, even though it is another illusion. For the greater part of the white highlands is either pastoral land which could not be used for peasant holdings, or the rainfall is too unreliable to support intensive cultivation, or else it is already producing more food than it could do under peasant methods, and therefore ultimately supporting more people. But these facts do not matter either to the peasant, who does not understand them, or to the educated young men, who do not believe them.

What with its political implications, and the attitude of the Roman Catholic church, birth control is an explosive topic, and one therefore to be handled like a thin-shelled egg by today's timid governments. Yet it remains one of the only hopes for a lasting improvement in living standards, indeed for avoiding great disasters and miseries. To apply death control so drastically without restraining births, to fill the human reservoir while stopping up its normal outlets, appears so great a folly, and to dispute the facts so wilfully and illogically blind, that human reason would seem to be a very dubious captain of our destinies if, as the scientific humanists tell us, we are henceforth to direct the course of our own evolution and, as a Jesuit philosopher has said, 'to seize the tiller of the universe'.

CHAPTER 8

Under Mount Elgon

I

'We are up against three tremendous obstacles—apathy:
couch: diet.' This was the opinion of Mr. Philip
Rimington, the agricola at present working in the human
ant-heap of North Nyanza. Apathy and diet are linked: the
couch grass appears whenever people break a *shamba*, and it
breaks their hearts.

In this area of high rainfall and soil fertility, couch does
battle with the whole idea of balanced farming. Whatever
grass you plant, in it comes and takes over, and the effort of
keeping it under is too great. If you dry its roots in the sun,
apparently, they make an excellent cattle food, full of
minerals, but Mr. Rimington said sadly that either the
people don't believe this, or find it too much trouble.

But of course he has his Better Farmers who have prospered.
One such was a tall, lean, well-brushed-looking elder called
Likhanga, whose seventeen-acre farm has been enclosed and
then planned by the local instructors. Here coffee is to be what
tea is to the Nandi, and many rules and inspections accompany
its growth. Likhanga had a permit for 175 trees, each to be
planted in enormous holes, on terraces kept clean as a slate,
and mulched with banana leaves. Likhanga showed them to
us with pride. A spray-team employed by the District Council
had just been round 'giving them medicine' against all forms
of disease. So far they had brought in nothing, but he trusted,
and meanwhile lived on the profits of bananas, which paid
the wages of two Luo labourers.

His two wives gave us tea under the trees beside his house
which was flanked by two round huts, one for each wife;
giggling shyly, they refused to join us, they were not educated.
One of the guests was Festus, a District Councillor and

teacher: a thin, intense-looking, voluble man with a reputation for doing battle with authority.

'The Government's programme is failing because of three things,' he cried, his eyes a-glitter. 'First there is money. No one can improve his farm without capital. The Government must give more loans. Now, if you get a loan, you must pay it back in four years and this is too short a time. Then, the methods are too complicated. Too much must be done. For instance, the Government insists on terracing the land. People do not understand this and far more explaining is needed. And finally, prices are too low. The Government should pay more for maize, and it should find other cash-crops.'

The agricolas agreed about the money. 'Of course we need more,' they said. 'Money for loans, money for staff to do the explaining, money all round—but Festus should say all that to his fellow-members of the District Council.' It is a constant struggle, here as elsewhere, to persuade Councillors to vote for agriculture any money at all. They want to spend every penny on education and, in this district containing over 350,000 people, have reduced the total for agriculture to £800 a year, although a tax on produce brings in more than twice as much.

In June, 1958, a Joint Loans Board was set up with capital derived partly from the Government and partly from the District Councils. Each district has a local board to review applications for loans to pay for small improvements such as cattle sheds, corrugated iron roofing, fencing, improved bulls, ploughs and so on. A shortage of loan capital is pressing and everyone hopes that the American I.C.A. and the World Bank may find this a useful employment for their resources.

Likhanga had borrowed £50 for fencing and a cattle shed, but needed so much more—for labour, for terracing, for water supplies, for corrugated iron roofs. 'Agriculture is like a daughter in the home, education is like a son; the son will get the biggest share, but a good father will not neglect his daughter . . .'

'What has happened to the Swynnerton plan?' cried Festus. 'Why cannot we be taken round to see what the money has been spent on? Where are the water schemes, the dams, the fences, the improvements we expected? All we can see are big houses for European staff and now we hear the plan has ended and the money run out.

'The Government is our father and our mother, it will look after us. You say it is short of money, but in England, I have read, there is a machine for printing notes . . .'

II

As you go north the land becomes rather less crowded, there are patches of combretum bush and scattered erythrina trees with their flaring scarlet blooms. Fear of the Nandi, who occupy the hills above, once kept it empty; now it is filling up, but belongs to a tribe called the Kabras who do not welcome infiltration by Maragoli. They have taken kindly to farmers' clubs, and I met the members of one. We sat, as usual, under a tree, men on one side, women on the other, at the home of Mark the president, an oldish Quaker whose living-room was adorned with holy pictures. For most of his life Mark had worked as a cook for Europeans. Then he inherited a farm and retired to put into practice as many as he could afford of the methods he had seen. He had a Sahiwal bull and regularly sprayed his seventeen cattle; he owned a plough, a chicken-house, a Rhode Island cockerel; the chug of a hired tractor breaking his land accompanied our talk.

'I will tell you the club's history,' Mark said. 'We began four years ago, with six members who wanted to help each other; we paid ten shillings each and bought seeds. Our maize was yielding very little then. Our first step was to fence our land and put up cattle sheds by working together as people used to, without payment. Then we ploughed, and put on manure from the sheds. We planted in rows, instead of everywhere. In one year we saw a big change, and I got twenty-four bags of maize to the acre.

'Then we bought wire netting for poultry runs and planted orange trees, pineapples and vegetables. The instructor helped us with everything, and the Veterinary department helped us with sprays and better bulls. Then the Medical department

15 The Rev. Daudi Mokinyo, a Masai parson, on his ranch; and some of the lions who share his country

16 Where tsetse flies keep out Masai cattle, grass, trees, rivers and wild game
still survive: and Sally the lioness enjoys a drink

decided to buy our milk; one of our members takes it on a
bicycle to the main road and it goes to Kakamega on the bus.
The money goes into a bank account and is shared out
between us, and now we have fourteen members.

'We do not let anyone join, only those who have enclosed
their farms and decided to follow these new methods. It is
hard work, but we see now that it pays. We are asking the
Government for a loan to make a reservoir and pipe water
to our farms. This will be a big thing. Now our main need is
for another cash crop besides maize.

'In the past,' this dignified old man added, 'Europeans
have come and taken photographs of us as if we were gorillas;
now I hope that they can see that we are people like everyone
else.'

Then the women spoke. All wore clean, neat cotton dresses
and head-scarves, and sat gravely listening until their turn
came. One, a schoolteacher, spoke excellent English, but it
was the older woman, Mrs. Mark, who did the talking, while
the younger translated.

'We have planted vegetables,' she said, 'onions and
tomatoes and carrots, but we cannot find a market; it is the
same with eggs; we cannot sell them. What can be done?
How can we benefit from our work if we cannot sell the
produce?'

The same story was told by a young woman who turned up,
on her own initiative, at a co-operative sugar factory I saw
later in the day: a schoolteacher with a husband and two
small children at home, she entered the office where the
manager—whose name really was Mr. Manager—was giving
us tea and said she wished to speak.

'Some of us, the younger women,' she said, 'are growing
European vegetables; if we sell them we keep the money,
and this is the only way we have of ceasing to depend upon
our husbands for everything. But how can we sell these
vegetables? At the market, people do not buy them. How do
you manage in Britain? Can you tell us what to do?'

Alas, I could not help her, for the answer to this cry for
markets, a desperate cry I heard everywhere, can lie only in
great social changes far beyond her power, or any individual's,

to invoke. It must lie in the rise of industries which will
support urban populations and draw people off the land.
Some 87 per cent of the Americans live in cities and buy from
the farmers who remain, and over 90 per cent of British
citizens are urban. Yet in both these rich countries, despite
all the resources of science and high levels of efficiency, despite
the immense market on their doorstep, farmers must be
subsidized to survive.

What hope of expanding markets can be offered to peasants
in a country where 95 per cent of the people live on the land
and are self-supporting, leaving only a tiny market in the
towns? 'You must wait,' was all I could truthfully have said
to this young woman, 'until industries thrive and perhaps
half the population has left the land.' Meanwhile, as her
vegetables so hopefully planted grow to waste, so do the seeds
of emancipation, germinating under a soil of age-long female
subjugation, find scant encouragement. Onions had become
for her the symbol of freedom. I could only wish her well.

III

The farther north you go, the less crowded does the land
become: it is not such good land, mostly a thin layer of soil
over murram and combretum bush with erythrina trees and
even a few euphorbia candelabras, which signify dryness. Yet
the rainfall seldom falls below fifty inches; the ground fails
to hold moisture. Maize is almost the sole crop. This worries
the experts, partly because it exhausts the soil and partly
because the price of maize is falling. Only when you get to the
northern extremity of this province do you find promise—
to the east, on the slopes of Mt. Elgon, from coffee; on the
west, on the borders of Uganda, from cotton.

Coffee is a dangerous crop. There is a danger that prices,
which have risen like a rocket, will fall like one that fails to
stay in orbit. And there is a danger that disease will damage
or even wipe out the crop completely, as happened to the
Europeans in Sotik.

Nothing, of course, can stop the price of coffee falling if
world markets so react; these decisions, if they are decisions,

are made in Brazil and in New York, not in Nairobi or even in London. I was told that Brazil is holding off the market, to bolster prices, a quantity of coffee equal to forty years' Kenya production. An even greater threat lies in the discovery of a synthetic flavour which, if it develops, will enable people to drink ground wheat, for a quarter the cost, under the impression that they are enjoying the finest blend of *arabica*.

If prices fall, it is always the lower grades that suffer most. An agricola put it like this: 'We think Africans could produce coffee at a profit after Europeans had been knocked out, because their costs are so much lower. But with one proviso: they must grow *good* coffee. There's no future for the low-grade producer, African *or* European.'

Coffee here grows under the conditions that have been described already in relation to tea: in small patches cultivated by illiterate peasants ignorant of its treatment, often by nature haphazard and lazy. It is heir to a great many diseases, which can be held off only by regular treatment at the right time. The plan can succeed only if coffee growing is closely and consistently controlled. And, at the present rate, about three million new trees are being planted every year by Africans. A free-for-all would unquestionably meet with disaster.

Yet no colonial government can stand over the peasant with a big stick and an eviction order. If the growing of coffee, or anything else, is to be a success the control must be exercised by the people themselves. And they will do this only if they understand the necessity.

Throughout Kenya, co-operative societies are the chosen method for the exercise of control. All coffee growing is organized through growers' co-operatives which are in turn advised by agricolas. District Councils have passed rules for whose breach people can be prosecuted. The co-operatives themselves have legal powers, and every grower is obliged to join them. If this elaborate structure were to be dismantled, it is unlikely that coffee growing would survive the first cold economic blast.

IV

In Elgon Nyanza I met the directors of the Chesikaki
Coffee Society, eight elderly men elected by members of the
eight groups into which the society is divided. We sat on the
veranda of their factory which houses a pulping machine.
Outside were concrete tanks where the beans in their coats of
'parchment' ferment for several days, the sluices where they
are washed and the hessian trays where they are dried ready
for bagging and transport to Nairobi. The president was an
elder with a deeply lined, sculpted, rather ugly face which
reminded me strongly of a deceased uncle of mine whose life
was devoted to horses; his ears were pierced, his delivery
deliberate and weighty, his words were translated by the
secretary, a young, good-looking bearded man—beards are a
sign of advanced political views—with a reputation as a
footballer.

'We began to plant coffee in 1952,' he said, 'but it was not
successful, and in 1955 this society was formed with thirty-five
members. We borrowed money from ALDEV to build this
factory, about 31,000 shillings. By 1958 we had 850 members
and were buying over half a million pounds of cherry which
women carried in on their heads.' Ripe coffee on the tree
looks like holly berries, only a bit larger; inside each red
'cherry', whose flesh must be removed by pulping, lie two
hard beans wrapped in a 'parchment' skin. 'Our factory
manager was told to pay only for good cherry and to reject
anything bad,' the president continued. 'Last year we sent
away 983 bags of parchment coffee. We took a cess of ten per
cent and paid back all the loan. Now we take eight per cent
which pays our expenses. In addition, we grow coffee seedlings
which we sell at a small profit. Every member must buy his
seedlings here.

'Our troubles? First, there is theft. People steal our seedlings.
Then, our members are angry when the manager tells them
to throw away some of their cherry. Now we have a manager
who was a prison warder. Since he fought one or two of the
angry farmers, people are afraid to argue with him.'

132

All the societies are united in a Union which has lorries to collect the beans, sheds to store them and a staff to move them to Nairobi, where they are sold at auction with all the other coffee, whether grown by Africans or Europeans. The various African Unions are members of the Kenya Coffee Planters' Union which handles all coffee grown in the country by members of any race. This district alone has over 10,000 growers, with about 2,000 acres of coffee between them in plots of a few hundred trees.

v

In July, 1957, the local agricolas resigned their previous direct control over the societies to the newly-formed Elgon Nyanza Farmers' Co-operative Union, which embraced fourteen coffee societies in the district. Almost at once, standards began to deteriorate and in the following season the proportion of Elgon Nyanza coffee to reach the three top classes fell sharply. So did prices, of course, and the growers began to complain: but instead of blaming their own slackness, the cry of 'discrimination' was raised. Europeans in Nairobi, they said, were discriminating against African-grown coffee.

Things went from bad to worse until, in October, 1958, the D.C., Mr. Winser, summoned a *baraza* and told the growers that, unless there was a change of heart, he would cancel the powers of the societies and restore government control. In a leaflet he explained:

'The coffee industry in Elgon Nyanza has reached a critical stage.

'Despite advice tendered by the Government, the following state of affairs exists because of the failure of the co-operatives to act on this advice.

'There are many cases of bad husbandry which lowers the standard of the crop, e.g. failure to prune: failure to plant shade trees: failure to mulch: failure to manure: failure to spray: failure to prevent theft of seedlings: failure of members to pay their shares: failure to impose penalties on members who do not comply with co-operative regulations.

'Constant advice has been given. The response has been very disappointing. . . .

'It is the primary task of the Government to govern. This includes seeing that people increase in prosperity and that money is available for development.'

Mr. Winser then warned the growers that no one would be able to get new seedlings until he had put his plantation in order, and that no factory would have a licence unless it was properly run. Anyone who had not paid up his co-operative share was not a member and could have his coffee rooted up. And the societies must pay their contribution to the central Union, to whom they owed about £9,000.

'The Union is UMOJA,' the appeal concluded. 'The Government wants to help the co-operatives. The Government wants the co-operatives themselves to look after the coffee. But if the co-operatives cannot do this, the Government will have to take over. The Government will provide advice, support and loans to the Union. The societies are asked to follow this advice and pay their shares. It isn't difficult. The Union is UMOJA. Umoja is strength! Umoja is wealth!'

This appeal, followed by action, led to some improvements. 'But I wouldn't say we are out of the wood,' was Mr. Winser's summing-up.

It is an observation widely made that Africans in authority, when answerable not to some superior authority (as chiefs to the Government) but to their fellows, will seldom insist upon awkward and unpopular measures. And the difficulties of so doing are greater than most Europeans recognize. Like veins under the skin, a complex network of relationships underlies the surface of life. Omukasi fails to mulch his coffee properly; one of the committee elders is negotiating for Omukasi's daughter on behalf of his son; if there is trouble about mulching, Omukasi will take offence and refuse to part with his daughter. But the girl is with child already, a child that should belong to the committee elder's clan. How much more important is this than a detail about covering tree-roots with old banana leaves! As for coffee prices in Nairobi, that is something quite remote and uncontrollable, the business of Europeans; to suggest that it depends upon putting old banana leaves round the roots of a tree is far-fetched. Even if banana leaves *are* beneficial, Omukasi's few head-loads of berries can hardly influence the matter. The question of the marriage is obviously an infinitely greater one, and the women will not keep silent about it; the committee elder simply cannot afford to offend Omukasi by making a fuss about his mulch.

That may be how things work, and it is all very understandable; it is also difficult to run co-operatives on those lines. It is arguable that most people would prefer a more direct, authoritarian system, by which Omukasi was ordered to mulch his coffee by the agent of a Government not concerned with marriages and the network of relationships, so that awkwardness between neighbours and relatives would not arise. Nevertheless it is the policy of the Government to foster co-operatives as training-grounds of democracy: an honourable policy, but only a confirmed optimist would see much future for them, at least as maintainers of quality, were the ultimate direction of an outside authority removed.

After our meeting we adjourned to the president's house, which commanded a superb view over the rolling foothills of Mt. Elgon and towards its forested peak. His senior wife, a well-proportioned mother of nine with a soft, gentle voice, a gay blue dress and a manner charming, dignified and self-possessed, served us with tea. All the family, it transpired, were strict Quakers and would not touch alcoholic drink in any form. 'But your husband has two wives,' I remarked. 'Don't the Quakers object?' She looked blank. 'What is wrong with that?' I asked her if she had been pleased when her husband took a second wife. She roared with laughter at such an idiotic question. 'Of course I was glad, she helps me with everything.' Polygamy solves the baby-sitting problem, anyway.

VI

The Teso people are bisected by the border between Kenya and Uganda, but they do not appear to mind. Here you are about as far as you can get from Nairobi and the political temperature is low. In the whole district of Elgon Nyanza, land enclosure has proceeded of its own volition, during the

last six months, to the extent that within a year nearly all its
habitable lands will be marked out into farms averaging
about fifteen or twenty acres.

Chief Alexander took me round in his Consul—he has a
farm of five hundred acres, so does not have to rely solely on
his official salary—and we passed at regular intervals traces
cut in the bush and flagged sticks, each indicating the boundaries of a farm. Already the people had planted sisal hedges
in the traces. Under a tree we met the land elders, locally
called the *lokalip*, who had brought all this about.

There had been a plague of land cases, the senior *lokalip*
said; people had wasted their substance on litigation, so chiefs
and elders had asked: 'How will you pay your children's school
fees if you go on like this?' The people had agreed to exchange
fragments and to mark out straight lines.

'Now this has been completed and the people want the
land to be surveyed and registered.' A thin, energetic man
in a white robe acted as spokesman: he was *lokalip* Antonio,
under whose vigorous leadership demarcation of every holding
was completed among the Teso in five months. All the
Government did directly was to insist on straight lines, and
help lay out roads.

What about inheritance? That set off the usual discussion,
the outcome of which was that a man might give his eldest
son a portion of the land but tell the other sons to seek a living
elsewhere. 'We know the land must not be subdivided, and
that on little *shambas* the soil gets tired and people cannot
live.'

'Visitors' flannel,' commented the district officer laconi-
cally. 'They mean to subdivide.'

We lunched with the Radia family who operate a cotton
ginnery, oil-extraction plant and soap factory which gives
employment to about 150 people and provides the sole
local outlet for the cotton crop everyone is anxious to foster.
The luncheon was based upon a succulent curry full of spices
flown from India to Nairobi and thence by rail to Malakisi,
to be skilfully blended by the sari'd ladies who did not come
to share the meal. Fruits pickled in heavy syrup and sweet
confections were rounded off by cardamom seeds which left

a sharp, clean spiciness on the palate. One of the sons of the house had studied engineering in Bombay and brought home a lovely bride from India, all in white, who looked about fourteen. After the urban bustle of Bombay, this isolated spot in the bush must have appeared as a station on the Roman Wall to a sophisticated Etruscan.

The factory was efficiently run but seemed like something in the early days of the industrial revolution, with gins fed by hand—no electricity—and soap wrapped very slowly, bar by bar. 'A machine? Yes, of course there are machines, but it would cost £10,000 to erect one and it is far cheaper to wrap the soap by hand.'

With us, to inspect the factory, came an eager fellow-journalist, the self-appointed Bungoma correspondent of the *East African Standard*. 'He used to wander about telling stories for his keep, like a medieval troubadour, except that he didn't sing. A rare bird—a man apart, possibly a little fey.' So I was told. Then he married a schoolteacher and could not roam so much, but is still at heart a wanderer and question-asker. In his largely self-taught English, he started to send stories to the *East African Standard* and some were worth printing. He seems to have a natural flair for news. 'My last story was about a rat that stole ten thousand shillings,' he said with justifiable pride. 'The Indian thought he was being burgled and hid in the room. The notes were locked in a drawer. Then he saw a rat carrying one away and discovered a secret passage into the drawer.'

Now Mr. Hezekiah Wepukhulu has applied for a British Council bursary to study journalism in Britain. He will make good use of it, should his application succeed.

VII

Five years ago Bungoma was just a ridge on the plain below Mt. Elgon's foothills; now it is a thriving town with shops, a stadium, schools, Indians and twenty-six Europeans, all civil servants. Its glory is a hall built in modern style for the District Council by a young architect in Kitale at a cost of £26,000, with handsome panelling in Kenya timbers, probably the most imposing rural council hall in the country. In a district where the average annual income per family is 214 shillings—the highest in the province, in North Nyanza it is only 42—this seems a lot to pay for a hall.

Are the people proud of it, or do they grumble at its extravagance? A bit of both, probably; now the Councillors have got used to their imposing chamber, they feel it adds dignity to their deliberations. Most of their money, as usual, goes on schools. They have a scheme whereby the Council provides timber and corrugated iron for the roofs, and the buildings are put up by the citizens, who work without pay. Scores of primary schools have appeared in this manner, every one packed with blue-clad children.

'What will they all do?' I inquired of the District Councillors whom I met in their red and blue hall. Unemployment is rife among the semi-educated, who hope for and expect office jobs which simply do not exist in Nyanza, or indeed anywhere else.

The Councillors shrugged their shoulders. 'That is our greatest difficulty. We need industries. There is nothing here.'

Another added: 'And soon there will be no more land. Then they must take it from the Europeans.'

The Council was a lively body, the usual mixture of one-third government nominees and two-thirds elected members. The nominees, mostly chiefs, did not seem to be yes-men by any means. The chairman of the finance committee was one of the chiefs: fluent, incisive, portly, quick and commanding, he gave an analysis of the situation in Elgon Nyanza that was balanced but by no means complacent.

'Our most pressing need, next to industries, is to find capital to improve our farms. Look at the poll-tax graph: in 1956, over 3,000 people had paid by the end of January; in 1957, only 2,000; last year the number was less than 1,000. We must find ways of getting money into the district. I have been a chief for twelve years and I am worried and puzzled.'

An elected Councillor and teacher—they are nearly all teachers—echoed his words. 'And then, another trouble is, our schools are too academic. There is not enough technical training. If we had more boys who could use their hands, they could improve the farms; as it is, they must leave the district to find work, and now they cannot find it even outside.'

Then the secretary of the coffee co-operative union spoke. 'The Government has not spent enough on capital improvements. Nor has it done enough to encourage cash crops. And then there is discrimination. There are many rules for Africans who plant coffee, some of them are exaggerated, and Europeans do not have the same rules. This is unfair.'

It is quite true that certain coffee rules, designed to safeguard the crop's health and quality, are not applied to Europeans—for example, that which ordains that every tree must be planted in a hole 'three by three by three'. Europeans, it is felt, can, or at any rate should, look after themselves. If their trees do not thrive, that is their funeral; whereas if African hopes are dashed, and four years' labour thrown away, the whole project will collapse. But it is hard to put this over, and many dismiss it as one more argument to explain away one law for whites and another for blacks.

A canon of the church then spoke, an old man, erect as a tree, with more of the bearing of a sergeant-major than a divine. 'Every farmer,' he announced, 'is given three boxes: one is called Central Government, one is called District Council, the third is called Location Council. These he must fill. And those boxes become heavier and heavier until the farmer is weighed down by them and crushed. The Government should show him how to fill those boxes, but all they say to him is dig! dig! dig! dig! DIG! DIG!' Loud applause endorsed this plaint.

'The coffee union secretary is right,' cried another Councillor. 'The rules are too harsh. I live on Mt. Elgon, and if I am to grow coffee I must clear the heavy bush. But there is a rule that no one may burn bush or forest. How can I clear my land unless I can burn?'

This question electrified the canon. 'What is this,' he cried, 'about burning on Mt. Elgon? What about the grazing for my cattle which are pastured there?'

The annual income of this council is about £250,000, but although it has been in existence only for some four years it has run into plenty of trouble. A previous treasurer was

arraigned on twenty-one charges of forging tax receipts, and
left the coffers empty. Then a contract for a stadium was
awarded, against impassioned official advice, to a builder
whose only qualification appears to have been that of race;
the stadium cost £13,000, and the first serious storm blew
its roof away. Although the African builder was bound by
contract to renew the roof he went bankrupt, and there the
roofless building stands, rotting quickly away, a sad white
elephant. Now this District Council, equipped with a financial
adviser from the Mitcham borough council, has made local
history: it has become the first in Kenya to divest itself of its
official chairman and to elect an African Councillor to that
office. Others are expected soon to follow suit.

VIII

Almost everything a farmer in the province of Nyanza can
grow will be bought, stored, graded, moved and sold by a
body called the Nyanza Marketing Board, one of whose
main buying centres has been set up at Bungoma. Before it
existed, everything was in the hands of Asian traders. Sometimes they bought up the whole crop at harvest time, stored
it, and then sold part of it back to the people for food, in
the hungry season, for three times the price. What the Board
has done is to reduce the Asian trader's share of the market
to less than one-fifth, to encourage the growth of maize
co-operatives and to foster the African trader, who now
handles over half the produce. This they have achieved
mainly by giving short-term loans to African traders. The
Board's inspectors visit every market and sample every sack
of produce they buy. Naturally the rejection of poor quality
stuff has caused bad feeling and the Board is often unpopular,
but their policy has paid, and the whole of their last maize
shipment to Nairobi fetched top prices.

At the head of this successful enterprise is a man who
learnt his trade not in any academic chair or government
office, but by collecting old bones from all over Nyanza,
even hippo's from the lake shore, grinding them, and selling
bone meal to European farmers during the hungry thirties.

So there is not much Mr. Stanley Everett does not know about Nyanza province and its inhabitants. Agents of his Board, African or Asian, buy at the markets on commission, then the grain is fumigated, dried and stored until someone on the end of a telephone in Kisumu sells it to people in Uganda or Tanganyika or the Belgian Congo, or in London, Hamburg or New York.

By far the most important crop is maize, which accounted last year for over £1 million of a total of £1½ million handled by the Board. One-tenth of the Board's income is put into a stabilization fund to support any crop that may suddenly go into a decline.

The stabilization fund has already proved useful: a sudden spurt in China's groundnut production (from 2¼ to 7 million tons) collapsed the price by 17s. 6d. a bag, but the Board was able to cushion the shock to growers who had never even heard of China, but would have been quick to see in this disaster the machinations of Asian traders or of Europeans. Smaller fluctuations can be cushioned by storage; egg prices normally fall, for instance, during Ramadan, and millet prices just before the cotton harvest in Uganda, when everyone has run out of money. These Nyanza farmers are perhaps more fortunate than they realize, first in finding a buyer for almost everything they grow, and secondly in getting as fair a reward for their labours as the vagaries of world markets will allow.

CHAPTER 9

South Nyanza

I

WHEN Mr. Rimington was a boy his father, a D.C., was posted to Kisii, the headquarters of South Nyanza district. The family set out from Kisumu in canoes with their baggage, and chanting paddlers took them down the papyrus-fringed lake to a little fishing village on Homa bay. The D.C., his wife and two children then walked about seventy miles through grass that met above their heads until they reached the Kisii *boma*. The last incumbent had been speared, though not fatally, by Kisii warriors, and the one before that, the first administrator, had died of blackwater fever. When Mr. Rimington inserted the key into the lock of the mud house he had inherited the door fell in; white ants had eaten it away—they had even gnawed down the flag-pole.

All touring then was done on foot, no roads existed, and ponies died from tsetse-borne trypanosomiasis. Mrs. Rimington and her children stayed behind in the *boma*; they had no choice. Kisumu lay beyond a number of unbridged rivers. Now and again a doctor visited them on tour, but a runner might take three days or more to reach headquarters. Elephants and all forms of game abounded in the bush-clad, fertile, steamy river valleys and the forested hills.

I reached Kisii from Kisumu along an excellent road in two hours and found a thriving township with over sixty Europeans, a comfortable hotel, new bungalows and offices. The only relic of the past is a humble little mud building, looking like a tramp in a garden suburb, which is the old *boma*. In 1914 it was captured by the Germans after a battle whose casualties, German and British, lie together in the graveyard. There is not a wild animal within fifty miles, except reptiles—the head agricola, Mr. Victor Burke, killed seven cobras on and around his veranda in one week. During the Emergency, while at Meru, he had captured a Mau Mau general; both seem a far cry from farm plans, but he took it all in an easy stride.

Near the *boma* the population is almost as dense as in Maragoli. This is the country of a Bantu people, numbering about 270,000, who have some skill in the making of animal figures from a soapstone which can be worked with a knife and hardens in the sun, and of stools set with beads. They have occupied the rich, fertile highlands, leaving the Luo to manage with the low-lying plains near the lake. Although the two tribes have lived cheek-by-jowl for several generations they scarcely ever inter-marry and will not share the same schools. It is not only people of different races who resist integration, it is people of different tribes as well.

Practically the whole of the Kisii highlands are now enclosed by hedges of Mauritius thorn and all the steep hillsides—they are very steep—stepped with narrow bench-terraces made by laying armfuls of trash, such as maize stover, across the slope. When it rains—which it does frequently, the rainfall being about 70 inches—top-soil comes down to mingle with the trash and form a little bund. This process continues until a series of benches comes into being. Thus the rain does most of the work for the Kisii, rather than their picks and muscles.

II

Gilbert, a young, English-speaking instructor trained at Siriba, took me to see some of the farmers. He wore his beret at a dashing angle and evidently took much pride in his work. We came first to a man with five wives.

'This man is a good psychologist,' said Gilbert. 'He understands how to control his wives. This is difficult in a polygamous family because the senior wife wants the biggest share. This husband doesn't allow that. All share equally. Also, they all decide what is to be done together; he listens to them, and does not merely tell them what to do.'

The wives confirmed this. 'When the coffee money comes

in we meet together,' said the senior wife, 'and agree on the most important things to be done. First come school fees and taxes. Then things needed for the farm. After that, each of us gets something for her labour, perhaps twenty shillings, and the rest goes into the bank.'

Each had her train of five or six children and a baby on her back or on the way. Their husband was an elderly man with twelve acres, inherited from his father, which supports them all: 420 coffee trees produce the necessary cash, and a herd of six cows, one bull and thirteen sheep and goats graze the rich star-grass pastures. His sheep, he said, were kept mainly for sacrifices.

What sacrifices, I inquired? Circumcision, marriage contracts, illness or ill-fortune, or the visit of a relative. 'But when a mother-in-law comes, that is a big event, and then an ox must be slaughtered.' With five mothers-in-law, these must be expensive visits.

'When my mother-in-law came to visit me soon after I was married,' Gilbert added, 'I had to get leave to greet her. A man must never neglect his mother-in-law.' I asked how long she had stayed. 'Hers was a short visit, about one year.' 'That would seem a long visit to a European.' 'Oh, no, it is not long; sometimes a mother-in-law stays two years; it is as she pleases.'

Five wives, twelve acres, at least a dozen sons—what would follow his demise? 'Each wife will get her share of the land and her sons will inherit it.' Simple arithmetic suggests that in the next generation the fragments will be down to fractions of an acre and the whole work of land reform undone.

Gilbert quite agreed. 'The customs of the people are at war with the needs of the land. Until recently there was land for everyone because the Kisii took it from the bush. There was a system for dealing with the land. First were the *etureti* elders, the heads of clans, who gave permission to any landless man to cultivate for his lifetime. No one could buy or sell land, but they could exchange or borrow pieces. All disputes were settled by the *egesaku* elders who dealt with groups and listened to appeals from the *etureti*. If a man refused the

17 'Water is the mother of us all': a sand river in Ukambani, where you must dig to find moisture

18 Dams are the first step towards recovery, and the Kamba people help to make them with voluntary labour

judgement of the elders he could use the *rigio* oath to curse
the land by throwing down a pot with holes in it, and then
no one from his own clan could cultivate there.'

III

In the coffee and pyrethrum belt farms of nine, ten, twelve
acres are the rule, but down below in a location called Kituti
the average holding is little more than two acres, the rate of
stocking two beasts to three acres. Further sub-division is
impossible, in fact many holdings ought to be pooled. It is
the old story. And, while Progress marches on, some administrators are gloomy.

'Consolidation will be a flash in the pan,' one of them
opined, 'because it hasn't sprung up from the people, it's
been imposed. The crying need is for some outlet to drain the
population off the land. In Europe, an industrial revolution
accompanied enclosures; people found employment in the
towns. They can't here. That's the vital, all-important need—
to start industries on a scale no one has dreamed of. Yes, we
lack minerals and cheap power. But what about modern
industries that don't need minerals, things like plastics,
artificial fibres and so on? Even on a smaller scale, we could
do more. There's plenty of sugar-cane, for instance: how
about making rum? Industrial alcohol? We need a new
approach. . . .

'Meanwhile, there's still some land available, this overcrowding is in pockets. The country's honeycombed with land
barriers. For instance, these people have their eye on the
Masai reserve. There it is, an area nearly half as big again
as the whole of the white highlands and producing nothing
at all.* Some of it's arid and the Masai have turned it into
desert, but there's also splendid agricultural land. Open it up,
let the Kisii and the Luo and the Maragoli pour down there.
There are 83,000 Masai on fifteen thousand square miles.
They'll have to disappear.'

Some attempts to relieve pressure by siphoning people on

*The Masai reserve covers 15,232 square miles, land alienated to
Europeans covers 11,579 square miles.

to empty lands have failed. In the south of the district is an almost uninhabited area called the Lambwe valley, fertile and well-watered with a rainfall of over fifty inches. ALDEV spent a lot of money there in clearing bush, putting down bore-holes and getting rid of tsetse fly, and in 1952 they invited Luo settlers in on fifty-acre plots. Very few came. It was too far away and too dangerous, with buffalo still lingering in the valleys and all sorts of unknown perils in the hills. ALDEV spent more money, cleared barriers against tsetse, made roads, and reduced the plots to twenty-five acres. A few local Luo trickled in, but still scarcely any from the overcrowded areas farther north.

At last the Government decided to open the valley to people from other tribes who badly wanted to come, Maragoli and such. The Luo were appalled, and protested strongly. The Lambwe valley lies in their land unit and, although they did not appear to want it themselves, they were determined that no one else should have it.

Either the scheme must be closed down, said the Government, or it must be opened to men of other tribes. The Luo did not hesitate to choose the first alternative.

IV

Kisii is the oldest African coffee-growing area in Kenya; as long ago as 1933, the first nursery was started by the District Council. But in 1936 an outbreak of coffee berry disease wiped out the plantations on the European farms at Sotik and all the trees had to be uprooted and replaced with a disease-resistant variety called Blue Mountain. Only this, or a new variety called K7 bred at the research station near Nairobi, may now be planted in Kisii.

There is no better coffee land in the country, with its deep, rich volcanic soil and its ample and reliable rainfall, and the growers are proud of their achievements. There are 10,000 of them, organized in twenty-five co-operative societies—the standard pattern. From a small start in 1942 the Kisii Co-operative Union has progressed to handle £155,000 worth of beans, and in a few years this figure will rise to over

£1,000,000. Its instructors circulate continually from *shamba* to *shamba* to exhort their owners to care for the trees, under the eye of committees elected by the societies' members.

Nevertheless the quality, as in the north, has been declining, and now only one-third of Kisii coffee qualifies for the first three classes. The reasons are the same as elsewhere. 'They must learn to be tougher with each other,' said the European coffee officer. Can people learn to behave in a different way in their economic lives from the way they choose to behave socially? That remains to be seen.

Another weak point in Kisii economy lies in their livestock. 'Farming is advancing on one leg,' remarked an agricola. The veterinary station concentrates entirely on the local breed—no Sahiwals or exotics—to show what can be done when they are properly handled. Several native cows have trebled their previous yields solely through good management, and their daughters show even greater promise.

It was a pleasure to see their neat, small-boned calves, each in its clean compartment, sleek and twice the normal size, simply because they get enough milk. They need only about half as much milk as an exotic. The parties of Kisii farmers who come continually to see round have one basic lesson drilled into them: make sure your calves get enough to eat through the mother. On these lush pastures it should be easy, yet very few practise what the vets preach. These pastures mainly occupy the higher zones, above the coffee belt, and here one sees now and then a patch of white pyrethrum flowers. I met the members of a flourishing co-operative society of growers who have already planted, between them, a thousand acres of the daisy, mostly over 7,500 feet where very little else will thrive.

v

'This is the finest location hall in Kenya,' said Chief Zachariah with pride. 'We of Kituti location raised all the money ourselves; it cost £5,000. Now the people gather every Monday morning and we discuss any business anyone wants to raise. And people come here to pay their taxes: the district tax, the location tax, and the special education rate, in all 29 shillings.'

The location, a subdivision of the district, is an active unit of government; it has an elected council presided over by a chief, and a staff of clerks and officials. A rural district council is its nearest British equivalent. The chief is a cross between clerk to the council and its chairman, but is paid by the central Government. Chief Zachariah is a member of the Coffee Board of Kenya which markets £10 million worth of coffee annually and, at his Monday gathering, he reads out the weekly coffee market reports sent up from Nairobi.

Above the location council stands the District Council, equivalent of a British County Council. The clerk to the South Nyanza council is a local notable, Mr. Paul Mboya, M.B.E., the author of a number of books on Luo custom and on local government. A heavily-built, affable person, he presides over an efficient office full of maps, files, reports, clerks and typewriters, and will conduct visitors through a council hall hung with oil paintings of chiefs, past and present. He must get tired of being asked if he is related to Kenya's nationalist leader. The answer is that he is not. Some thirty years ago, when he was a Seventh Day Adventist minister, he visited Rusinga island in Lake Victoria. A son was born to the parishioners with whom he spent the night.

'It is a Luo custom to name a child after any distinguished visitor who may be staying at the time,' Mr. Mboya remarked. 'So he was given my name. His father was a teacher in a Seventh Day Adventist school.' I asked him whether the beaded cap which Mr. Tom Mboya often wears is really part of traditional Luo costume, as the nationalist leader claims. 'It was worn by old women,' he said. And added: 'Here we do not oppose the Government, we work with it. But what does Tom know of our needs? He does not come here, he stays in Nairobi. How can he represent us when he does not come to ask us what we want?'

VI

West of Kisii the hills decline, in stages, into the lake basin, and in place of deep star-grass pastures and high fertility you once again encounter coarse, sandy soil, twisted combretum bush, flat-topped thorns, tufted grasses and flatness with bumpy little hills. You are back among the round euphorbia *bomas* of the Luo. Their hefty, black, snaggletoothed, small-eared appearance is unmistakable, and the upright, masculine look of their pipe-smoking women.

I met a group of sugar-growers at a little factory, run by the agricolas until such time as they can get a co-operative going, which makes jaggery. This is simply cane juice boiled up in vats and set in moulds, whence it emerges in brown lumps the shape and size of Christmas puddings. The Luo are not very anxious to form co-operatives; they take the line that these things should be done for them. 'The Government should pay more for cane, the price is too low,' said a spokesman. 'And we need more factories. Is there to be a white sugar factory? It was left to the Government to decide. . . .'

The story of the white sugar factory is a sad one. Very large areas of south Nyanza, which runs to over 3,000 square miles, are suitable for cane-growing, and a biggish industry could be developed, but refineries cost a great deal of money—at least a quarter of a million pounds. Both in Kenya and Uganda the sugar industry is in Asian hands. A respected and efficient Asian firm from Uganda displayed an interest in South Nyanza, and the Government encouraged it to draw up a scheme. But no firm could invest a great deal of money without a guarantee of regular cane supplies. To depend wholly on peasant production would be too risky; at the best it fluctuates unpredictably and at the worst a disagreement about prices, or even a political storm, might at any minute lead the growers to withhold supplies. The Uganda firm therefore stipulated that they must lease from the Luo, for a generous rent, 2,000 acres on which to grow their own reserve of cane.

The offer was a fair one in the Government view and they urged the Luo to accept it, but the usual cry was started of a plot to steal the land, and it was rejected out of hand by the District Council. So the cane potential of the district languishes. Moreover the price paid for such cane as three small jaggery factories can absorb is only one-third of that which could be paid for cane treated in a white sugar factory.

VII

Chief Zephaniah entertained me on the veranda of his well-built, European-style house to a lavish feast of fish-and-chips and an iced cake baked by his wife, who leads the local Maendeleo club. The chief was large and black and strong and with him was an instructor even larger and stronger; one can see why this location is in the lead—it would be rash to disobey either of these progressive gentlemen. Here the agricolas' message is to plant early, which makes all the difference to the cotton crop—they reckon yields could be increased tenfold merely by following a few simple rules of husbandry. And they would like to see a thousand tractors, instead of three, at work on these plains.

We called on a Better Farmer, Ishmael Juma, an oldish cotton grower with four wives. His senior wife invited me into her hut, built in the traditional Luo style; round, mud-walled, without windows. Inside was a circular wall of hurdles enclosing the central fire and three cooking stones. In the space between the inner and outer walls the wife and her small children slept on Kavirondo matting. One section was divided off to make a store, and in it was a pile of cotton, her own personal share of the crop. Each of his wives, said Ishmael, received the same share, and each grew the food to feed her own children.

'Do your wives ever ask you to build improved houses?' I inquired. 'They do so every day.' 'And what is your answer?' 'That I will do so when I have the money. I have put in for a loan, but there are many things to spend it on—a cart, labour to put up fences, a water tank. . . .'

Water is a difficulty: plenty of rain falls, but it runs away untrapped. Now a campaign to build self-help dams is under way. The plan is so to site the dams that every homestead will be within two and a half miles of one, and that for each dam the people build themselves, ALDEV will build another.

We passed a self-help dam on which the people were

150

working lustily and with apparent enjoyment. Some were hacking at the soil with their short-handled hoes, the shape of a wish-bone; others were scooping the earth into round metal basins called *kerais*, and gaily-clothed girls were carrying these vessels on their heads along the barrier to deposit the contents at the farther end. Everyone from one *jokokwaru* was there, old women and young girls, chiefs and children, working each according to his capacity and singing away like birds.

At evening, on the way home, we called upon a colony of pelicans in a single fig-tree growing in a gully, about twelve miles from the lake. The birds flock to this particular tree, and no other, to nest and to spend the night, commuting every day to the lake for the fishing. The tree's branches and the ground beneath are white with droppings and the foliage alive with these giant birds, like huge white fruit among the leaves—a bird-watcher counted over seventy.

Pelicans appear to be such cumbrous, gawky, lumbering creatures that it was astonishing to see how gracefully they came in to land on a nest, braking with their wings and judging speed and height to a hair's breadth. They drifted down into the nest like a leaf on a breeze. As we watched, the western sky behind them turned smoky red and then a deep, sultry, reddish-purple as if half the world was on fire, and the birds' white plumage was tinted with the glow. A purple haze enveloped the sky and the birds went on circling and settling in with a good deal of talk and flurry; one could imagine them as great white spirits coming home to their ghost-town—smelling distinctly fishy, and sometimes arguing over whose perch was which. Nearby is a small market called Oyugi's after a giant hero of olden days; but no one I questioned could remember any stories of his deeds.

CHAPTER 10

Masai Herds and Mara Lions

I

THE Masai have won respect by their contempt for civilization and all that it has offered them. For half a century Europeans have been tempting them with all the material bribes, indeed even non-material ones, for which every Bantu and Nilotic people is avid. There is scarcely an African of the fat lands who would not sell his soul for a school certificate. The Masai have rejected school certificates with a proud and lofty disdain.

Will a certificate fatten a bullock or swell the belly of a cow? Masai hearts are with their cattle; they desire no finer destiny for a son than to walk in the dust of a larger herd than his father's. The young man who dreams of glory sees fine white bulls and brindled cows and green grass knee-high, he does not see the stone bungalow, the shining motor-car, the well-cut suit, the framed diploma so alluring to his darker fellow-countrymen. He likes to wear his hair in matted pigtails smeared with red ochre and rancid butter, to stand with one foot against the other knee, to eat a compound of bullock's blood and curdled milk, to carry his long spear and to keep his women in their beads and coils and fly-infested mud burrow as his ancestors did—those ancestors whose lion head-dresses and painted shields filled the hearts of lesser breeds with terror, and won the right of conquest over the steppes of eastern Africa from their northern Somali deserts to their southern tsetse bush.

For the Masai have pride, and pride is a quality we recoil from in ourselves and half-admire, half-deplore in others. An Englishman today must stamp with the hob-nail boots of equality upon the little shoots of pride that cannot help but spring up in his heart; but when he sees the fine, free growth of it in others, an envious respect attacks him. For

Westerners the Masai have become the symbol of a vanished aristocracy, a lost cause they can afford to keep as a household pet who has the spunk to stand up to its master.

The Masai way of life is certainly doomed. For a while it may continue, but nothing in the end can resist the pressures of Western materialism. The British have protected it by freezing a tribal pattern of land ownership, enshrined in a treaty to which the Masai hold with all the desperation of a man clinging to a raft when the waters are rising. That treaty, which confirms them in possession of their grazing-grounds 'for ever', was made to keep out Europeans. Now it is no longer white settlers who threaten them, but black ones. Will a treaty made for the one purpose serve for the other? Only while the British enforce it; when politicians of the land-hungry Kikuyu and Luo peoples occupy the seats of power in Nairobi, the borders of Masailand seem unlikely to remain intact.

For here lie the last reserves of fertile, well-watered and unused land in Kenya, hitherto protected by the strongest guardian of the land in Africa: the tsetse fly. In the last ten years, modern techniques of mastering tsetse-borne diseases, and the tsetse fly itself, have reached a point where all this land could be thrown open to settlement. The question now is partly one of expense, and partly of politics. The Masai themselves do not cultivate. So long as their treaty with the British Government holds good, they will resist to the last man the opening of their land to settlement by the cultivating tribes.

II

The Tanganyika–Kenya border cuts through the Masai's territory, most of which is open, semi-arid grassland useless for any purpose other than seasonal grazing by scrub cattle, even if water could be tapped by boreholes. But in the west, where Masailand approaches Lake Victoria, and on the Mau escarpment's south-western slopes, soil and rainfall would support a sizeable population of cultivators.

The Masai, numbering about 85,000, keep about one

million head of scrub cattle, and 660,000 sheep and goats.
They *could* export fat steers and lambs, but have done next to
nothing to improve the quality of their animals. This is
because they do not need the cash. There are old men living
in mud hovels with little but ear-rings, a spear and a blanket
who could at any minute realize several thousand pounds
for their cattle. Scarcely one of them could not afford a motor-
car if he wanted one, probably a Jaguar at that. The plain
fact is they do not want motor-cars, or beds, or kitchen sinks,
or radios, or refrigerators, or washing machines: they just
want cattle, which they have, and which the processes of
nature will increase for them without their having to do any
disagreeable work.

It is an *impasse*. The whole machinery of modern society,
modern trade, modern development, has been halted by the
Masai's refusal to keep up with the Jones's, or the Kamaus
in this case. It is like a great Britannia aircraft grounded by a
midge in the works. Modern civilization runs on avarice as
cars on petrol, and if there is no pump where you can fill up
with avarice, you simply stay where you are.

But even the Masai are not really free of avarice: it merely
takes a different form. If they do not want bicycles and
trousers, they do want more cattle, and this has led them
into a great error. Instead of rejecting everything the West
offered them, they accepted the hypodermic syringe of the
vets. First of all the vets put an end to rinderpest, and then,
rather less successfully, dealt with various other diseases that
were keeping their herds in check.

No doubt it would have needed superhuman self-denial on
the part of the Masai to have rejected this magical means of
ending the periodic epidemics that had wiped out all but a
rump of their cherished herds. Yet these were the means by
which nature had kept herds and habitat in balance. Vegetation, controlled by constant factors like rainfall and soil
structure, cannot multiply as creatures of the animal kingdom
can, and do. The fact remains that to accept the vet's syringe
was fatal to the Masai, and to offer it to them, as the Government did, without also insisting upon some means of keeping
down the livestock population, was an act of remarkable

imbecility—or perhaps not remarkable, since nothing has been more characteristic of the half-century of European intervention in Africa than the slap-happy introduction of bright, well-meaning ideas by enthusiasts of all kinds, without any regard for their long-term consequences.

Anyway, vets controlled diseases, livestock multiplied and their hoofs and mouths destroyed the precarious grass cover of the plains. The result is that, except where the tsetse fly remains in control, the Masai are living in country poised upon the edge of deserthood. Some of it has gone over the edge, some hovers on the borderline, some has not reached it yet. And so pressure mounts upon those regions that are still protected by the tsetse fly.

Overcrowded people outside want to get in, overstocked Masai themselves want to take their herds where grazing is still rich and deep. If either succeed, unless they adopt very different methods, they will destroy those regions as surely as they have damaged their present inheritance. Agricolas and vets do not want to see these last remaining areas opened up without strict control. But governments are terrified of controlling anyone by what may be represented as harsh measures, and administrators have inclined to caution since the Masai speared to death a D.C. who was persuading them to sell some steers. So the matter, like many others, rests in a state of suspended flux, and everyone hopes for good rains.

III

Down on the Kenya–Tanganyika border, not so very long ago, there lived an Englishman who kept in touch with the world by carrier-pigeon. For three or four months of the year no vehicle could reach him, and even in the dry weather it was a long, hard, bumpy seventy-mile journey from Narok, where the road ends. The aeroplane has changed all that. An hour's pleasant flight from Nairobi brought us comfortably to rest beside a tributary of the Mara river.

First we flew over the Mau, that range of mountains forming the south-western wall of the Rift Valley. Covered with forests of cedars and olives and, higher up, of bamboos, the

Mau is the source of all the rivers watering the western half of Masailand, Kipsigis and part of the Rift Valley. The birthplace of innumerable streams, it is, in theory, protected by its status as a forest reserve.

Looking out from the small yellow aircraft expertly handled by June Wright, one of the best commercial pilots in East Africa, one could quickly see how different theory was from practice, here as elsewhere. In a forest reserve no one is allowed to fell trees, cultivate, start fires or graze livestock. In less than half an hour, I counted seventeen active fires and saw the shambles created by innumerable others. Whole ridgebacks of the mountain, sticking up like black spines, were as bare as slag-heaps and already runnelled and creased by gully erosion. Older fires were still smoking in some of these devastated areas; one could see the forest being eaten into like a great fur pelt attacked by moths.

As sure as fate, one day there will be no more water for cattle in the streams below. 'God is punishing us,' will say the Masai: but it will not be God, it will be themselves. The streams are already shrinking and the Masai are driving their herds farther into the hills to find grazing. They cannot take cattle into forest and so they burn a way in. They are creeping upwards, spreading destruction as they go in order to escape the consequences of destruction they have already caused.

Other fires are started by honey-hunters who burn down trees to smoke out the bees. Often, in the forest, you can see blackened hollow cedars and olives killed by fires tucked into the roots. If the foliage is dry and the wind right, the fire will spread and get out of hand.

And then there are 'acceptees': a clumsy term given to men of other tribes who are settling in Masailand, family by family, with the permission of Masai elders. They are tenants: but it is very unlikely that they will ever go.

In South Nyanza and in Kipsigis it is reckoned that upwards of two thousand families a year are crossing the southern border into Masailand and Tanganyika. In recent years a good many Masai have married Kikuyu or Kamba wives because so many of their own women are sterile; at one time there was quite a trade in Kikuyu girl-children, exchanged for cattle. The Kikuyu and Kamba have brought in the habit of eating ground maize. And so when a man of some other tribe asks a Masai elder if he may cultivate a patch of land, and offers in return to supply maize, the elder will often agree. The cultivator will clear his patch and grow a crop; next season, he will ask permission to bring his wife and family; soon his cooking-stones, his household goods, his thatched hut are installed; he is there, probably for ever. His daughters may grow up to marry Masai men. That is the way the Masai doom will overtake them—as a people, as a warrior race.

Some of these acceptees, used to the cold, are creeping up into the Mau, burning the trees to make their *shambas* as they have done before in other places. Their actions are illegal, but there is no one to enforce the law and no one dares to do so. This country the Masai know to be theirs. If they agree to let people cultivate in the forest, who is the Government to gainsay them? Attempts to remove intruders might well be met by force, and that is a thing no Government dares to contemplate. It was an attempt to use force, after all, for the ultimate good of the people, that led to the Hola disaster. If the tenant were to be hurt, and the Masai to be angered, and a fracas to arise, denunciations of colonialist oppression and tyranny would thunder from the benches of the House of Commons and repercuss all through the Secretariat. So the Mau forests burn.

IV

From our camp on the Talek, a tributary of the Mara, Dr. Philip Glover showed us a little of a tsetse research project which combines the excitement of scientific discovery with that of tracking in the old-fashioned, footprint-in-the-sand way. A tough, enthusiastic and handsome young man called Jungle Smith, helped by several veterinary scouts, has cut traces in the bush to make a grid three miles square. Each trace has been cleared of vegetation so as to leave a path receptive to the footprints of animals.

Each morning, scouts patrol the grids with notebooks in which they enter every spoor they see. By about eleven o'clock the numbers and variety of every animal that had entered or left during the night had been recorded. From these notebooks Mr. Smith plots the movements of the game and eventually produces charts which show the numbers of each species that has visited the grid over the year, so that their seasonal behaviour can be observed. In the last six months about fifteen different species have been identified.

The next process is to capture flies in nets. Once you know the habits of your particular tsetse—there are eight species hereabouts and these were *Swynnertoni*—they are surprisingly easy to spot taking their ease in the bush; they cling underneath the branches of thorn-trees, and the trick is to peer against the light until you see their silhouettes. Each fly is then squashed on paper and dispatched to a laboratory in London where its blood is analysed with such accuracy that the kind of animal it has last fed on can be diagnosed. The object is to discover more about the relationship between game and insect, so as to arrive at ways of controlling tsetse flies which do not involve, as most current methods do, the wholesale destruction of animals and vegetation.

Before this work was done—and it is new in Kenya—people assumed that all forms of game acted as host to the tsetse and must therefore be wiped out if areas were to be cleared for cattle-ranching. This was the theory behind the appalling slaughter that has taken place in other parts of Africa in the interests of tsetse control. Kenya has never used this indiscriminate policy, but in Southern Rhodesia over 600,000 game animals have been shot by tsetse control officers working for the Government. These modern blood analyses have revealed some unexpected facts. Of all the flies squashed on the Talek and subsequently analysed, nearly 49 per cent had fed on warthog. Next in order came giraffe—a long way behind with 14 per cent; then buffalo with under 10 per cent. And at the very bottom of the list were waterbuck, bushbuck and impala, each with one single squashed fly out of over four hundred specimens.

The conclusion to be drawn is that many of the species mowed down with the rest in battues of indiscriminate slaughter need never have been shot at all. From a 'tryps' point of view they could have safely been ignored, at any rate until the researchers had discovered whether the fly, deprived of its normal food, would switch to other species. And tsetse flies are, in general, very conservative.

It seems to be a rule that people who enjoy their work grow fond of whatever creature, object or device they work with. One can understand shepherds becoming fond of sheep, or engine-drivers of locomotives, although it has always surprised me to find how attached sanitary engineers, for instance, appear to become to drains, or helminthologists to tapeworms. Following this rule, Jungle Smith had become devoted to tsetses; one of his amusements was to let a fly settle on his arm and bury its proboscis in his flesh, and to watch it gradually swell like an inflated balloon as it filled its belly with his blood. Then he gazed after it with affection as it lumbered off, replete, for a nice sleep, and no more blood-sucking for a couple of days. The gorging process took about two minutes.

v

Until the recent discovery of drugs which kill trypanosomes in the blood of infected animals, almost the only effective way of tackling tsetse-borne disease was to clear the bush so as to drive away the flies. The pioneer of this method—or rather methods; it became a complex science—was Mr. C. F. M. Swynnerton, for many years Game Warden and Director of Tsetse Research in Tanganyika and the father of the author of Kenya's present agrarian plan. For twenty years, bush-clearing held the field. Often it was found sufficient to cut down certain types of bush only, because of the fly's conservatism: each species likes so much shade, no more and no less, or certain kinds of tree.

All this time the fly was actually spreading. During a slow build-up of knowledge millions of flies were examined, weighed, fed on different foods; their wing-beats were counted, their rate of respiration graphed, the humidity of the soil in which they pupated was tested, their least preference or idiosyncrasy carefully recorded; thousands were marked with luminous paint to trace their movements; all over East Africa, people bicycled about the bush with sacks on their backs to attract them and grew to pensionable age catching them in nets, digging their pupae out of the sand, keeping them in test-tubes and cages, even studying micro-organisms which appeared to be their enemies.

Seldom has so much careful, detailed, expert study been given to one kind of insect. Some of the many facts discovered have been used ingeniously. Tsetse flies, for instance, probably mate only once in their lives. A current experiment is to expose a number of pupae to controlled doses of radiation which sterilizes them, and then to release the males so that gradually the fly population will die out.

The expense of bush-clearing is its principal handicap, and the quick regeneration of the bush. By itself, it could never have conquered tsetse fly in Africa. In recent years, chemists have discovered how to synthesize drugs which kill the trypanosomes in the blood, and which will prevent infection. The main drug in use at present, Antrycide pro-salt, will protect cattle for about four months.

No one doubts that, in time, the chemists will improve on this, and cattle-owners like the Masai will be able to take their herds anywhere they please. The battle is not yet wholly won; trypanosomes have already shown a tendency to develop resistance to the drugs, and there will no doubt be disappointments and setbacks. But, by and large, it can only be a matter of time before areas like the Mara are opened to hungry herds from overstocked pastures elsewhere.

Several experiments are under way to discover how things could be managed so as to avoid disaster to the land, and at the same time make a profit for its custodians. One such is the Ol Choro Oirowa ranch which the vets are running on behalf of the District Council at Narok. On some 21,000 acres young beasts were to be fattened and sold at a profit, but profits have been shy because of various setbacks, such as an outbreak of pleuro-pneumonia and an army worm invasion. Now it seems that the acreage is too small and the Masai have so far refused to enlarge it. So the vets have not yet succeeded in bringing home to the Masai cattle-owner the basic fact that

19 'Walking hat-racks' pick a bare existence off thornscrub but, on properly managed ranges, grass recovers and beasts grow fat

20 Before and after treatment: hillsides in Machakos, eroded by over-cultivation, regain fertility when terraced and enclosed

good management on modern ranching lines will bring him in hard cash.

I saw the ranch mainly from the air. Lines of bush, cleared by bulldozers dragging giant chains between them, lie neatly along the contour like windrows in a hayfield. Soon the six or seven thousand acres that have been cleared will be fenced, and so managed that star-grass will cover them and steers fatten twice as quickly as they normally do. The snag, of course, is the Masai indifference towards cash.

Yet even here the seeds of change begin to germinate. There are schools now in all Masai centres, Masai students at Makerere, the start of a trickle of Masai teachers, doctors, administrators, vets. One has a Cambridge degree in geography, one is a Legislative Councillor. The shell of Masai indifference has been pricked.

The puncture so far is tiny, but time will enlarge it and one day, not so far away either, the whole shell may crack. Already a Masai parson, the Rev. Daudi Mokinyo, has fenced off 2,000 acres of communal grazing where he fattens steers bred from improved bulls, has a simple milking bail and makes ghee. Elsewhere, half a dozen other Masai have fenced in grazing land. When the railway took a pipeline off Mt. Kilimanjaro, they set up watering points for Masai cattle along its course, and in return one section of the tribe, the Il Kisongo, agreed to operate a pasture-management plan, financed by a grazing fee, which is acting as an entry-point for new ideas.

When these movements spread, as they seem bound to do, the doom of the game will be accomplished. For game cannot co-exist with modern pasture management. Unless the Masai come to see game as an asset of high value, it will go here, as it has on European farms, and for the same reasons: it will go down before the fence, the improved pasture and the need to keep the land free of disease.

VI

To admire pictures in the National Gallery, cathedrals of the Middle Ages or the antiquities of Greece is considered praiseworthy, and proposals to burn the pictures, blow up the cathedrals and destroy the antiquities would certainly provoke an outcry of shocked dismay all over the world; funds would, if necessary, be raised to preserve such treasures. I have never heard it denied that the wild life of Africa in its natural surroundings is of surpassing beauty, one of the few sights left in the world that lifts the heart with wonder and fills the mind with praise. Yet anyone who protests against its widespread destruction, often by the cruellest of means, is liable to be thought a sentimental crank. 'Ah, well, the interests of human beings must come first. . . .'

Which human beings, one may ask? The only humans to count are assumed to be those in the immediate vicinity who, having destroyed their existing pastures by allowing their beasts to multiply to excess, now wish to apply the same process to fresh pastures hitherto occupied—and preserved—by wild animals, even though these may lie in a game reserve which attracts people from all over the world. What about the visitors who enjoy looking at the animals? Are they not humans too? And what about future generations of Africans who will themselves, if they are able, relish these sights? Anyone who doubts that Africans enjoy, in the deepest sense, their heritage of wild life should study their folk-lore and legends, which are very largely taken up with animal tales, or note the minute observation, indeed the loving eye, which older Africans, like countrymen everywhere, bring to bear upon their natural surroundings.

And if beauty is no passport to survival, the animals have economics on their side. They provide a raw material, for one thing, in a part of the world that cries out for industries and lacks the wherewithal to build them on. Like all industries, tourism has its depressing aspects but, duly encouraged, it can scarcely fail to proliferate as freely as marrows on a rich dung-heap. Already it comes third in order of importance and, with the prospect of packaged airline tours from countries where wealth and leisure are increasing year by year, it might easily rise to the top of the list, bringing needful dollars and employment.

Tourists will not come to look at views or to admire

triumphs like hydro-electric schemes: they will come to look at animals. If there are no animals, very few will come. It is as simple as that. If one has an oil-well, it is unwise to let it gush out wastefully over the sand; if one has animals, it is unwise to kill them off.

There is another, even stronger, argument, based on the twin facts that game animals, as I have mentioned, do not destroy their habitat, and that they are edible. Why not use them as a source of meat? They cost nothing to keep, they seldom die from diseases, you do not have to dip them, to inject them with Antrycide, to drive them from place to place to find grazing, or feed them in times of drought. On top of everything, they provide a sport. To hunt is a traditional African pastime; whole tribes exist who do very little else; to end the possibility of hunting is to extinguish one of the very few exciting diversions that remain in a world becoming daily more drab and ridden by routine.

This seems a simple proposition, and from time to time people have advanced it, but until very recently no one has taken it seriously. Now that it is almost—but not quite—too late, the idea is gathering force. A scientific study by Dr. A. N. Harthoorn of Makerere has shown that buffaloes convert poor pastures into protein much more efficiently than cattle do, besides paying no attention to 'fly'. Why kill off the buffaloes and replace them by less efficient, more delicate herds of cattle? Why not let the buffaloes stay where they are and take an annual 'crop' by shooting under licence a number calculated by experts not to damage the replacement capacity of the herds? This is, in effect, the same as culling herds of cattle, or taking off an annual draft of steers. It is game farming, a science that has been developed with great success in the United States, Denmark and Sweden. There is absolutely no reason why it should not be developed in Africa, except inertia, indifference and timidity.

So far the only practical step in this direction has been a scheme drawn up by the Kenya Wild Life Society to allow a tribe called the Waliangulu, living near the Tsavo National Park, to shoot elephants and keep the meat and ivory. The genesis of this scheme was the need to check poaching, which annually destroys hundreds of elephants in and around this large but barren, almost waterless, stretch of bush and plain. An anti-poaching combined operation between Game department and police in 1957, which lasted nine weeks, brought to light in an area about twenty miles by twenty-five the bodies of 1,280 poached elephants, over a hundred of which were babies who died of starvation after their mothers had been killed. Since money and staff cannot be found to stop the poaching, the only hope appears to be to legalize it, and so endeavour to keep it down to a level that will at least allow the animals to survive.

VII

In Tanganyika lions are threatened with extinction but on the Mara, where game is still under tsetse protection, they rule the bush-clad gullies and thorn-studded plains. We saw our first lioness within half an hour of leaving our shady camp on the Talek river. She was sitting under a bush beside a stream and three small cubs rolled about beside her; disregarding them, she gazed out over the plain with that detached, contemptuous impassivity of lions, her eyes focused on the far horizon. Deliberately, slowly, she turned her glance towards our Land-Rover and stared straight through us, her eyes hard, opaque, lapidary as cornelians. Then she withdrew her glance, a glance neither fearful nor angry, interested nor concerned—a glance of utter indifference—and resumed her watch on the horizon. She looked thin and hungry. Was there a hunt in progress somewhere beyond our sight? Or was she waiting for a signal? She sat in a penumbra of mystery, a very monument of dignity. There is nothing in the world so full of dignity as a lion.

Beyond the gully lay an open sunlit plain knee-high with red oat grass, which grows here wherever bush is kept down by fire. The Masai burn these plains every year to encourage fresh pasture for their sheep, which do not mind tsetse flies; their cattle, which do, stay out. Without these fires, the red oat grass would succumb to stubborn, vicious forms of bush like *Acacia pennata* and *Euclea*. Vegetation here is in a state of balance easily upset. Fires, correctly timed, are beneficial; oat grass is beneficial; even man can be beneficial when he exercises moderation. The trouble comes when the balance is upset.

This was explained, as we bumped along, by Dr. Philip Glover, chief zoologist to the Government and in charge of all the tsetse work. 'I've seen it all before in British Somaliland,' he said, 'which once had good forests, some permanent rivers and a lot of wild animals. Today the forests have gone, the country's been over-grazed till scarcely any good grass remains and the desert has come in in many places. Three years ago they found the skeleton of the last elephant in Somaliland. It had died of starvation and loneliness.'

We were looking for Major Temple-Boreham's pets. Just as a shepherd knows each sheep, so can this game warden recognize every lion on the Mara; he has seen them as cubs, followed their youthful adventures, watched them take their mates and in turn produce families. In particular we were looking for Sally, a lioness Major Temple-Boreham, who has been in Masailand for twenty years, has known for twelve or thirteen of them.

We found her in the shade of a thorn-tree, lying with her face on her paws. It was a hot afternoon and she was panting gently; her age showed in her thinness and in the scars of old adventures on her sides. We drove to within a yard or two and Major Temple-Boreham placed a *kerai* on the ground near her nose, and then filled it with water. Sally did not even raise her head, only the black tip of her whippy tail flickered now and then. We drove off a few paces and stopped the engine. Sally got slowly to her feet, strolled with that deliberate lion's prowl to the bowl, lay down again and lapped until the *kerai* was dry. 'It's a longish way to water and she's getting old,' said Major Temple-Boreham. 'She's always glad of a drink.' Once, he said, he even got out of the Land-Rover, picked up one of her cubs and fondled it while she looked on.

In a camp pitched in a grove of tall, umbrella-like acacias near a sandy river, another cub—I think it was Sally's granddaughter—romped around playing with the dogs while we drank our tea. Would it, I asked, have to end in a zoo?

'No, I shall turn her loose with her relations,' he replied. But would they accept her? Wouldn't the human smell turn them against her? Major Temple-Boreham said not, if she was young enough. 'Besides, they know my smell.' Certainly these Mara lions appeared not only to have no fear of humans, but an acceptance bordering on friendliness.

The Mara is a sanctuary surrounded by dangers. If animals go south, as many do, they cross the Tanganyika border into an area where they lack all protection. Here large organized gangs kill for meat either with rifles or, more often, with steel-wire snares. Often these are set in the gaps in a system of staggered thorn fences into which the animals, once they stray, have no hope of escape; and stray into it they must, as the fences are constructed near water-holes whither, in dry weather, they are bound to make their way. Game rangers have found systems of thorn fences set with snares five miles long, capable of killing literally thousands of game animals in a season. A conservative estimate has put the slaughter of game animals for meat in Tanganyika at over one million annually.

The cruel part about these snares is that sometimes their owners do not visit them for days at a time, so the trapped animals die slowly from strangulation or are eaten alive by hyenas. Game rangers have on occasion spotted snare-lines by a long black cloud of vultures in the sky. Other snares are fastened to heavy logs which the antelope or giraffe must drag about while the wire digs into its flesh to make a festering wound. Sometimes the poacher takes a knife to hamstring a trapped animal and then releases it, to keep fresh until it is wanted. In the Nairobi game park I watched a lioness with a snare round her neck rubbing herself against boulder after boulder in an effort to free herself; even in this agony she was calm and self-controlled, and did not fly at the cars which clustered round her like bluebottles round a lump of meat. Eventually a game ranger put a bullet through her head.

On the Mara, we saw a buffalo with a leg broken and festering: possibly the wire was still taut inside the flesh. With it was another, able-bodied buffalo who seemed to be keeping it company away from the herd, perhaps until it died;

both were bulls. They made off through the bush; had the injured beast charged in its pain and desperation people would have shaken their heads and said: 'Buffaloes are dangerous brutes—treacherous!' They are far less dangerous than bulls in English farmyards, which do not wait to attack until they are in pain and wounded.

It is strange, this great to-do about the savagery of animals. They can be made dangerous, as a rule, only by alarming or injuring them, otherwise their one desire is to hide or to escape. One cannot say that unprovoked attacks on humans never happen, but they are rare and, when they do occur, often due to some old wound or injury—with the exception of an occasional bout of elephantine hysteria, possibly caused by an appalling toothache due to an abscess under the tusk, or of man-eating habits among old lions no longer able to catch anything more appetizing. It is infinitely less dangerous to walk through game-inhabited bush than to drive along an English highway. Lorries charge far more often than rhinos, sports cars are more lethal than whole herds of buffaloes, a motor cycle is a great deal fiercer than a lioness with young. By instilling fear, one can *provoke* almost anything into anger, even a cow. It is time the myth of the dangerous wild animals of Africa came to an end.

VIII

The morning we had to fly back to civilization we went to look once more at Major Temple-Boreham's pets. It was not long before we found a big, dark-maned lion sitting regally under a bush on the crest of a small knoll whence he could command a wide view of the surrounding countryside. A herd of tommies tail-wagged unconcernedly within fifty yards, topi and zebra cropped the turf, the newly-risen sun was mild as honey in the heavens, dew glistened on the grass. Through binoculars we soon observed two other lions strolling in our direction across the plain.

Then a pack of wild dogs gathered round: mangy creatures with a mean, cringing appearance, spotted all over like plum duff and evidently lousy, for they frequently sat down and scratched. It seemed unfortunate that man's chosen companion should have descended from such curs, or at any rate be so closely related; they did not compare at all favourably with the lions, or the silver-backed jackals that trotted gracefully across the turf. As for the little bat-eared foxes we had just seen darting down their holes and then popping up again with eyes bright as berries, theirs was a charm of quite a special order; how much better had they been the ancestors of mankind's favourite pet!

Bored with the unresponsive Land-Rover, the pack went off to taunt the lion under the bush. He paid no attention. A lioness advanced and they ran off to prance round her, making short rushes, getting up close and then darting away. She lay down on the crest of the knoll about twenty yards away from the lion. The dogs sat down to scratch and then began to yelp and prance again. Two more lionesses approached, lean and tawny, walking with a swift deliberation, silently and with a purpose of their own.

The wild dogs began to hunch together, rather taken aback. At some unseen signal, two of the lionesses suddenly bounded with tails lashing towards the dogs, who turned and fled. Halting a little way off they wheeled and made several short, yelping charges at the lionesses, like street urchins taunting a policeman. This game went on for some time until the dogs, evidently feeling that matters had gone far enough, loped off and disappeared. The lionesses lay down and yawned.

We watched a little longer, for it began to seem that something was in the wind. I could not say what gave us that impression; perhaps it was a suspicion of nervousness among the tommies and topi grazing nearby. They did not move away, but they were restless; they kept taking a few mouthfuls, raising their heads and staring about them, moving on a few paces, resuming their meal, wagging their tails and then repeating the performance; they did not settle down. Then over the horizon came more lions. They walked towards us with their slow deliberate padding step as if answering some summons, and that indeed is probably what they were doing.

The dark-maned lion, still under his bush, let out a sudden

roar and several of the approaching beasts answered him. Then he and one of the lionesses struck up a duet. The lion's roar is one of the most impressive sounds in the world: not unduly loud, although it carries far, it has in it all the menace, majesty and might of the wild, a tremendous power of suggestiveness, and it vibrates somewhere inside you as drums do at night in the distance, when a dance is on.

The lions sat one on each side of our Land-Rover and roared across it, paying no more attention to us than to a clump of bush. I expected the tommies and the topis to get out while the going was good, warned by these fearful gusts of sound, but they merely went on grazing and walking about, though with the same restlessness as before.

We could now count seventeen lions, all lying down, all facing in the same direction and strung out in a wide arc across a hillside, with a bush-clad gulley at the bottom. That they were acting in concert, to a plan, was undeniable. Who had framed the plan? The dark-maned lion who had first roared? Or had it formed itself like a web from the strands of hunger in the lions, was it a rhythm that arose in them as it must in birds when they wheel in the air, or in ants when they stream across the countryside? The hunt was up, some zebra or topi would soon satisfy their need.

It was extraordinary to see the unconcern of the animals towards the lions and the unconcern of the lions towards our Land-Rover, which sat in the middle of the arc, full of humans, completely superfluous and ignored. Had we been able to stop, the hunt would have unfolded before our eyes on this sunlit morning, amid the green grass and the sweet rolling pastures under a china-blue sky. But, with that idiotic slavery of humans to their self-invented scale of time, we had to go; appointments awaited us like a prison sentence in Nairobi, an hour's flight and many centuries away.

Here and now the lions were masters and ignored as irrelevant the squatting humans in their metal box, but one day, not far distant, the tide of humans will come in like an army of soldier ants to strip the bush and slaughter all the animals, and the last hungry lion will slink away or die with lead in his guts, to provide for the man who pressed the trigger

of his efficient mechanism an ego-flattering saga and a rug
for his sitting-room floor.

IX

For about the first twenty minutes we looked down from
our little yellow aircraft on the trackless country we had
bumped across in the Land-Rover, greener than ever after a
heavy storm. Strips of thick bush writhed about the landscape
and the Mara hid itself in a deep belt of forest, now and then
showing a glint of water as it twisted its way towards the
lake. A large herd of buffalo speckled a hillside like a flock
of battle-grey beetles and our shadow flickered over them
without disturbing their peace.

And then the country changed quite suddenly, almost as
if a line had been drawn: vegetation vanished and we were
flying over desert, so it seemed. A livid grey desert creased
everywhere with swirling gullies like an old, old, withered
face; there was a stark and corpse-like look about this carcass
of a country, the blood-stream of its rivers dried, its flesh
rotted away. Here and there were speckled patches with a
tinge of green about them, as if a pepper-mill had shed its
dark flecks on to a lime-green and biscuit-tinted cloth; these
were Masai herds and flocks picking up a living, God knows
how, on the relics of their pastures. Beneath us the withered
land was pimpled here and there with circular *manyattas*, some
deserted, some a focus for the sheep and cattle that spread
out round them in a coagulation of dots.

We were out of the fly-belt and over what had once been
the great Masai plains and was now, it seemed, the great
Masai desert. We saw it at its worst, at the end of the dry
season; after a few good storms the writhing empty sand-
gullies would fill and water come down in spate to strip more
soil from naked hillsides. Then the herds would find pasture,
but how do they survive meanwhile? This is the time when the
weakest die of starvation, or of exhaustion during long treks
to find water and a bite of thorn-bush to eat.

One can see that there is no room left here for wild animals.
One can see with what desirous eyes the Masai must look

towards country still protected by the tsetse fly and by the forest. And one can see how precarious is the last stand of the vegetation, resting at best upon a fly that science has all but overcome. If the Masai take their cattle to the Mara, unless there are great administrative changes the vegetation will go, as it has in the rest of Masai country: first the game will go and then the bush, trees, grass and finally the streams and soil itself, to become brown, bare, pock-marked with gullies like the sliced, dust-bedevilled, sun-sodden Loita plains that we flew over on our return to Nairobi—like a bit of the moon almost, a hot moon, peopled by men and women whose stubborn pride has kept their dignity and betrayed their heritage.

CHAPTER 11

The Dry Lands of Kitui

I

WHILE I was in Kitui, in the country of the Kamba, two animal-catchers were trapping rhinos on a licence which carried the condition that for every one they sold, one was to be taken to the Northern Frontier District and released there, in the hope of restocking an area where rhinos have been all but exterminated. These Kitui rhinos—who themselves survive in very few places—were lassoed from a truck, and seven were crated and taken up to the Northern Frontier.

I inquired later about their fate and Mr. George Adamson, the game ranger at Isiolo, kindly supplied the following details:

'The experiment has so far been a success. The rhinos very quickly made themselves at home in their new country which, compared with their original home, is a rhino's paradise: plenty of food, a permanent little river to quench their thirst in, and less danger from poachers. One of the seven died soon after release from some mysterious complaint.

'Stuffy—rhino No. 2—was liberated on 13th July at the same place as Bernadine, rhino No. 1. But unlike her compatriot, Stuffy was full of fight from the moment she stepped out of her crate. Without hesitation, she put her head down and charged. My Land-Rover refused to start properly. Fortunately, her attention was diverted to the other Land-Rover which had got under way. She gave it a glancing blow and set off in pursuit, chased it for a couple of hundred yards and then disappeared into the bush.

'There is every reason to believe that Bernadine has settled down in her new home. As was to be expected with such a comely young rhino, it was not long before she aroused the interest of a surviving local blood. A few weeks ago one of my scouts saw her with an escort.'

172

Poachers with their snares and poisoned arrows will be her worst enemy. Rhino horn is worth up to £5 a pound and a good horn will weigh 40 lb., a fortune to any poacher. Moreover, Somali traders are always at hand to take the horn across the Ethiopian border or down to the coast, whence Arab dhows smuggle it with negligible risk to India.

To judge from the birth-rate one would not suspect a need for aphrodisiacs in India, but apparently the demand is insatiable. The potency of rhino horn in this respect is simply an illusion. Yet, to feed human lust and ignorance, this ancient species, defenceless for all its thick hide and short temper, is in danger of imminent extinction. There are said to be no more than a thousand left in all Kenya and in Tanganyika also it is on the danger list. Once the numbers of a species sink below a certain level, it passes the point of no return. The rhino is very near this point and, for lack of money to enforce the law, and because of the spreading out of population, its numbers dwindle year by year. One can only hope that Bernadine and Stuffy will manage to survive.

II

I have always thought it must be pleasant to be a Kamba because everyone is inclined to like you. The first Europeans who passed through Ukambani (as Kamba country is called), on the caravan route to Uganda, praised the inhabitants' friendliness and hospitality, and to this day most Europeans can hardly speak highly enough of the people. They make excellent soldiers and seem to possess an inborn talent for machinery; other Africans do not react against them as they do so often against the Kikuyu or Luo. Their great weakness is the drink, but in this they are not alone.

The Athi river bisects their country. To the west lie the steep, well-watered hills of Machakos with their close-packed inhabitants; to the east, the great dry plains and bushland, covering nearly 12,000 square miles—about the same as the whole of the European Highlands. Here life rests mainly on cattle and is a constant struggle against drought. In the east of the district people grow their crops on an annual rainfall of six or seven inches: an area called Ngomeni had four inches last year.

The key to existence is the preservation of water, and there are two principal methods: trapping it by dams, and catching it on terraces. Dams and terraces, those are the edges of the sword of Progress in this part of the world.

'And manure,' said Justus, the first model farmer I visited. 'Nothing can be done without manure.' Justus is a hospital orderly on the point of retirement after thirty years. All his savings have gone into his small estate near Kitui, where a belt of high rainfall confers upon smallholders a chance of success.

Three generations gathered for a cup of tea in the sitting-room of his neat brick bougainvillea-swaddled bungalow. The senior age-group was represented by a large framed photograph of a thin old man sitting very stiff and upright and staring down at us with a buttoned-up expression, as if he had relied upon his will-power to fix his image for posterity.

The old man was about ninety, Justus said, and had visited Nairobi, to have the picture taken, for the first time since 1914. 'He thought his eyes were playing tricks, but in spite of all the buildings he was able to point out where tents had been pitched before the railway arrived. When he was a young man he fought the Masai, they used to come to raid our cattle.' (They still do: last year they stole 388 cattle partly from Europeans, but mainly from the Kamba.)

What did the old man think of modern times? 'Our people imitate Europeans too much. Our ways are different and instead of copying white men, we should have developed along our own lines. And he thinks that things have been made too easy for the young men.'

I asked his grandson, Justus's eldest son, if he agreed, but he shook his head and said 'I do not know.' His meaning, I think, was that he would not say, for he was a teacher twenty years of age who had passed his school certificate. He had that look about him, a sort of quietly smouldering discontent, that infallibly indicates a dedication to politics, and Justus said sadly that he took no interest in the little farm.

He sat on a sofa underneath the portrait of his grandfather: the old man of the past who had fought the Masai before the coming of Europeans, and the young man of the future teaching mathematics and history who may become a lawyer or a Cabinet Minister, linked by the careful, hard-working son and father who had climbed a ladder that was alien but that he had accepted. It was sad that the son, who had already climbed so much higher, seemed so much less happy, less companionable, less adapted to the life into which he had been born. Even at twenty he was a disappointed man because he had so far failed to get a place in a university to which he felt he had a right, and had been cheated out of by some hidden, inimical agency. He was trying still, and no doubt in time would either succeed or accept a limitation shared by the great majority of his fellow-humans in all parts of the world.

Would he, as the eldest son, inherit the farm? Justus had six sons so far, and would leave the land to be divided among them according to Kamba custom. But he had only fifteen acres. Could six families support themselves on that?

'One or two will have to buy the others out. Our custom is for the elders of the clan to divide the land among a man's sons. That is a good custom, and I shall follow it. Now I will show you my banana pits. . . .'

These kill two birds with one stone. At the bottom of each terrace you dig a line of pits to trap the rain-water and in them you plant bananas, which will not normally thrive in dry lands. Bananas yield a good income—8 shillings a tree a year, Justus said—and provide also wind-breaks and shade.

III

Tobacco is a new idea that has spread since its introduction by Mr. Paul Kelly, a D.C. remembered for his energy in tramping on foot over the greater part of Kitui and preaching with untiring ardour the doctrine of dams. I saw tobacco growing on the farms of two brothers. The elder, a Master Grower, displayed proudly his brick-curing barn, the very latest idea—a bold one also, for the flue-curing of tobacco is a tricky affair. The temperature has to be exactly controlled at different levels in cycles of ten days to treat each batch of leaf. Normally experts employed by big producers supervise flue-curing but, with the faith that characterizes all these Kenya projects, Kamba growers having only a few acres of leaf are being encouraged to build their own barns.

A very old man in rags was in charge of Mr. Samuel Mulandi's barn; he had a chart of instructions which a schoolboy read out and translated. The cured leaf, soft and springy like a horse's nostrils, was done up in neat bundles according to grade to await the lorry of the East African Tobacco Company which collected the leaf from the door. And the price was good.

Mr. Mulandi kept a herd of twenty cattle mainly to provide the tobacco with manure, and employed six men to look after his two acres of leaf and his other crops like pineapples, onions and maize. He reckons to clear at least £500 a year when his thirty-two-acre holding is fully developed. Next door lives a brother, much poorer because he had to buy a holding, whereas Samuel inherited his. All he could afford was seven acres of very badly eroded hillside from which all the topsoil had been stripped by others, who grew maize on slopes year after year. Makau, this brother, helped by one thin, work-scarred wife, terraced every bit of it himself and planted grass on the sides of the terraces to feed his half-dozen cherished cattle.

'Wheelbarrows have made my land fruitful,' he said, a gleam of dedication in his eye. 'I borrowed three wheelbarrows from Mr. Meadows and put all the manure on my terraces. They would grow nothing before, only a few stalks of maize smaller than a child; now the maize is taller than a man; without the wheelbarrows, how could I have done that? Now I am going to grow some of this tobacco. And I have built a dam to help my cattle: for is not water the mother of us all?'

IV

About three years ago terracing by group labour caught

21 Women are the principal land reclaimers in Ukambani: terracing by *mwethya* groups

An instructor at work

22 A Better Farmer's wife offers salt to her Better Cow, while her son is not quite sure of the intentions of the Better Heifer

on like a fever all over Kamba country. These groups are called *mwethya* and consist of members of a single clan. The custom is an old one that has revived, more or less spontaneously, in response to the need.

A young man showed me with pride a silver cup his *mwethya* group had won for the most energetic terracing in the district. He is the owner of a chain of five small shops, including a butchery and a beer-hall, and is investing his profits in a twelve-acre farm on which he employs ten men and grows heavy crops of maize, onions and groundnuts. Twice a week, in the season, he drives forth in his car to lead a *mwethya* group with song and dance; he is a great improviser of lyrics. His wife has a framed certificate for the best Better Home in these parts.

About half the maize land in the Kitui district has been terraced by *mwethya*, all without machinery and without money changing hands. Until five years ago, the district imported maize to feed its 220,000 inhabitants every season, and almost every other year had to accept famine relief. Now the district is not only self-supporting but, in good years, has become a small exporter of maize.

All these farmers were full of hope and buoyancy—all except one, who was sad and silent, almost submerged in a pair of gumboots as large as waders. While his neighbours extolled tobacco and thrived on its profits, he was debarred from planting any by his Christian Mission, founded by Americans, which forbade smoking and frowned on the leaf. Nor could his wife take part in *mwethya* because the women dance as they dig, and that too is forbidden. This poor man seemed crushed under all these prohibitions, and showed us a cotton-like plant with a red flower which dyes the water used by his Mission in place of Communion wine. One can only suppose that the parable of the wedding feast has been expunged from this Mission's copies of the Gospels.

V

Most African women are more reserved than men; their hard life and habit of obedience combine to make them cautious and they do not display their personalities until they have ceased to be strangers. One of the liveliest exceptions to this rule, if rule it be, is an old woman—she must be about eighty—called Kisembe, whom I met on the shores of an enormous dam. It was the right place to meet her, for this was her dam: she built it. By sheer force of personality she recruited about five hundred women and girls who scooped out every grain of earth with pick and shovel, carried it on their heads to form the barrier and, in three months, completed a cavity which now holds 25 million gallons of water.

Kisembe arrived at the head of a file of gaily dressed girls who intoned a marching song. Wrinkled like a June apple, she wore a red tarboosh, a boldly striped scarf attached to it by a safety-pin, and a yellow *shuka*. Her history is a strange one. When, in 1898, a great famine ravaged the country, followed by smallpox, she lost first her only child, then her husband, and finally the brother-in-law who had inherited her. No African woman is ever without a family but she, it seemed, repudiated hers, and lived alone in the old style of Kitui house, a cigar-shaped hut like the Masai's, made of plaited grass.

'I have no children,' she had said, 'so all the Kamba are my children'; and she became a leader among women, someone set apart, a little queer, but respected. And in old age came this dam, which will be her memorial. I asked why it was built by women, not by men.

'The men had gone away,' she said, 'to Mombasa and Nairobi, to seek work; and the women who were left here in Migwani had to walk as much as eight miles to fetch water, and back again. And then the D.C. called on people to make dams. That was *bwana* Kelly, he went about and planted sticks and said: the dam should be here.

'But the young men who had not gone away would not do it. Why? There was the Migwani Youth League; they were defying the Government. They were disobeying the chiefs. Even our chief here, Kasina, who is wise and strong. So I called upon the women to build the dam, and they came, and we built it. And now everyone is glad.'

Kaliluni lay beneath us, a big lake, with watering-places for cattle: perhaps a reproach to the young men, certainly a boon to the women. Kisembe beamed at it proudly: surely one of the great women of the country, who can remember the days of the *murati*, the Arabs who came and took people to the coast, never to return. She has very little patience with the young politicians and they, probably, only the kind of respect for her one gives to a legend or an image from a past one wishes to forget.

In the hottest of weather Chief Kasina wears a pair of khaki woollen gloves and when you shake hands you feel the hardness of metal: both his own hands were chopped off at the wrists, in 1953, by a Mau Mau gang. His neck was almost severed too, and when he reached hospital no one expected him to survive. 'Dr. Carswell saved my life,' he said: besides, he had made up his mind. Once before, somewhere about 1890, his life had been saved by some clansmen who had rescued him from a raiding party of Machakos Kamba on the way to sell him and his mother into slavery.

He grew up and married in a country which had changed but little, apart from the ending of raids. Kitui was a far-off place that no one visited except ivory hunters and safari parties. In 1914 Kasina saw troops drilling at Thika and a Major Montgomery persuaded him to join the K.A.R. (This major later came to live in Kitui, turned Moslem and married a Bajun girl from the islands off the coast.) Kasina rose to become a regimental sergeant-major, collected many medals and, on his retirement, was appointed chief. In the second war he formed a committee of elders to supply meat for the Forces and himself visited the Kamba troops in Burma. The resettlement of the *askaris*, he said, was the hardest task he had grappled with during his chieftainship. And then came Mau Mau.

VI

The Kamba's attitude was one of the key factors in the Emergency. Their affinities lay with the Kikuyu, their country was full of ex-*askaris* accustomed to good pay and now unable to earn more than a pittance. Everyone was being told to terrace and make dams: hard, unpopular work that seemed to bring no immediate benefit. The seeds of Mau Mau had a good soil. In Nairobi many Kamba joined, Kenyatta visited their country and the Kikuyu sent out (as it were) evangelists. Had the whole tribe turned Mau Mau the matter would have been doubly serious in that a majority of police and K.A.R. *askaris* were Kamba.

The staunchness and courage of chiefs like Kasina was therefore crucial. They did not waver and perhaps it was their strength, combined with the progress already made in the reclamation of Ukambani, that turned the scale. Gangs of Mau Mau, like that which cut off Chief Kasina's hands, did roam the country, but the people as a whole rejected their grisly doctrines. Now Chief Kasina in his woollen gloves farms 600 acres, has a tractor and a son as manager. The selection was perhaps difficult; he has twenty sons and nearly as many daughters, the progeny of six wives.

As a reward for their loyalty, the Kitui Kamba were given £10,000 by the Governor. They said at once that they would like to spend it on water. So it was put at the disposal of the Water Supply Organization, a body which buys equipment to build the larger dams, and puts in piped supplies. The District Council raises an annual water rate of 2 shillings per head of cattle which brings in £20,000 a year, and has just confirmed this for the next five years.

Already there are over 450 completed dams of all shapes and sizes in the district: big ones excavated by ALDEV machinery; medium ones dug by *mwethya*; rock dams, natural catchments in the hills into which water is skilfully conducted; and, perhaps most ingenious of all, sub-surface dams where you do not see any water at all. To make these, you build a barrier across one of the dry river-beds in which people find water for their stock by digging holes in the sand, and install a pipe well below the surface. Out comes a steady flow of absolutely pure water, filtered by the sand, which you can either trap in a tank or pump to a reservoir above. At Mwingi, in the district's dry north, a growing township depends entirely upon water pumped from a nearby sub-surface dam.

There is a danger that all these dams may, in the long run, do more harm than good. If people simply keep more cattle because there is more water for them, they will overload the grazing and destroy their pastures even quicker than before. The water will help them only if they themselves exercise restraint and limit their herds.

Kitui is badly overstocked. An annual take-off of ten per cent for the country as a whole, the very minimum to balance natural increase, would result in the slaughter of 600,000 cattle a year of which half should come from the Masai and Kamba between them. Last year, instead of 300,000, only 60,000 were taken off from these grazing-grounds, and Kitui's contribution was less than 8,000. It should have been ten times greater. Foot-and-mouth disease quarantine restrictions were partly to blame. Livestock population is piling up dangerously and the dam-making is 'an act of faith', say the agricolas.

VII

All over Ukambani are what is known as *mangalata* lands. When asked to define them an agricola said simply: 'They are the bottom', and that seems to sum up as well as anything these end-products of over-grazing by livestock. From the air they show up as great raw patches of mange. Depressed-looking thorn-trees prick up from their bare subsoil, but nothing else. They are brick-red and, until a few years ago, had been written off as bits of man-made desert that could never be brought back into use again. Even the most land-hungry optimist did not try to plant anything on *mangalata* lands.

But it now appears that, just as no soul is past praying for, so no bit of land, however battered and abused, is quite past redemption. In the last few years a system of reclaiming *mangalata* lands has met with astonishing success. It was evolved in another region by Mr. Leslie Brown, a world authority on eagles and a student of flamingo lore, and is now going ahead more or less of its own volition.

The first step is to keep out everything on four legs. The

local chief has power to close the area and anyone whose beasts are found there is fined. Once an area is effectively closed, natural regeneration will work wonders, but more has to be done on *mangalata* lands. A *mwethya* group is turned out for scratch ploughing, a simple process which consists of making shallow furrows in all directions—no nonsense about straight lines—with the simplest of little ploughs. Then along come men with seed gathered from natural grasses, mainly *Eragrostis superba*, which they strew down the furrows, followed by ox-teams dragging thorn branches to harrow it in, and then by teams who fence the area by laying branches end to end. *Mwethya* groups plant sisal alongside, so that when white ants have eaten the branches a permanent hedge will arise.

We came on several scratch-ploughing parties in the bush and a good time was being had by all. Everyone brings his team of four oxen, and those who have them bring their ploughs, and a lot of ground is treated before everyone knocks off at tea-time. When rain falls the *mangalata* comes out in a fuzz of green but no one may graze it until the chief, advised by his location council, gives the word, and then he strictly rations the number of animals. Scratch ploughing, terracing and dams could redeem the whole of Ukambani and make it as fertile as nature will allow. About 120,000 acres have been reclaimed: but there are nearly eight million acres in Ukambani.

We stopped near a patch of unhappy maize, raggedly existing on the flat, bush-covered, biscuit-coloured plain, and walked across crumbling, sad and dusty clods towards a girl listlessly hoeing in the hot sunshine. Beside her was a boy of four or five wielding a hoe almost as large as himself. She looked up at our approach and stood transfixed with horror; so far from even the smallest market or trading post, we must indeed have looked like something from outer space. And one arrives, too, with questions that go off like a lot of bombs: where do you live, what are you growing, how big is your family, do you go to school? Decent manners would require a day or two to get acquainted, a careful mutual probing, a sharing of the maize porridge or the millet gruel.

Tears rolled slowly down the girl's face; she was too frightened even to run away. If there are racial memories, the shadow of light-skinned strangers who had come so often to these parts, back through the generations, to seize girls like her, yoke them together and drive them to the slave-markets of Mombasa and Zanzibar, must have fallen over her mind.

The chief who was with us knew her family and after the shock wore off she was able to conduct us to the hut she shared with a widowed mother. Inside were two beds made of sticks, a few gourds, some pecking hens and that was all, beside the three cooking stones. They lived off this bit of *shamba*, unterraced, unmanured, squeezed dry—no cattle—no cash-crop—no *mwethya* even. An uncle looked after them, but he lived some distance away. Her mother made a few shillings by gathering fibre from wild sisal plants, retting and drying it, and making ropes to sell in the market. The girl had not been to school, she was helping her mother; she had an older brother but he had gone away, there was no work here, he had not returned. . . .

VIII

The Yatta is a long tongue of uninhabited land running north-west to south-east parallel with, and on the left bank of, the Athi river. The reason no one settled there was lack of water: pastures are good and rainfall adequate. Also the Yatta was a buffer state. Old battles are recalled by several place-names: Mwakini hill, from *mwaki*, meaning fire, where the Kamba lighted beacons to warn of the approach of Masai, and Mwita Siano, a river, which means 'empty out the arrows'.

In 1934 the Morris Carter Land Commission awarded this area of 110,000 acres, which they called B2, to the Kamba, while recommending that it should remain technically Crown land. ALDEV put in dams, the Kamba flooded it with cattle and by 1947 it had become so denuded that it had to be closed completely to livestock. When the veterinary authorities reopened it they imposed strict controls, and now they are using the area to improve the quality of Kamba herds. A man who sends a heifer down to B2 must normally leave her there for about eighteen months. During that time she is served by a Sahiwal bull, calves, and is served again; she returns to her owners with a calf at foot and another inside her, both half-Sahiwals. For this he pays a grazing fee of 10 shillings a year for the cow and 5 shillings for the calf.

In spite of grumbles at the fee, the scheme is popular. The plain looked so green, it was hard to believe that only twelve years ago it had been virtually a desert. B2 is divided into five enormous paddocks, each with its water supply provided by ALDEV and each grazed for three months in turn. It was carrying about 8,000 head of cattle but could support almost twice the number, under control, if more water could be found or conserved. The aim, eventually, is to use it as a ranch to fatten Sahiwal-cross steers, but that must wait until the cattle population of the rest of Ukambani has been stabilized.

IX

The Yatta furrow started, as so many things do, with an idea that everyone thought silly, and which came to a farmer in the Thika district called F. J. Jordan. The silliness lay in the expense, not in the technical aspects, for this was in the early 'thirties when the treasury was empty as a drum. Probably the furrow would still have been a diagram stacked on a dusty shelf had the Mau Mau Emergency not come along. Civil servants, in search of work for idle hands, turned up the scheme, hurriedly examined it and set detainees to work upon it in December, 1953. The original scheme was to dig a 25-mile channel estimated to cost £25,000; the outcome was a 40-mile channel which cost around £300,000.

Like the track of a slug in a garden, the furrow winds about hither and yon in a seemingly vagrant manner, actually in one of great exactitude: the fall is only one foot in 2,500. You cannot take a furrow where you like, it must go where the contour line leads you and this one led into some most inconvenient places, through veins of solid gneiss, across reaches of porous shale and very seldom across a nice, straight-forward stretch of easily-dug soil.

Most of the furrow was dug by hand and over 18 million cubic feet of earth were shifted. At one point the excavators came upon a collection of bolas stones: rounded lumps of granite, rather larger than cricket balls, which Stone Age hunters looped together with thongs and hurled at the legs of wild animals. Alongside the main furrow runs a second smaller one, a shadow furrow as it were, to take storm water off the hills, otherwise floods would overwhelm the main furrow. At intervals, all the way along, concrete fly-over bridges are provided to conduct storm water over the furrow and discharge it harmlessly into the bush below. The engineers had to make these strong enough to stand the weight of hippos, which emerge occasionally from the Thika river for a stroll.

What is the furrow for? 'To bring water to a hundred miles of country that has never had any water before,' said Mr. George Classen, the senior ALDEV engineer in charge. 'It will open up about 1,500 acres for potential irrigation and a quarter of a million acres for grazing.' Twenty million gallons a day go down that furrow from the Thika and most of it is discharged into a dry river-bed leading to the Tana called the Muthangauta. Now, for thirty miles, the Muthangauta flows again, and the Kamba are moving down there with their cattle. The rest of the water travels on to the Yatta plains and discharges into the Mwita Siano.

Already there are new settlers coming in. They are supposed to wait for an organized scheme but, as we drove through thick acacia and combretum bush sealing over a coarse murram soil, we saw little clearings and thin spines of smoke; water brings life; it will not be long before the whole length of the channel is peopled, and herds and flocks move on to pastures that have lain fallow for centuries.

By the furrow's head-waters¹ we picnicked under trees beside a pool where the Thika's clear, fast-running water divides about an island and tumbles over rocks towards the hot Tana valley far below. Six years' hard struggle with the furrow were just ending. It had been a far tougher task than anyone had expected, and had cost ten times as much. Had engineers and planners known what they were up against before they started, they probably would not have started at all; as with the Perkerra scheme, there was no time for preliminary surveys and experiments, survey parties were often only just ahead of excavating gangs.

Moreover the economics of the furrow are dubious. The carrying capacity of the plains on to which Kamba cattle will now spread is only about one beast to ten acres, or sixty to the square mile, and it will be many years before the beasts themselves are worth more than a few pounds apiece. A return of about 10 shillings an acre is the best you can hope for—hardly enough to support a furrow that has cost nearly £8,000 a mile. There is hope of irrigation, but so far only on paper; what will grow, at what cost, how it can be sold, these questions are all unanswered; and the experience of Perkerra is not encouraging.

So altogether, as an economic proposition, the Yatta furrow is a doubtful starter, taking water at high cost through uninhabited bush to plains of low potential value.* Despite all this, the engineers who built it are happy. For one thing it has been a hard job well done; for another, some instinct is satisfied by seeing water flow in dry countries where none has flowed before. Once you have got it flowing, there is no knowing what may be done—always provided the channel is well maintained, which will not be easy.

The Kamba, too, are pleased. At the official opening of the furrow on 16th September, 1959, Chief Timothy Munai no doubt had to say the right thing, but I suspect that he was speaking from the heart and for his people when he observed:

'When we first heard of this canal, we thought it was only words—we did not believe that it was really possible. . . . Beginning today, water will flow through a country that has been dry since the beginning of the world. Beginning today, every homestead between the Thika river and the Thatha

*This is partly a matter of book-keeping. In the U.S., a large part of the cost of such projects is charged to flood control, power development and recreation, leaving only about 30 per cent to the farmer, who has a ten-year moratorium and then repays the capital over 40 years without any interest charges, which would double the cost to him in that period.

hills, and every homestead between the Tana and the Tiva, will have water close by. Beginning today, the rivers and streams will flow with water instead of being beds of sand and stone. Beginning today, we shall not fear the failure of the rains.

'We cannot begin to understand what wealth will be brought to us by this canal, for there has been nothing like it in the history of East Africa. We only know that yesterday Yatta was a poor and troubled land and tomorrow it will not be so, but a land of wealth. This the Government has done for us. No man can ever live in Yatta now who will not see every day this great proof of the wisdom of the Government and its care and help for the Kamba people and who will not, if he is an honest man, know to whom he owes the water by which he and his cattle live.'

CHAPTER 12

Machakos Miracle

I

Iᴛ is said that when Mr. Tom Hughes-Rice came to Machakos in 1951 to take charge of the latest of many attempts to restore life to its dying land, he announced that all he could do was to sit on top of a hill and weep.

A great many people had wept over Machakos, and it had buried many hopes. This district was a classic example of all the worst agrarian evils of modern Africa: red, bare hillsides stripped of their vegetation and soil; rivers degenerated into wastes of sand; cattle like walking hat-racks; people burning cow dung for lack of firewood; women toiling miles to muddy holes they shared with goats for dribs and drabs of water. The picture in this district was grimmer than in any other because so much of it consists of very steep hills easily ravaged by heavy storms; because of a long dry season which parches the land; because all the forest cover had gone, even from atop the highest and steepest hills; and because there were three times as many cattle as the land would hold.

By the middle 'thirties, Machakos was permanently on the dole. Before harvest, every year, the Government had to distribute maize while starving people waited for their own skimpy crops to ripen. Until as recently as 1950, the Government was giving out on average 200,000 bags of famine-relief maize every season.

The war made things worse. When in 1946 Mr. Creech Jones, then Colonial Secretary, toured Machakos an account of his visit read:

'He drove mile after mile through hillsides and plains swept bare in many places to the solid rock, through areas where there was not a vestige of grass, through acre after acre of

dead and wilted maize. . . . A fair comparison can be made
with parts of British Somaliland—sand rivers lying between
bare red hills; in some places flat plains so worn out there
was no grass, and sand rather than top-soil. . . . Mr. Creech
Jones expressed the opinion that an immediate, imaginative
and forceful plan would have to be evolved.'

Many people had expressed that opinion. Since nothing
could be done until the livestock population was at least
halved, a de-stocking drive had always been on the programme and in 1938 the Government had decided, after
long and nervous hesitations, to put compulsion into effect.

The result was even worse than they had feared. The
Kamba refused to part even with the boniest of the walking
hat-racks and marched in large numbers, men, women and
children, to Nairobi, where they settled down in the grounds
of Government House. With some difficulty, they were moved
away to the race-course, but further than that they refused
to go, and they remained deaf to all appeals until the authorities gave in. Compulsory de-stocking was dropped like a hot
brick and never mentioned again.

In the later stages of the war Sir Philip Mitchell had
another plan drawn up and announced a 'D-Day' for Machakos on 1st January 1946. Two of the scheme's proposals were
to terrace eroded hillsides with caterpillar tractors, and to
resettle some of the landless at Makueni, an area in the tsetse
belt. So suspicious were the Kamba that both these excellent
intentions failed. Hysterical Wakamba threw themselves in
the path of the tractors and (after a visit to the district by
Jomo Kenyatta) everyone boycotted Makueni. And the land
went from bad to worse, if that was possible.

II

No wonder Mr. Hughes-Rice sat on a hill-top and wept.
General opinion then held that nothing effective could be
done until many thousands of families had been moved, in
order that the worst areas could be closed completely to
humans and livestock. One assessment put the number of
people to be moved at 50,000, others at up to a quarter of a

million, but there was no unused land to move them to, except some under tsetse bush. Mr. Hughes-Rice was told that no large-scale population movement could be arranged and that he would have to persuade the Kamba to regenerate their land despite its congestion and overstocking, and despite the repeated failure of persuasion over the previous twenty years. Added to that, a great many *askaris* had recently returned from the wars by no means in a biddable frame of mind.

A few advantages could be set against all this. The first was an outstanding Commissioner in charge of the district who was determined to push the reclamation project through. This was Mr. John Thorp, now Governor of the Seychelles. The second was a particularly good set of chiefs, weaker ones having been discarded during the war. A third was money: the Government was at last prepared to back its officers with funds.*

In these matters everything hinges on staff. There must be enough men, they must be good enough men and they must get about among the people to win confidence and trust. The trouble had always been a shortage of officers, who lived mainly in their headquarters at Machakos impaled and frustrated by paperwork. Administrators and agricolas had complained about this for years. Now, at last, new officers began to arrive, and Mr. Thorp and his team were able to decentralize.

Young administrators, agricolas, foresters and vets were sent out not merely to tour their districts but to live in them. Bungalows were built and they set up new centres out in the locations, much more closely in touch with the people than anyone in the central *boma* at Machakos could hope to be.† This setting up of small posts at strategic points throughout the district, which proved perhaps the key factor in success, was later adopted in Kikuyu country after the

*In 1946 ALDEV was allocated £3 million for reconditioning African lands and for African resettlement. By 1955 it had spent £2.4 million of this, of which one-third had gone into the single district of Machakos.

†Machakos district covers 5,614 square miles and in 1946 had a population of 356,000. (In 1918, the estimated population was under 200,000.) By 1959 it was about 428,000, with 300,000 stock units.

Mau Mau Emergency broke out, and played a major part in overcoming it.

By 1955, although a vast amount remained to be done—as it still does—the nut on which so many teeth had broken had been cracked. Hillsides were turning green again, raw red sores were healed, the walking hat-racks had diminished in numbers and turned back into cattle, streams were flowing in valleys where they had not flowed for twenty years, the people were alert, co-operative and reasonably contented—about as much as human beings ever are.

III

How had this been achieved? To see the answer I went to the place where reclamation started: the Makavete square mile. In 1949 it was chosen as typical of the worst *mangalata*, scored by gullies and without a blade of vegetation apart from the usual little twisted thorn-trees whose bark had been gnawed by goats. The carrying capacity was put at one beast to thirty acres.

Mr. George Cowley took it over and an African 'betterment team' went in, each of whose members had specialized in one particular aspect of the work, but all of whom had been grounded in their colleagues' subjects at a Jeanes' school course. The team's commander was a district assistant, Mr. John Malinda, and everyone who knew the story assured me that his was the major part in its success. He threw his heart into the task and was able to convince his people that this was their opportunity, not a sly official trick to steal their land. The team's first achievement was to persuade land-holders in the Makavete square mile to join *mwethya* groups.

'*Mwethya* achieved three things in Makavete,' I was told by Mr. Reginald Spooner, now head agricola in Ukambani. 'They are like the three stones that support the cooking pot. Terracing: grass planting: closure of the land to stock. Once the people applied those three remedies, the speed of re-generation astounded us all.' Experts had talked gloomily of ten, fifteen, twenty years. The job was done in two.

'By 1951,' Mr. Spooner said, 'the right-holders were

grazing parts of Makavete at the rate of one beast to the acre. If you remember, the rate was thirty acres to a beast before. And those two years, 1949 and 1950, were two of the driest in Machakos since records began. They were drought years. And yet by 1951 the grass was waist-high.'

The Makavete square mile is now fully terraced, cattle are back in larger numbers than ever before, and I saw thick grass everywhere. We made our usual calls on Better Farmers, mostly oldish men living on or near the old caravan route from Mombasa to Machakos along which the foot safaris had passed before the railway. One of the farmers pointed out a fig-tree in whose shade the tents had many times been pitched; another said he had a treaty, treasured in a biscuit-tin, between his grandfather and the Imperial British East Africa Company. This must have dated back to before 1895, when the Chartered Company handed over to the Foreign Office. 'It recognized my grandfather as the paramount chief,' said its inheritor. 'I ought to be the chief now.'

These men had largish holdings—one of a hundred acres— for the land, however much improved, is thin and light, and the rainfall indifferent. One farmer sent oranges to Nairobi through a co-operative and grew popcorn, perhaps to end up in the cinemas. Another had poultry in a deep-litter house and was chairman of an egg co-operative. They were living well and making money. To realize that all this country had been bare as a board only a few years ago was almost impossible. And the treatment was so simple: merely common sense, manpower and an end to years of futile suspicion.

Mr. John Malinda showed me round, looking proud, as well he might; the respect with which he was greeted was evident. On the dusty bush-track we picked up a woman agricultural instructor who wanted a lift. 'What do you think has pleased the women most?' I inquired. 'The water,' she replied. 'The dams. And now the water is clean.'

IV

I drove for several days about the Machakos district and saw with prolonged astonishment that the triple formula

23 Settlers transplanting rice on the Mwea-Teberre irrigation scheme

24 The peaks of Mount Kenya: and far below, threshing rice on the irrigation scheme, Embu district

discovered in Makavete—terraces, grass-planting, closure to stock—really does work everywhere. Of course, there are still bad patches: but, generally, I saw grass, sometimes deep grass, and this was about as surprising to anyone who remembered Machakos before as it would be to find an oak wood sprung up at Charing Cross.

'In fact, in places we are *understocked*,' said Mr. John Peberdy, the local agricola. 'Our main problem now is bush regeneration. It's gaining on us in places.'

Had there been extensive de-stocking? Are there fewer cattle now than before?

'No, we think about the same number of cattle. But when we closed areas to livestock—and a lot *were* closed—the goats and cattle simply disappeared.'

They were not sold, or not many of them. No de-stocking rules were made. Some were sent away, illegally, to other places, but by no means all.

'Most of them were kept in the homesteads,' Mr. Peberdy said, 'and never allowed to graze. Once a day they were driven to water along routes which the chiefs laid down. All this was done on a location basis; the location council decided when to close an area, gave out the boundaries, and then the chief enforced it all. Anyone whose cattle were found grazing in the closed areas was fined. The District Council made the rules, the location councils and chiefs enforced them. We scarcely interfered.'

What did cattle live on? No one seemed to know. Scraps from the roadside, leaves and twigs of trees, maize stover brought in from the *shambas*, weeds, almost anything. They must have lived on air. They got very thin, Mr. Malinda agreed; but then, they had been thin before. Live they did, somehow, most of them, to emerge when the grass had got established and find a feast awaiting them.

Is there not now a danger that they will increase again, and start once more to overgraze the pastures? And that the whole cycle will begin anew?

Yes, said the agricolas, a very real danger, especially since the marketing of African cattle is far from satisfactory. Quarantine restrictions and prices the Kamba consider too low combine to bottle up the herds. No laws prevent the Kamba from ruining their country all over again, and population pressure is increasing all the time.

'Our great hope now is that they've seen with their own eyes that their country *will* recover, if they give it half a chance. They know now it's something *they* can do, not just some order from the Government. We say to them: "Well, it's over to you. Go back to your *mangalata* if you want to, and your famine relief, but do you really think it's a good thing?" They've grasped the point.

'Things *should* go on all right—unless the politicians work up the old suspicions again. . . .'

There is an Akamba Liberal Party in Machakos, with a paid-up membership of less than fifty, which censured the local Legislative Councillor for his refusal to join with his colleagues in condemning the agricultural policies of the Government. The district's annual report observes:

'During the year the *malaise* that has infected the national political scene has crept into the district from Nairobi. People with a mainly urban background, and little appreciation of the immense revolution that has been brought about in the day-to-day life of the district, are spreading abroad their doctrine of opposition to the policies and discipline which the Kamba leaders have so successfully adopted to save their country.'

Since 1955 there has been no famine relief in Machakos: in 1958, a maize export of 20,000 bags. People and land advance towards an equilibrium. And there are few things in the world that can be more easily upset.

v

'Full of thin cows and fat spivs,' someone said of Kangundo, a part of the district as tormented topographically as if nature had whipped it up with a beater. Now that Machakos is 'on the tarmac' it has almost become a dormitory area for Nairobi and even enjoys such benefits of civilization as gangs of motorized thieves.

We looked from a hill-top down over a series of narrow bench terraces like many flights of steps to heaven, and on a bowl of greenery checkered with brown. 'This used to be a famine relief area,' said Mr. Peberdy. '*Mangalata*. Gullies. Hat-racks. The lot. Now it exports maize and beans and the coming thing is coffee—already our most valuable export, although it's been in production only two years. But 76 per cent in the top three classes and a first prize at the Royal Show. . . .'

Before reconditioning, the average maize yield in this valley was one to two bags: now it is six, and the best growers get up to fifteen. Soil fertility and rainfall are there, it is just a question of human common sense. 'Early planting and manure, that's all it is, once you've got in the terraces. Simple? Yes, but . . .'

I met Chief Uku, who deserves much of the credit for the state of Kangundo today. In his youth he worked for Mr. Robert Barnes, with Colin Maher the pioneer of all soil conservation in Kenya, and with his own hands and eyes made and saw the great changes. When he became a chief he made sure that in his own location the gospel was followed. His light-skinned face was wrinkled, resolute and command-ing. 'He is a strong character,' one of the African agricolas said with admiration. 'He was in Legislative Council for three years and never spoke.'

In Machakos a grand new hall is going up for the District Council. To lay its foundation stone, the Councillors invited the three men they thought had done most to bring their country back to life and found its new prosperity. One of these was Senior Chief Uku. Another was Mr. Onesimus Musyoki, B.E.M., who started as one of Colin Maher's levellers and is now an agricola and District Councillor.

The third was Major Frank Joyce, C.B.E., who for nearly fifty years farmed at Kilima Kiu on the borders of the Machakos district, and for about thirty of them worked quietly, persistently and with energy, gaiety and judgement towards getting Ukambani back on its feet again. He was one of the driving forces behind ALDEV, on whose Board he sat from its start in 1946 until his death, while on its business, early in 1959. On a quarter of his own ranch, set aside for his labour force and their stock, he demonstrated how the Kamba could manage for themselves if they followed simple rules which he understood and practised. Starting before the first war without capital—his initial venture was to capture ostrich chicks, which grew up to yield tail-feathers of commercial value until the market collapsed—he and his partners built up Kilima Kiu from an uninhabited, waterless stretch of plain and bush to become one of the most productive milk-and-beef-producing ranches in East Africa; and the Kamba, who like everyone else respect achievement, knew that the advice he gave was as correct as the manner in which he gave it was endearing. No reward pleased him more than this invitation, a year before his sudden death, from the District Council in Machakos, nor could there be a more fitting memorial. Frank Joyce's first love was the land, and his greatest happiness lay in putting right the wrongs that had been done to it.

VI

It was a surprise to hear the sound of hunting horns piercing the clear air of the Machakos hills. From a hill-top, looking down over the shadowed valleys, we saw signs not of a chase but, it seemed, of a fair or gathering: banners fluttered, brightly-clad people clustered in some rhythmic activity, the sound of song and drums came to our ears and, as it seemed, the clang of armour.

A dance, perhaps? A ceremony of harvest or of circumcision? We descended the hill. A cloud of red dust hung above a line of dancing women each with a shovel in her hand. As the women sang, they thrust with their shovels, flung the earth on to a bank and struck the backs of their shovels together, two by two, all in one continuous, fluid, rhythmic motion, while their bare feet stamped out a sort of jig. They wore bright dresses and gay head-scarves; they were plump and vigorous and cheerful; they made their own music while they worked. Each group had a gay banner bearing the name of its clan, like the colours of a regiment.

A musician walked up and down blowing lustily on a horn with a very long bamboo stem fitted into a bent-round mouthpiece, which must have taken a tremendous amount of lung-power.

At the beginning, *mwethya* groups were drawn from everyone who lived round about in the *itui*, the parish (like a *kokwet*). People did not work with a will, and it was John Malinda who tried the experiment of calling out to work not *itui*-dwellers but members of a clan. Although often it meant travelling farther people liked it better, and soon developed a spirit of clan rivalry. In *mwethya* everyone has a part to play; old men make pegs to mark terrace lines, old women mind babies, the young and active wield pick and shovel, musicians play, headmen supervise. Now the clans compete for the reputation of being the fiercest and for doing most terracing in a day.

'This group is particularly fierce,' an instructor said, indicating a line of young women throwing the earth above their heads and clinking shovels with tremendous gusto and abandon. I asked him to translate the words of their rollicking song:

> The *askaris* used to be strong and bold as lions.
> They went to fight and they were fierce as lions.
> But now it is we who are strong and bold as lions.
> Now we are strong as the *askaris*.
> Now we are stronger than the *askaris*, stronger than lions.
> Yeh! Yeh! Yeh! Stronger than *askaris* or lions.

The men's part in this seems mainly confined to making music and looking on. 'The women would not let them join,' said my informant. But groups that are less fierce do so: we saw a few working later on.

The countryside seemed alive with *mwethya* groups. There is plenty of work for them before the goal of terraces on every slope is reached. The Government's part is to provide levellers who peg terraces on the contour; location councils provide the shovels, and the rest is free. The main difficulty now is to keep up enthusiasm. Before a man's land is terraced he is glad enough to send his women, but once his turn has come he wants to keep them working at home, knowing that he himself has nothing more to gain.

VII

We picnicked on a hill-top among the bracken, over 7,000 feet up, with yet another eye-assaulting view over innumerable hills and twisting valleys down towards the plains that run almost to the Indian Ocean. On a clear morning Kilimanjaro's white table-top can be seen above a scarf of cloud, but later in the day a heat-haze veils it. Over to our left lay the rocky peak of Nzaui, like a lion crouching, known in caravan days as 'the gateway to the highlands', a sign to weary porters that their long, waterless marches through deadly heat and jagged rocky deserts was over, and that a land of cool nights, fresh mornings, clear water and ample food lay ahead. Lugard, writing in 1890, called Nzaui the Mighty Custodian, and said it 'looks like an old friend, and in its great giant massive bulk seems like a tower of strength and of comfort. It stands out as a worthy guardian to the higher lands, and chaos of range on range and peak on peak, which go to form the central lands in the very heart itself of the Dark Continent.'*

In the seventy years since he wrote that, the complete destruction of the forests has had a most disastrous effect upon the rivers, which now dry up every year for six months or more. It took twenty years to get the Kamba to agree to reafforestation, and it was not until 1954 that they 'set aside' any hill-tops for this purpose. Before that, despite years of propaganda and a chronic shortage of firewood, the total acreage of trees planted in the Machakos district, which covers over $3\frac{1}{2}$ million acres, was a little over 3,000 acres in dribs and drabs here and there. Now the target is 50,000 acres; of this, just over half has been set aside by the Machakos District Council, and 7,500 acres actually planted. Although most of the cost of planting—at least £250,000—is to be paid by the central Government, the forests will belong to the

* *The Diaries of Lord Lugard.* Ed. Perham and Bull, Vol. I. Faber and Faber.

District Council which will enjoy all the revenue, and get the first returns from thinnings after eight years.

From our picnic on Makuli hill we looked down on dark-green vistas of Christmas trees, for nearly all the plantations are of exotic softwoods, not the native trees of Africa.* Perhaps only sentimentalists feel sad about this, as they do in Britain when they see native oaks, beeches and ash give way to nothing but softwoods. But there it is; Christmas trees are a great deal better than no trees, and their resinous scent freshens the mountain air. Forty-three hill-tops are due to be afforested, but the pace is slow because of shortage of money; work on these precipitous hillsides, without roads, is expensive and difficult.

Mr. Onesimus Musyoki had come up from Makueni, shimmering below us in the haze, to talk about his work there on the resettlement of landless Kamba. It began as long ago as 1945 with the clearing of tsetse-sheltering bush to make way for settlers from the overcrowded Machakos hills, who began to trickle down there, reluctantly, at the end of 1947.

Mr. Musyoki, then an instructor, had the task of trying to persuade the settlers, who had been set against it all politically, to take up 70-acre plots. One of the many facts discovered by trial and error was that 70 acres was far too much for one man and his family to cope with. The plots were progressively reduced in size to 20 acres and even that is now believed to be, on the whole, too large. On too big a plot, back creeps the bush and with it tsetse fly. 'That is still happening,' said Mr. Musyoki: and what is more, the trypanosome carried by the fly has developed a resistance to drugs, so that many of the Makueni cattle are dying. The only permanent remedy is to reduce plots to a size a family can look after well enough to defeat the bush, perhaps to ten acres.

At first, the carrying capacity of Makueni was put at ten acres to the beast but now it is clear that, with proper

---

*Mostly *Pinus patula*, with other spp. of pinus and some *Cupressus lusitanica*. In the lower areas, below 5,000 feet, two spp. of indigenous hardwoods have been included in the programme, viz. *Terminalia brownii* and *Brachylaena hutchinsii*.

management, this can be cut to about two acres to the beast—a 'revolutionary discovery', the experts say. The cost of settling a family down there has been cut rather less drastically. At the start, the cost worked out at £632—it would almost have been cheaper to have shipped them all to Britain and taken flats for them in London. By 1958 it was down to £149 per family, still too high to make re-settlement a practical solution for the overcrowding problem on any but an experimental scale. Over £300,000 has been spent on Makueni and it holds 2,075 families—the full complement at present: Kamba objections have faded out and now there is a waiting list of applicants.

VIII

During the twelve years or so since Makueni started, a fundamental change has taken place in expert opinion about the right way to reclaim land. What Mr. Richard Hennings, formerly ALDEV'S guiding spirit, called the 'obsession with over-population and the need for more land', has virtually vanished; the truth has dawned that land is not so much over-populated, except in certain places, as under-used. It is much more a question of wrong practices and too little skill than of too many people. As Ukambani demonstrates, you can reclaim land without moving out its inhabitants, without finding new land for them, without costly, uneconomic schemes like Makueni.

Four things have helped to dispel this 'over-population obsession'. One is the demonstration in the Makavete square mile that eroded land can be restored in two years, not in two generations; another the discovery, at Makueni and elsewhere, that a family can make its living off a much smaller acreage than had previously been thought; a third, the proof from these Machakos hills that land can be re-claimed while the people continue to live on it; and, finally, the realization that a prosperous peasantry can support a great many people who do not actually work on the land, such as traders, transport owners, craftsmen, clerks and many more.

And so emphasis has swung from the need to settle people on new land to the need to develop the land they already have. Of course, that does not mean no new land is needed, or will not be needed in future. Many settlement schemes are on foot, much settlement is taking place without schemes at all, and the process will doubtless go on, as the population multiplies like bacteria, until the whole of Africa is as fully developed as Surrey.

Makueni has some way to go, as we could see from our summit, before it is at all like Surrey; the struggle at the moment is to keep the bush at bay. But nearly all the wild life has gone. Mr. Musyoki told me that 1,078 rhinos were shot by hunters employed by the Government in that 780 square miles below us, besides 78 elephants and 30 buffalo. 'I used to go without shoes,' he said, 'so that I could get up a tree quicker when I was chased.' Luckily he came to no harm.

Below us, in another direction, lay an experimental ranch owned by the District Council from which the first shipment of steers on the hoof went off, a few months ago, to the Persian Gulf. The whole area is being paddocked and Sahiwal bulls are leaving their stamp on the small Kamba cattle bought for the foundation stock. Boreholes, rotational grazing, wire fences, cattle dips, truckloads of steers going off to be canned and sent abroad. . . . Money for the District Council to put into new schools, health centres, ambulances, community development. . . . Progress marches on, Surrey catches up; soon at this rate the old peak of Nzaui will look down on fields and market gardens, cattle sheds and villas, garages and television aerials instead of bush, game and an occasional long file of porters winding its slow way down to the coast.

IX

On the pavements of Nairobi, and of other African cities, even in some of the big stores of London and New York, you may come across the neat wooden images of animals and elongated Africans fashioned by carvers of the Kamba people. Nowadays these carvings have penetrated everywhere, they appear at all trade and agricultural shows, they adorn mantelpieces in many countries and have a fresh, naïve charm of their own. I have often wondered how these carvings came into being: whether certain families produced them, or master-carvers with their own schools, and to what extent they followed an old tradition. And so in the Machakos district I took the chance to inquire.

They emanate, it seems—and emanate in thousands—from a single village called Wamunyu, near the border of Machakos with Kitui. A stout, aldermanic chief explained that it had all started with a single *askari* who had learnt the craft in Dar es Salaam in the First World War, and returned to his native village to practise it. There was no Kamba tradition of wood-carving, he said, before that. And an anthropologist who studied Kamba customs in 1911 and 1912, Gerhard Lindblom, wrote in his treatise: 'No sculpture in wood or any other kind of ornamental wood-carving is found.'* Thus Chief John Wandare's account is confirmed.

This *askari* taught some of the young men of his clan and gradually the craft grew. An original family compound has expanded into a sizeable village made of low brick buildings grouped round a square. In the veranda of every building sat a group of carvers, mostly quite young boys, whittling away with small knives. It is mass-production without machinery. Perhaps a carving expert could detect subtle differences between one elephant and another, between the innumerable antelope lying with their fawns at foot, between the various rhinos and tortoises and giraffe-headed salad-spoons, but to the ordinary eye they appear identical. Yet there does not seem to be any pattern laid down, still less a master-carver in charge of it all. Marketing is organized by one or two traders who buy at flat rates from the carvers, dispatch their wares in batches to agents in the towns, or at the coast for shipment overseas, and supply the wood, which may be one of the olives, or a species called *Brachylaena hutchinsii* which used to grow locally. Wood is getting short, so great is

* *The Akamba.* By Gerhard Lindblom. Archives D'Etudes Orientale, Uppsala.

the demand, and now it must be brought from far away.

Here is an example of an industry built up without any outside help at all. From design and workmanship to marketing, all is indigenous; there are said to be Kamba agents living in places as far afield as Johannesburg and Salisbury. Wamunyu is almost the only village in Machakos that now supplies no recruits to the K.A.R., for the young men have a home occupation. Exports of these carvings from the district are worth about £150,000 a year.

Like most arts that get commercialized, it is losing its virtue, or so it seemed to me. The trader for whom many of the carvers were working displayed their latest models, and instead of sticking to their little antelopes, which have great charm, they were launching forth into complicated groups of baboons and of human beings, which lacked the delicacy of their earlier work. Perhaps museum experts of the future will pay high prices for early Wamunyus, now mostly in the homes of retired officials who worked in Ukambani between the wars.

CHAPTER 13

Consolidation in Embu

I

FROM the air one sees that civilization is order: a pattern imposed upon a shaggy landscape. To some extent it is simply straight lines. We flew across livid plains pale with drought and sunshine, where cattle-tracks, rivers and gullies bitten by erosion lay in sweeping curves or corkscrew convolutions, like long hair tossed back on a vast terrestrial pillow. Then we came suddenly to a patch of squares, as if we had an aerial view of the Red Queen's chess-board. The landscape had been laid out with a ruler, it was patterned with black and green rectangles, streaked by lines and dotted with neat toy compounds.

This was the Mwea-Teberre irrigation scheme, lying on the plains south-east of Mt. Kenya. Like Perkerra, like the Yatta furrow, its origins lay in finding work for Mau Mau detainees to do. Men came from the Sudan to run it and Mr. Rodney Dew, the director of irrigation, is from the Gezira. Technically it is sound; the question is, what can be grown at a profit.

We drove for miles along tidy bunds enclosing square plots, each of one acre. Four of these make up the standard family holding. The tenants were cutting their paddy with sickles and carrying it in golden bundles to a heap where the women, dots of colour in their printed cottons on a blue and yellow landscape, beat them out against stones and gathered up the ripe grain in bags. All this was simple, primitive and serene. Lorries would then collect the bags and take them to a central factory which dries and cleans the grain, and then off it would go to the railway station. Harvesting cannot be mechanized because the ground is too soft, having only just been drained, and, in any case, hand work is cheaper.

204

We stopped on a bund and watched the rice being cut and threshed on the sunlit plain under an enormous cloudless sky. A group of tenants was harvesting together. One was an old man whose clan, he told me, owned hereditary grazing rights in this area—it had been uninhabited but formed part of the grazing reserve of the Embu people—and so he had been given a four-acre plot. He had never seen rice before, it was a new thing, but he had followed the instructions and now he liked it very much, it was bringing more shillings than maize or beans.

A much younger man was there and went on working while we talked. When I asked where he had come from, he answered politely that he had been in Tanganyika until Mau Mau, when he had become a detainee. The camp he was in was one for bad cases, terrorists and the like, so he must have been an active oath-taker. He had passed, he said, through the rehabilitation 'pipe-line' and been given a plot, and had brought his mother, brother and sister, who helped him; he, too, was pleased with rice, which was bringing in good money.

The work is hard but the rewards satisfying. All tenants were landless men—that is a condition of tenancy—and they get their four acres free, with all its bunds and channels, and a house in a village, but after their third season must pay a water rate of £10 an acre a year. The return they get depends mainly on their energy. Their principal fault is a failure to transplant the paddy in time. One old man who did everything he was told got a yield of three tons to the acre. When the pay-out came after harvest he went off, in dazed astonishment, with a wad of notes amounting to £150, having never before handled more than 20 shillings in his life.

After that pay-out, a flood of applications for tenancies arrived. The average yield so far is four times higher than the Indian and Burmese average and, unless the price falls, the management reckons that, after all deductions, tenants should average about £140 a year. Their housing is free and they also get land for nothing on which to grow their food. The water rate ought to pay the running costs, which include a European supervisor for every 1,200 acres of paddy, and a headquarters staff.

The project is by no means completed. We came upon a cloud of dust in the midst of which were several D6 caterpillar tractors making irrigation ditches. There are reckoned to be 14,000 acres of soil suitable for irrigation and up to date 2,230 have been levelled; if the money holds out, and the rice can be sold, the scheme can absorb new tenants at the rate of 600 a year and build up to about 30,000 people.

The trouble is to sell the rice. Even at its present stage, developed to less than one-fifth of its capacity, the scheme produces half the rice consumed in the country. Once the local market is saturated, the rice must be exported, and its costs of production do not allow it to compete with India and Burma. What happens then? Export at a loss, limit the scheme, switch to some other crop? How will the tenants react if they find their rewards dwindling, while their costs rise?

II

As we drove around to see the irrigation headworks on the Nyamnindi and Thiba rivers, the villages where the tenants live, the experimental farm that tries to find new crops, the driers and cleaning machinery, the offices and tenants' ledgers in which each man's transactions are recorded; these and other difficulties were explained to me by the experts in charge. Like most troubles, they go back into the history of the scheme. It was started in the usual hurry and at one time 3,500 detainees were at work here, living in camps which now stand empty and decaying behind their rusty barbed wire. As at Perkerra, no preliminary experiments were made. This resulted in two basic and very expensive mistakes.

The area set aside for irrigation consists of two kinds of soil, one black, one red. The black soil is an obstinate kind of viscous clay, hard to work and left alone by native cultivators; the red soil is extremely fertile, easy to work and will grow almost anything. The men who started the scheme put most of their faith in the red soils. The rainfall in this district is about 25 inches, which is marginal; irrigation was expected to make for heavy, certain crops and two of them a year, one planted in the short rains, about November, and the other in the long rains, in April. Throughout most of the fertile parts of Kenya, two crops a year are the rule.

The first thing that went wrong was the red soil—the first to be levelled, bunded, and drained. The irrigation water, instead of soaking in to gratify the crops, simply ran through and vanished. Costly work was wasted and the red soils had to be written off for irrigation purposes.

So of the 30,000 acres earmarked for the scheme there remained only the 14,000 acres of black clay. As these turned out to be well suited to irrigation and to grow excellent paddy crops, the attention of the management was switched to them and there seemed to be every prospect that they would reward it.

In the spring of 1958 all the black soil that had been prepared was planted with paddy and the crop, harvested in September, proved a dismal failure. Most of the ears were blind. Only then did the managers realize that the cold, cloudy weather which generally follows the long rains in July and August had inhibited pollination of the flowers. The paddy had grown splendidly, but developed scarcely any grain.

So planting in the long rains has had to be abandoned and now there is only one rice crop a year, planted in October, just before the short rains. These were called the millet rains in old parlance; in the long rains people planted beans only, never grains. There was a clue here, had the experts followed it up, but they had no time for caution and experiment. Now the managers are stuck with two problems for which they have at present no solution: what to plant on the red soils? And what catch-crop to plant in the long rains on the black, so as to get their two crops a year?

At an experimental farm, two young scientists are trying everything they can think of on the red soils—Chinese pumpkins, citrus, asparagus, onions, tomatoes, even coffee and tea. The most promising so far is hibiscus, whose fibres might replace imported jute for sack-making. If the costs could be kept low enough, the technical problem could probably be solved by overhead sprinkler irrigation, on the principle of little and often. As for a long-rains crop on black soils, there is an interesting possibility—fish.

The idea would be to flood the plots immediately the rice was off, and stock them with tilapia fingerlings. The fish would have five months to grow before the plots would need to be drained. Manure is their favourite food, it seems; for this, cattle would be needed; experiments in how best to keep stall-fed cattle, which would also be a source of milk, meat and profit, are under way. When the fields were drained ready for the paddy, the fish would be harvested. How to market them is still unsolved, but the prospect of working out a system of fish-farming has made everyone hopeful at Mwea-Tebere. 'At any rate,' the manager remarked, 'the tenants would have plenty of kedgeree.'

III

The game that formerly inhabited these plains has gone, but bird life has to some extent replaced it. Herons fish in flooded paddy-fields, cranes pick among the cracked stubble, storks flap overhead with dignity, geese in their V formation honk by, waders paddle, many other kinds of water-loving bird rise from field and bund as you pass by. The most pleasant sight I saw was a dam covered with purple water-lilies and circled over by flights of whistling teal making their sad, haunting cry.

But one species of bird has become a serious menace to the scheme. This is the Sudan dioch, or *Quelea quelea aethiopica*, a drab-looking finch that in recent years has taken to going about all over Africa in gigantic flocks—a single one, in the French Sudan, was estimated to contain eight million birds—and settling upon any large expanse of crop it can find. The damage has been getting worse year by year and in certain places, such as northern Tanganyika, is said to be more severe even than that caused by locust swarms.

25 Two types of settler: an Elgeyo farmer on the cold uplands of the Cherangani mountains and a Meru family on the Giaki plains

26 Marking out a new farm for a Kikuyu landowner: a consolidation committee with measurer at work

To every pest modern science and human ingenuity between them can, given time and money, find an answer. The Tanganyika Government was the first to employ a bird control officer in the shape of Mr. Tony Haylock, whose own wheat farm had been devastated by these *quelea*, and he has worked out a technique of blowing up the birds in their roosting-places with drums of high explosive and oil. At Mwea-Tebere the diochs nest in a particular swamp into which it is impossible to penetrate in order to set the drums, so the method is to spray them from an aeroplane.

I did not see this done, but heard it described with a somewhat ghoulish respect. The pilot has to fly at dusk when the birds have settled in to roost. He has to take his aircraft across this swamp in semi-darkness, the most tricky time of day, at a height of ten feet: and the swamp is studded with ant-heaps a good deal more than ten feet high. He has to do this in cold blood with a drum of a deadly poison at his back—Parathion, a substance developed during the war so lethal that a single splash on the arm would kill a man.

The pilot's name is 'Timber' Wood and he is forty years old. In the war he won several 'gongs', but the men on the scheme reckon that nothing he did then needed as much skill and cold courage as these flights in darkness that skim the surface of the swamp with lethal spray spurting out below him. They say he killed at least three million birds last season. As each bird will spoil, rather than eat, two ounces of grain daily, he probably saved over 2,000 tons of rice and every tenant owes him about £50. It is unlikely that any of them realize this, or would therefore subscribe to his memorial.

IV

So closely are the Meru and Embu sub-tribes related to the Kikuyu that it is sometimes hard to tell them apart; differences are those of degree and circumstance rather than of ethnology. The great belt of territory occupied by these peoples, circling Mt. Kenya and stretching across to the hundred-mile-long range of the Aberdare mountains,

is divided into five districts of which Embu is one. Kikuyuland as a whole amounts to about three million acres, supports about 1½ million people and contains some of the most
fertile, best-watered and richest country on earth.

As the people multiply, it becomes impossible to find land
for every Kikuyu, Embu or Meru individual. No doubt, as
Kenya develops, many more will earn their living, as in all
advancing countries, by other means than with hoe or cow.
If all of England's forty million people shared out Britain's
dwindling agricultural land, we should be down to half-acre
plots, and belong to one of the world's poorest nations,
instead of one of the world's richest. Africa will diversify also,
and is in fact doing so; but there are many difficulties and,
in the meanwhile, many landless people who lack qualifications to earn their living in any other way.

In the Embu district there are perhaps as many as 10,000
landless individuals. Only a very few of these can be given
tenancies at Mwea-Tebere.

'People say land consolidation is creating a landless class,
but that is not true,' said an agricola. 'Land consolidation
merely recognizes the existing position and brings it to light.
It does not take land from anyone who already has it. But
it gives us a chance for the first time to size things up properly.
And, in the long run, it provides the best hope of creating
employment.' Before the end of 1961 all inhabited Kikuyuland, including Embu and Meru, will, barring accidents, be
divided into smallholdings, fenced and registered.

Consolidation in Embu, as among the Luo, is done on the
basis of the sub-clan, here called the *mbari*, rather than the
individual, but the object is the same: to leave everyone
who has a claim to land with his own holding which he can
then enclose, improve, enjoy for his lifetime and leave to his
sons. Here is a brief outline of the system: this part can be
skipped by anyone not interested in the machinery of getting
things done.

These are the various stages:

 1. A committee of all elders of the *mbari* meets to decide
    upon the *mbari* boundaries.

2. These elders call a meeting of the whole *mbari* and explain what is to be done.

3. A boundary-walker—a clerk from the district office—beats the bounds with the elders and prepares a sketch-map.

4. All objections are called for and noted by the clerk.

5. Large committees, twenty to thirty elders from each *mbari* (numbers discourage bribery) meet to hear and settle disputes.

6. If this settlement is not unanimous, the dispute is laid before an Arbitration Board. In Embu, up to the date of my visit, only forty disputes had been so referred from over 10,000 settlements.

7. A planning committee is set up among the younger, educated men of the *mbari*, such as teachers, instructors, traders, clerks and so on.

8. All the departments likely to want land for future use put in their bids to this committee. These bids cover foreseeable needs for schools, roads, health centres, community centres, markets, coffee factories, tea nurseries, churches, playing fields, cemeteries and other purposes. Generally this comes to between three and five per cent of the area.

9. The planning committee divides the residue of the land between all the claimants in that *mbari* according to agreements as to acreage already reached by the elders.

10. The names of the claimants who have been allocated land are put up on a notice-board in a public place for one month.

11. Survey teams go out with the *mbari* elders and the published lists, and allocate the *shambas* on the ground to the people on the lists, according to their agreed acreages.

12. Teams of volunteers from each *mbari* go out to plant boundary hedges.

13. Lists of those who have been allocated land go up on the notice-board for a further month and any disputes are dealt with.

14. Once everything is settled, the lists are closed and every land claim is registered for a fee of 5 shillings an acre. The register is kept under lock and key in the district office and a copy goes to a central register in Nairobi.

That is as far as the matter has got in Embu. When the district is finished, some 275,000 acres will have been demarcated into about 48,750 farms; the average holding is in the region of six acres.

The register of owners shows all encumbrances on each piece of land including the names of all tenants who are found in all Kikuyu districts and collectively are called *ahoi*. As consolidation proceeds every such tenant, and every man whose claim is too small to be agriculturally sound, is either offered land on a settlement scheme or given a quarter-acre plot in one of the permanent villages that are being developed all over the province. Here he will have a chance either to follow some trade or profession, or to work for one of his land-owning fellows.

No one who has a valid claim to land ownership will be left without a registered title, and no adult Kikuyu, Embu or Meru in the whole province need be left without either a title to land, a village plot, or a farm in a settlement scheme.

v

The twin objects of consolidation are these: first, to give a man a workable acreage all in one piece; second, to give him security. But this, agricolas constantly tell you, is only the first stage: a laying of foundations. The administration carry out consolidation and the agricolas and vets take over when this is done. Then comes their big task: to get good husbandry understood, accepted and practised by the people.

The basis of this is the farm lay-out and the farm plan. The farm plan is what agricolas most value and want to introduce, but it is complicated, or at any rate appears so on its piece of shiny blue parchment with all its contour lines and figures and, in one corner, a most elaborate chart showing what every field is to grow for the next ten years. It did not surprise me in the least to learn that only the most educated farmers took to these plans. I could well imagine what some of my Wiltshire neighbours would say, confronted with a plan like that by someone from the Ministry. A simplified version called a farm lay-out is more suitable for ordinary folk and of course much cheaper, for it can be drawn up quickly by an African instructor. The farmer gets it free and it can be issued to large numbers of people in a short time.

Farm lay-outs are not compulsory, but in the Central Province, where everyone was moved into a village during the Emergency and needed permission to move out while it lasted,* farmers were not normally able to settle on their land until they had accepted the principle of these simple plans. Most of the farmers I spoke to valued them highly and appeared to be carrying them out.

A farm lay-out will suggest to you where to put your homestead and sheds, to site your paddocks on the contour, the best place for a firewood plantation and a famine insurance such as cassava, where to plant your cash crops, and where to grow your food. The basic principle is that all arable land should spend about half its life under grass, generally on a seven- or eight-year cycle.

This may sound simple, and so it is, but to people brought up in the practice of shifting cultivation it is revolutionary. And for centuries shifting cultivation has been the norm for almost every East African farmer. A family would clear the bush and take a crop for as long as fertility lasted—not long, as a rule, in the tropics, in some regions only two or three years. Then they would clear another *shamba* farther on and let the old one revert to bush. Land was bush-fallowed for four, five, up to ten years, until population pressure began to cut down the resting period and so over-strain fertility and damage the structure of the soil.

The system was rather like a Mad Hatter's tea-party, with fresh ground in place of clean cups. The tea-drinkers moved round faster and faster and had reached a point where the crockery never got washed and much of it was broken.

*It ended officially on 12th January, 1960, having started on 20th October, 1952.

This traditional system worked well enough when people were thinly spread over the ground. When they started to accumulate, it broke down, and the only way out lay through enclosure. Because this idea is so obvious and familiar to Europeans, we tend to forget what a complete reversal of the natural order it was to most East Africans. For the first time they were faced with the stark fact that if they used their acres wastefully, they could not escape retribution by moving on.

The speed with which they have accepted this is amazing. Many cling to farm lay-outs as to lifebuoys in a sea of doubt. The next stage is to encourage them to carry out the basic practices of good husbandry, such as manuring, planting in rows, ploughing on the contour, rotations and grass leys. It is no good simply lecturing people: they must see for themselves. So the Government has started six major Farm Institutes and the more enlightened District Councils are following suit with smaller ones in various places.

One such is the Kianyagga Institute, near Embu, for which one *mbari* gave twenty-five acres and the local inhabitants raised nearly £1,000 by subscription. It is managed by the local agricola but supervised by a Board of Governors consisting of three chiefs, three schoolmasters and about half a dozen ordinary elders of the clan. At the Institute, where I met them, we sat on benches on green turf among simple mud-and-wattle, whitewashed buildings housing an office and some precious half-bred Guernsey calves destined to become Better Cows kept by the Better Farmers, who take three-week courses in batches of twelve. They bring their wives, who learn how to rear calves on the bucket and keep the milk clean—and learn faster than men, the Governors admitted, especially about 'germses' and bringing up calves.

This is indeed a progressive district. Parts of it are flat enough for tractors and a unit sent here to demonstrate caught on so well that the District Council keeps three tractors to plough on contract for the Better Farmers—of whom at least forty round Kianyagga are probably making over £750 a year. The co-operative has over 800 members whose produce it buys, bags, grades and markets. Pineapples are all the rage at the moment. A Nairobi canning firm sends round lorries twice a week to pick them up from roadside collecting points and they bring in a return, with luck, of £50 an acre, so long as they are grown at the right altitude.

Embu was one of the first districts to grow coffee, and the earliest plantings date from 1935. The first co-operative was registered in 1946 with 118 members; now the Embu Coffee Co-operative Union of eleven societies has over 12,000 grower-members, last season the district exported over £250,000 worth of beans and 4,000 new members are joining every year.

The Union's chairman, Mr. Marchus Njiru, is also one of the three African members of the Coffee Board of Kenya. 'Our members complained that European coffee was sold first and so made the best prices,' he said, 'but I have been to many auctions and have told them this is untrue; in any case, African coffee is fetching higher prices than European.'

The manager of the factory which Mr. Njiru showed me was an ex-sergeant of the K.A.R. and when he commands growers to take away inferior cherry he is promptly obeyed. The committee members borrowed £2,300 from the Government and have repaid it by docking one-fifth of the pay-out; now they are clear of debt, but with over 1,000 members— they started with 23—increasing their plantations, and new ones joining almost daily, the factory will have to be enlarged, more staff taken on, the seedling nurseries expanded. . . . It was a success story, and no wonder the chairman and his committee were proud.

Here among the green Embu ridges with their deep red loam, their tall trees, their neat productive little farms, their innumerable sparkling streams, one feels as if the world cannot go wrong; but it is alarming to reflect that all this prosperity and enthusiasm, this sense of achievement and faith in the future, rests upon a tight-rope of prices that might snap at any moment and plunge the growers into gloom and a feeling of betrayal by the Government. The

Embu people know nothing of this, and their one idea at present is to plant more of these profitable trees.

VII

As soon as you get into a Kikuyu district, you notice how much the people seem able and willing to do for themselves. Perhaps this is partly because of the lead they have secured in schooling. The educational harvest is now starting to come in; students are returning from Makerere and from Britain with all sorts of qualifications and, though they prefer jobs in Nairobi if they can get them, those who join the Civil Service must go where they are sent, and a few actually want to make their mark in their own land.

The Principal of the college at Embu that trains agricultural instructors for the whole province is such a man. Mr. Paul Thiongo, son of a Canon, studied for eight years at Reading and Cambridge, and his wife also has lived in Britain and taken courses—in fact, he receives 'inducement pay' with regular spells of leave in Britain. The fifty young men Mr. Thiongo is to turn out yearly will be thoroughly grounded and inspired with the importance of their task, but his trouble is to find entrants of a high enough educational standard. He had hoped to make the Cambridge school certificate a condition of entrance, but there are not nearly enough certificate-holders to go round and he is obliged to take boys without any secondary schooling. Every year about 3,000 children in the Central Province sit for the examination which concludes their eight years' primary and intermediate course, and offers access to the secondary courses. Some 1,500 pass, but there are places for only about 300 in secondary schools and another 300 in teacher-training colleges. For the rest, there is at the moment no future in the educational system. About a thousand frustrated youths are turned loose in the Kikuyu districts every year.

CHAPTER 14

Meru Settlement Schemes

I

IF I were asked to pick the district of Kenya which excels above all others in beauty, variety and generosity of soil and climate, I think I might choose Meru, which runs from the high cedar forests of Mt. Kenya, lost in mist and pinched with frost in the sharp starlit hours before dawn, down to the dry and baking plains of the Northern Frontier.

Possibly—I am not sure of this—it is the only district where you can travel in a day from an altitude of 9,000 feet in the bracken down to 3,000 feet or less on the rim of the desert, and where rainfall varies from over 100 inches in the tropical rain-forest of the Nyambeni hills—a Tarzan film was shot among their lianas—to about 10 inches near the camel zone. In extent this single district comprises over 3,000 square miles—nearly one-third as large as the so-called white highlands. Ice-clear streams run off the mountain, game still lingers in the bush and the deep loam is as fertile as any in the world.

With a population of under 400,000, Meru is not yet over-crowded. Empty bits of Africa can still be found. But it is filling up—partly with its own Wa-Meru people and partly with an overspill from areas where population pressure is higher. Its speciality is settlement schemes for the landless in undeveloped reaches of bush, forest and plain.

Everyone is proud of these schemes, because of their success and above all of their economy. Lips curl with pitying contempt at the mention of Makueni. Meru believes in do-it-yourself settlement with no more outlay than the pay of an officer and one or two instructors or guards. The cost per settler is about £6 a head—except in a settlement to which a 23-mile-long furrow was taken from the mountain, through forest much frequented by elephants, who played havoc with the furrow until engineers built several bridges, fringed with stakes, for their benefit. The elephants used the bridges until one of these collapsed, and then boycotted the remainder.

Meru is a strange blend of old and new. There is an active District Council but the indigenous machinery of government still operates on parallel lines. The agricolas told me that if they want to get a measure accepted by the people they do not press for District Council by-laws, they ask one of the Councillors to raise the matter at the Njure Ncheke, an assembly of elders which meets under a sacred tree and now and again, if the members want to, asks the D.C. to attend. Many of the Njure Ncheke elders are also District Councillors, so the two systems operate fairly smoothly side by side.

The women of Meru still carry heavy loads of produce on their backs, with leather straps biting into their foreheads; they still inhabit the old, round, windowless thatched huts of immemorial tradition, foggy with wood-smoke; the girls are circumcised, even those who go to boarding schools; on winding forest paths among the yellow *cassia* and the white clover one might be back in the Africa of fifty years ago. Yet Meru has three women on the District Council, the best-run coffee co-operative in the country, a thriving artificial insemination scheme and, in Meru township, an all-African company that runs a modern filling station, has the agency for several kinds of motor-car and employs a European manager. There is even a Meru man in Moscow, teaching a Swahili accent, among other things, to his fellow-students.

Under the old Meru custom, boys lived for two years after circumcision in the bush in huts centred round an elder who instructed them in the laws, customs, traditions and skills of their tribe. This custom has been adapted in an ingenious way at a training centre for boys started by the District Council. An instructor has replaced the elder as the focus of each group and the boys live under strict discipline imposed by an ex-sergeant of the K.A.R. These are lads who have completed eight years' schooling and failed to get into a secondary school. They are the disgruntled, often the bitter and frustrated, with no land, no trade, no prospect of jobs to match their own estimate of their abilities.

Here at Gitoro they receive a short, brisk training in a few simple skills and are taught some English, which is the bait: to learn that, boys will put up with almost anything. After their basic training, some continue as apprentices. I watched them learning how to tan and dye local leather and make it into boots, bags, belts and other useful objects. The officer in charge hoped they would set up as leather-workers in the new villages, and perhaps form a company of tanners to supply the boot and shoe factories near Nairobi. The District Council supports the school, but it can deal only with a fraction of the eligible boys. Every year the number of youths with no skill to offer rises and the economy, while it is expanding, cannot expand fast enough to keep up.

II

During the Emergency, most of the land along the forest's edge, all communal grazing, was 'closed': anyone living there was moved to a village down below. At the end of 1955 it was reopened, and 18,000 acres of it set aside to absorb 'villagized' families who wanted to return and were approved by a committee of local people. Their leader was Chief Stanley, an energetic, middle-aged man a-bubble with enthusiasm for his fenced green pastures in the clean, cedar-sharp air of high altitudes, commanding an eagle's view down the shaggy flanks of the great mountain and over plains that shimmer northwards to the Ethiopian frontier.

With its high rainfall, and grass that never browns, this must be as fine a dairying country as any in the world, and now it is to be proved as such by butter-yellow, pioneering Guernseys. Chief Stanley has three such and his thin face was alight with pride when he regarded them. He records their yields in an exercise book and sells their rich milk to his neighbours for sixpence a bottle. This is fine potato country, also, and his first crop came out at 25 tons to the acre. Pyrethrum thrives at this altitude, over 8,000 feet; lucerne for the cows lies across the hillside like a green collar; the Chief keeps three sows and a boar and does a brisk trade in weaner-pigs which last year brought in £400. Now he is trying European fruit trees: pears, apples, plums.

'Everything will grow here,' he said proudly, and his nine acres gave a wonderful impression of bursting fertility, of work and care, of happiness. The calves in their little paddock came prancing up to suck my fingers, their mothers quietly chewed a satisfying cud, piglets lay stretched out voluptuously in the sunshine, the Chief's four workmen hoed potatoes gently on the terraces. It seemed like a model of the good life, the successful farmer, the contented home. The Chief's wife agreed. 'It is good here because we have plenty to eat and I have a large *shamba*,' she said, 'and workmen to help me cultivate.'

About 250 settlers have so far been established on this particular scheme, which will hold perhaps a thousand families on farms ranging from eight to twenty acres. Or, rather, have established themselves: the only requirements are that they must observe the basic rules of good husbandry, and build their houses to a standard laid down by the Medical department which provides for windows, a separate kitchen, rather more cubic space than in the huts of tradition and no sharing with animals. Any extra services they get, such as piped water or artificial insemination, they pay for themselves.

III

It is the middle altitude belt in Meru, from about 4,800 to 6,500 feet, that is so thickly populated—the coffee belt; above and below, people thin out or have not yet penetrated, and it is here that settlement schemes are developing.

From Chief Stanley's we dropped by Land-Rover nearly 5,000 feet in less than forty miles, leaving the upland star-grass pastures and surviving native trees and arriving at thick bush and tall, coarse *hypharrenia* and guinea grasses. The Meru rainfall is remarkable. Even down at 4,000 feet, which in the Embu district would be parched and only usable under irrigation, you have here a 50-inch annual fall and a hot-house, forcing-frame kind of fertility, with moisture, heat and a great depth of volcanic soil.

Here is the Giaki settlement—'the best watered land in Kenya', I was told, with rivers coming off the mountain every mile or so. Until a few years ago it was uninhabited except for wandering honey-hunters and elephant poachers. This was the sort of country written off as worthless, largely because no one had ever examined it properly, while regions of far less native virtue and potential fecundity in the European highlands were called 'the best land' because a lot of capital had been spent on them. As soon as you cross the Meru border to the European district of Timau, the rainfall drops by at least twenty inches, bush gives way to eroded plain, ranching at the rate of twenty or thirty acres to a beast becomes the only sound form of land usage and smallholdings are out of the question.

Giaki was uninhabited because there was no land pressure, plenty of game and, along the rivers, tsetse fly infection from *pallidipes*. As there are no cattle, there is no erosion: here is a store of locked-up fertility. Out of a potential 40,000 acres suitable for settlement some 10,000 acres have so far been surveyed and marked out in ten-acre farms. All applications for land, and allocations of holdings, are dealt with by elders of the clans to whom the would-be settlers belong; no European is concerned unless disputes arise. The District Council pays for the handful of instructors who help the settlers to get started. The Government's only share is the salary of a settlement officer and the cost of tsetse clearance along the river banks, which pushes back both the fly and the game.

A tsetse officer expressed the view that all the cost and butchery of shooting game in places like Makueni, and in Uganda, had been unnecessary. 'A waste of life and money. As people come in, the animals go out. They're moving out now to the north where rainfall is lower and the land marginal. They must give way to man, but they needn't be slaughtered in the process.' This tsetse officer has one of the finest collections of wild life photographs I have seen, including some remarkable snakes. As an ex-sergeant-major of the

Gloucesters, wounded and captured at the battle of the Imjin River in Korea, Mr. Wateridge perhaps feels that he has seen enough destruction of life and would rather preserve it where he can. But feel as he may, he must play his part in driving the animals out of the haunts they have enjoyed since their species began, and in their eventual extermination by hunters and poachers, or by thirst and hunger in times of drought, on the fringes of the northern deserts.

On the Giaki settlement I saw an unusual way of housing labour: three men lived in a hut in the fork of a tree. 'It is safe up there from wild animals,' they said. They worked for an elderly couple who had emigrated from the highlands in search of better crops, and had given their own holding to a son. 'Look at the maize,' they said, almost with awe. 'Could you grow maize like that near the forest?' It was about eight feet high and the stalks thicker than a man's arm: a fifteen-bag crop, probably.

Although in their fifties, this couple were tending a plant they had never seen before. 'No, I do not know how to grow it,' the man said, 'but I do what the instructor tells me.' He showed us rows of well-weeded, healthy-looking tobacco plants. They will be cured in a dark hut by smoke from fires that smoulder in the ground, while pools of water in banana leaves create humidity, and a throat-choking, eye-stinging atmosphere kippers the leaf. Fire-cured tobacco is nothing like so valuable as flue-cured leaf, but much easier to handle, and the agricolas have found a market which should bring in £40 an acre, if everything goes according to plan.

Most things will grow here: the trouble is to sell them at a profit. The nearest railway station lies on the other side of the mountain and the roads are only tracks. Agricolas talked hopefully of a contract with a big canning concern to produce Michigan pea-beans—the baked bean we all know so well.

When bush-clearance has mastered the tsetse fly, there will be beef cattle. At the experimental farm, four Red Poll heifers, four Sahiwals and four Borans are in competition to see which thrives the best, and also to see what comes of mixed blood. A Red Poll–Sahiwal or Boran cross might combine the disease-resistance and thriftiness of the Zebu with the large frame and early maturity of the exotic. When the Red Polls arrived they escaped from the lorry and made a dash for freedom, pursued by the settlement officer and his men. Darkness fell before they were located and driven homewards. Only when they broke back and stampeded did the officer realize that he had been trying to escort four buffaloes into camp.

IV

With something like 23,000 growers, increasing by over 2,000 a year, Meru is the largest African producing district of *arabica* coffee. In Kenya as a whole, some 85,000 African growers now produce about one-quarter of the total crop, but this proportion will rise year by year as new plantings in African areas, at present proceeding at the rate of between 5,000 and 6,000 acres annually, come into bearing.

Meru holds the Coffee Board's cup for the highest proportion of first-quality bean, and has perhaps the most go-ahead of all the co-operative unions. A committee of thirteen, each elected by his local society, runs its affairs, and employs as manager Mr. Jack Benson, who started the first local society in 1938. Except for a war-time interlude he has been here ever since, guiding and advising the societies and now and then cajoling one back into the path of virtue, like some quiet, alert, tactful yet resolute sheepdog, grey-haired and blue-eyed, trusted by the Meru people after over a quarter of a century spent in their service.

What will happen when he goes? By then, he hopes, they will know the form well enough to run the Union by themselves. There are temptations. At the time of my visit, one society was trying to break away because its members thought they would get better prices on their own and, at the meeting I attended, one of the committee-men urged his colleagues to devote all the union's cash reserves to starting a secondary school.

Here, as elsewhere, the technical view is that the whole future depends on keeping up quality. The gap between the prices of good and of indifferent coffee is widening all the time. At present the pay-out is about sixty cents (roughly 7d.) a pound of cherry. If quality deteriorated it might be only thirty cents, a price that would arouse alarm, despondency and indignation among the growers, and barely pay their costs of production.

The secret of success with smallholders' coffee lies in personal attention to each tree. In Meru the average planter has less than 200 trees and the largest in the district, an ex-police *askari*, only just over 1,000. These bring him a profit, he told me, of 15 shillings a tree. His costs he puts at 3 shillings a tree, including the wages of six men who help him work his ten-acre holding, of which only two acres are devoted to coffee.

As recently as 1947, only one hundred acres were under coffee in the whole district; now there are about 8,000 acres, the crop brings nearly £750,000 into the district and less than half the trees are in full bearing. In ten years, if the present rate of expansion continues, more will be grown by Africans throughout the country than by Europeans. Yields here average 7 cwts., but good growers get a ton of beans to the acre or even more, which brings them in a cash return of about £350 an acre. The expansion of African-grown coffee is adding about £750,000 every year to the country's cash economy.

Above the coffee belt we bumped along a grassy track to see a farm called Marimba that breeds improved cattle for the bracken zone just below the forest. The hills around were brilliant with Kikuyu and star-grass; gorse-like yellow *cassia* bushes glowed on the ridges and the big mauve *vernonia* was in full bloom. For several months this high country is permanently swathed in thick mist and the livestock officer has a fire burning day and night to keep at bay damp that saturates the walls of his bungalow. The track to Meru, seventeen miles away, is too deep in mud even for Land-Rovers, and he and his wife and small children are cut off from the world.

In Mau Mau times, when the forest was full of terrorists, this can scarcely have been pleasant, but the farm never shut

27 Children of the new Kikuyuland: cabbage-picking for the co-operative, and first steps at school

28 A pioneer of land reform: Chief Muhoya of Nyeri. Below, a Kikuyu farmer receives title-deeds to his land

down, and the crosses between Guernsey or Sahiwal and the local breed of cattle which it sells cheaply to Meru farmers are much sought after. These highland pastures harbour surprises: for instance, a tendency among potatoes to turn black, due to an excess of aluminium in the soil. One day, if all goes well, tea will grow here, and creameries arise on the edge of the forest.

V

On the way back we met an old, white-headed, wrinkled man who said that he remembered when the track our Land-Rover was following had been used by Masai coming to raid Meru cattle from the plains of Timau and Laikipia. There was also an occasion, probably in 1895, when the spearhead of a Somali invasion from the north reached the flanks of the mountain, and a battle took place between these ferocious pastoralists and Meru warriors. In war, Somalis were far superior to Bantu cultivators, but only a small, and probably weary, detachment of Somalis had pushed up towards the forest and they were defeated after their leader, fatally speared, had perished on his knees, his arms held aloft by a lieutenant in a last gesture of respect to Allah.

As a fruit of this victory, the Meru gained the right to take rock-salt from a secret crater beyond the Uaso Nyiro river, in Somali country, and to this day, at certain times of year, Meru go with pack-donkeys down to the floor of this crater, 1,500 feet under the rim, to take the salt from its guardians who live in caves and allow no others to approach apart from members of the clan that owns the mine.

During these expeditions a Meru girl acted as my interpreter. Aged about twenty-two or twenty-three, she was attractive, fluent in English, intelligent, an efficient clerk and a devout Christian. To find any woman of that age unmarried and leading a bachelor girl's existence is most unusual, anyway outside the cities. A husband of the *shamba* without education, a pagan probably, could bring her little happiness, and in any case her family, having invested so much in a daughter's education, would feel entitled to a higher bride-price than such a man could afford. She is the natural mate for some young teacher, clerk, doctor or business man, but in Meru these are few; the cities drain off most of the well-educated, and many on the lower slopes of learning prefer less polished wives, on the practical grounds that they will work harder and demand fewer expensive dresses. So the highly educated girl, at this moment of transition, may be left out on a limb.

Perhaps my interpreter was content with her limb. She lived in a well-constructed terraced cottage built by the District Council for its officers. Two rooms, plus a kitchen and wash-room; bright cretonne curtains; the basic furniture; two Christmas cards on the wall; for company, a cat with kittens in an old tea-chest. No books, no radio, and it would seem few friends, for there are no other unmarried girls of her age to go round with and it is not an African custom for young men to take out respectable girls. She was a school certificate holder who had won a coveted place at the Alliance High School near Nairobi, the oldest and perhaps the best of the country's secondary schools. Now she was putting her education to good purpose, but at a sacrifice: the crowded warmth and security of family life had been replaced by the solitude of a clean, improved and civilized but empty room.

VI

A Muslim doctor in Nairobi once spoke to me in bitter terms about a substance he said was undermining the health of many of his Somali patients: a substance so highly valued that there is talk of chartering a special aircraft to fly it to Aden, where every family is said to spend on it an average of £1 a week. But European doctors compare mira'a, not with some vicious drug like Indian hemp or opium, but with tobacco.

The northern part of Meru is the source of supply. There is even a co-operative society to market the mira'a, undermined by Somalis who come down to a small trading centre called Kangeta to buy it under the counter for twenty cents a twig, or 15 shillings for a small bundle of twigs. To enjoy mira'a you must chew the bark within seventy-two hours of plucking twigs from the trunk of a tree about the size and shape of an old-fashioned apple, which grows only on the foothills of the Nyambeni hills.

No one has mira'a plantations but every wild tree has an owner, or a clan of owners, who profit handsomely and spend the money mainly on millet-beer—this is one of the most backward and remote regions of the country where alternative ways of spending cash are few. Mira'a tastes bitter but refreshing; its popularity in the baking heat of the north is understandable. It is said to shrink the stomach so as to counteract hunger, but I cannot say that it impaired my appetite for the excellent Danish lamb stew and chocolate éclairs I enjoyed at Lilliaba, in the far north of the district on the edge of Somali and Samburu terrain, where an experiment in reclaiming desert and then ranching it is under way.

VII

A long, hot journey across lava rocks and through stunted acacia bush ended at a tumbledown, two-roomed hut made of split logs, built during Mau Mau times for a warder in charge of detainees who were laying a pipeline from the hills. The rest of the camp has vanished: this hut stands alone and shadeless, and the white ants are demolishing it too. A surprise awaited us inside. The bare log walls were lined with books and heavily-framed portraits of Danish citizens in ruffs, brocades and army uniforms, and dark, heavy, antique Danish furniture filled the small living-room. Fascinating miniature mobiles swung apparently in mid-air, the threads by which they were attached to ant-eaten rafters being too fine to be seen. These had been made by Mrs. Middleboe from spikes of whistling thorn, guinea-fowl feathers and sealing-wax, and looked like small, strange birds in perpetual flight.

In this remote place, where groceries must come fifty miles by Land-Rover when they can, I had one of the best meals I enjoyed on my journeys, and a rum punch which made it hard to concentrate on all the details of the Northern Grazing Area project, which Mr. Hans Middleboe imparted in the form of a briefing with blackboard and diagrams. I cannot do better than summarize here what he said.

1. OBJECTIVES. To establish a permanent population where people have hitherto been nomadic; to open up that 80 per cent of the area hitherto unused because of lack of water; to reclaim the remaining 20 per cent which is badly over-grazed; to arrest the spread of man-made deserts. In a sentence: to turn the area into an economic asset instead of an increasing liability.

2. TERRAIN. The foothills of the mountain open out into a great arid plain, which in turn shades into a desert. Area about 244,000 acres; rainfall tapering down from 35 to about 10 inches, where a hundred acres may be needed to carry one beast. As herds must graze within reach of rivers, four out of five acres are unused, and on the grazed pastures erosion is terrible. During the rains, Meru men and boys drive cattle down from the uplands in order to rest their own pastures; no one lives on these plains. But just under the hills there is a belt of millet cultivation flogged year after year; this, too, is eroding; higher up, fires have destroyed bush and forest and the streams are vanishing.

3. STRATEGY. First, to open up some of the unused four-fifths so as to draw off stock from over-grazed areas; then, to start a series of simple grazing schemes.

4. FINANCE. So far, £40,000, half a direct grant from ALDEV, the rest half a grant and half a loan from the Meru District Council.

5. TREATMENT. To establish in the area four ranches, each based on a permanent water supply with the water roughly in the centre. On each ranch a prescribed number of livestock will graze all the year round, being moved from block to block in rotation. On each, an annual take-off will be organized through auctions, and each owner will pay a fee of three shillings per head of cattle to cover the costs of the scheme. The millet belt will also

be dealt with rotationally, and the banks of streams permanently grassed.

So far all this consists mainly of lines drawn on a map and of Hans Middleboe, who started the Sarora settlement in Nandi. The Meru are suspicious; they do not want their ancient customs interfered with, they do not want to sell their stock, they do not understand why it should be pushed around, and they certainly do not want to pay three shillings a head to anyone. The Government has no powers to compel them to agree to any of these things. It is a matter of persuasion, conversation, demonstration: a slow matter of patience, persistence and cunning. Mr. Middleboe, whose forebears invented Danish Folk High Schools, has all these qualities, and seems content to live, think, eat and sleep, if necessary for years on end, with the problems of the Northern Grazing Area.

One of these is unexpected: soil erosion by guinea-fowl. From the top of an eminence, looking down over a plain baked bare and over ferocious jutting boulders, prickly scrub, thorn-trees heavy with the nests of weavers, he pointed out a stretch of country that looked for all the world as if it had been ploughed and harrowed down to a fine tilth. All this had been done by the feet of helmeted guinea-fowl, who had scratched away all the grass roots.

Flocks of these plump, speckled fowl scuttled away into the bush as we drove by to inspect herds of dwarf humped Meru cattle who were standing up to their knees in liquid mud that was nominally a river. Every large acacia had a colony of weavers, yellow as canaries, whose cock birds build nest after nest, not just one or even two, and then try to entice a female into it. Weavers have no housing problem, but a great choice of empty nests. To build them seems to be an outlet for surplus male energy.

A small airstrip survives from Mau Mau days, and promptly at its appointed time a little Cessna aircraft settled like a stork upon it, watched by a solitary giraffe, the only wild animal I saw in the Meru district. From the air, bare eroded patches showed up like wounds and the gullied millet belt, the grassless earth, the cattle tracks to water, told the story very plainly. Here is a dying land that can be brought back to life by grazing schemes and water if the Meru will agree. In no time at all the hot northern desert fell behind us and a green candlewick of forest lay below.

CHAPTER 15

The Enclosure of Nyeri

I

THE forest belt at first was dark as fur, turned light green when we flew above the bamboos, and then we were over brown, tufted pastures with steep black gorges, winding streams like veins and queer giant groundsels on the end of tall stalks. Next came grey-brown, inhospitable scree, bare of all vegetation and all life, even that of birds, like (one imagines) a part of the moon. Yet some life there must be in the water, for the lakes caught up in gorges are green, from algae presumably; there is nothing to reflect but black towering rock-faces and a hard blue sky. As we approached Mt. Kenya's peak the rocks grew more and more savage, like the spines of prehistoric armoured beasts, snow gleamed among the cliffs and we came to glaciers, and to lakes black as the pit.

If you fly over a mountain it is hard to know exactly which the peak is, the whole surface below is so jagged and fierce, streaked with snow looking rather dirty, from wind-blown dust perhaps. Superintendent Bearcroft, the pilot, pointed out the Lewis glacier which leads up towards the peak of Bation, called after a Masai *laibon*, and there was a little hut on the snow and the dark speck of a man beside it.

How absurdly and unfairly easy it seemed to float above him sitting back in an arm-chair! One thought of all the people who had toiled up the scree and towering rocks and treacherous glaciers, of all the mountain-sickness, frostbite, snow-blindness and dangers—even with modern climbing techniques, Kenya is exacting. And here was I, without the least effort looking down upon the topmost peak on which Sir Halford Mackinder was the first human being, so far as anyone knows, to set foot, in 1899. It was certainly a very much more enjoyable way than his to get to the top, indeed over the top, of Mt. Kenya.

Light green, dark green, appeared below us, then un-clothed ridges with higgledy-piggledy little squares of *shamba* marked in green and chocolate brown: and then, before we landed, a detour to look down upon an amazing pale pink froth on the tops of the trees—Cape Chestnuts in full bloom along the Amboni river. Soon Nyeri hill came into sight, a curious lump of greenery, and we were down on the airstrip on the other side of the mountain.

It was in the three Kikuyu districts south and south-west of the mountain that the project of land consolidation started and has been carried through. In the districts of Nyeri, Fort Hall and Kiambu every square foot of land claimed by an owner has been brought together into compact holdings and each landowner has his valid title. Over a million acres have been dealt with and some 200,000 holdings registered.

II

The need for consolidation arose out of a custom far more developed here than anywhere else in the country—the fragmentation of land. A survey made in 1950 showed the *average* number of fragments into which each man's holding was split to be six to eight; some of the fragments might be seven or eight miles from his home. Individual cases were, of course, far worse than this. One man in the Nyeri district was found to have forty fragments, the smallest measuring 0·01 of an acre and some of them five miles from his homestead, adding up to just under twelve acres. Another had twenty-nine fragments amounting to three acres. The smallest fragment on record was a single banana plant. Yet a wife might have to walk five miles to tend this one small plot. In these three districts there was probably not a single holding all in one piece.

Before describing how this extraordinary situation has been dealt with, an outline of how it came about may be useful. It arose out of the system of inheritance of the Kikuyu people, which is typical of Bantu tribes. Two young officers, Mr. Tony

Sutton and Mr. John Golds, carried out a detailed study of a single area in Kiambu to discover how the complex land pattern had originated, and what follows here is a summary of their findings. They took as their sample an area of 1,880 acres known to its inhabitants as the *mbari ya Igi*.

Whereas most Africans, as we have seen, were able to take uninhabited land from the bush when they needed it, the forest into which the Kikuyu spread was already occupied, if only very sparsely, by people called the Aathi, small and primitive hunters who lived on game and honey. When the Kikuyu moved in, which in the Kiambu district was probably about 1830, they treated with the Aathi elders and, by paying goats and honey, acquired rights over certain stretches of forest—perhaps a belt between two glades, or a ridge between two rivers—regarded as the hunting ground of a particular Aathi family. The Aathi, of course, did not realize that the Kikuyu would cut down the trees and squeeze them out; they thought that they would share the forest's bounty with the Kikuyu, who would grow crops here and there in patches, to everyone's benefit.

When a Kikuyu acquired rights over a stretch of land this became his *mbari*, or family estate. Several people sometimes joined together to acquire a large *mbari*. This was the case with the *mbari ya Igi*; thirteen families shared it.

The head of a Kikuyu family, and its land authority, is the *murumati*. This office is inherited by his eldest son. After moving in to an *mbari*, the *murumati* divided it first among his wives and any married sons; if there was more land than they needed, he might allow a number of *ahoi*, or tenants, to cultivate. Sometimes these *ahoi* helped with the purchase price—about one goat to five acres—by lending goats to the family. These goats had eventually to be repaid.

Now the first complication arises: often an *mbari* was bought in instalments. This was the original form of fragmentation: each member of the family cleared and cultivated a strip of land in each instalment. A good many *ahoi* moved in, and it was perhaps at this time that the principle of redemption became established. That is to say, if one of the *ahoi* lent goats to help pay an instalment, the clan elders

233

could at any time return an equal number of goats to him and, when they did so, he had to pack up and go. It was bad manners, however, to give him notice openly; the custom was to surround his *shamba* with branches at dawn; when he saw them, he knew that he had received his notice.

In later years, this system of redemption blocked nearly all forms of progress. If a man could be evicted at any time by the return of some goats lent by his grandfather, it was obviously no good trying to plant a permanent crop like coffee or build a permanent house. If you did so, the clan elders would cock an eye at the improvements and, if they possibly could, dispossess you; endless cases of this nature came before the African courts. This system of redemption by simple repayment without compensation continued until it was stopped by a District Council by-law in 1952.

The *mbari ya Igi* was bought by thirteen families in seven instalments. In each of the instalments, all the wives of all the elders and their married sons were given plots to cultivate. Each senior wife chose her own, and the shapes were often peculiar. One was a strip three feet wide stretching nearly a mile from river to river. Another twisted about all over the countryside like a snake. An old man gave the explanation: when his mother was first married, her husband told her to mark out her *shamba* according to custom, and she was so happy that she ran joyfully about the countryside putting in pegs wherever she felt inclined.

Each time a man took a new wife, he gave her a piece of 'the man's plot' he had reserved for future use, and each of his senior wives gave her also a small piece of their own *shambas*. In return, she gave each senior wife a bit of the *shamba* she had just received from her husband. Since each senior wife would have a *shamba* in each of the *mbari's* seven instalments, every new wife would start off with eight separate plots. When her sons grew up and married, every son would receive a share of each of her eight plots. Finally, when the *murumati* died, each of his sons would receive a bit of 'the man's plot', as well as his share of his mother's different *shambas*.

When one considers the ramifications of this system, such as widows remarrying, and childless women's plots being split among all the other wives' children, and many other contingencies, one is amazed that the Kikuyu elders could keep a grasp on the situation at all. All the records were in memories, nothing could be written down; but so retentive are Kikuyu minds that every elder could recite the history of every plot and fragment in his family's possession, down to the number of she-kids dropped by each of the goats paid in his grandfather's time.

III

Nevertheless, land ownership and inheritance was the most fruitful source imaginable of disputes, feuds and court cases. As time went on, the flow of cases thickened until it threatened to silt up the whole stream of Kikuyu life. To waste of time was added waste of money, as a class of professional lawyers arose to batten on the illiterate. By 1952, it was reckoned that the Kikuyu were frittering away at least £100,000 a year on land cases.

The thing had got out of hand and the Kikuyu were the first to recognize it. Whenever I asked what had persuaded the people to accept such fundamental changes, I got the answer: 'We were tired of land cases. They were wasting our wealth. They were like a heavy load on the back of every man.'

But although many people thought this, perhaps almost everyone, very few dared to say so publicly before the rise and fall of Mau Mau. The political leaders of the Kikuyu opposed land consolidation bitterly and without scruple, spreading every lie and rumour to turn people against it on the grounds that it was nothing but a trick to steal their land. Most of the Kikuyu leaders, at any rate those with the intelligence of Jomo Kenyatta who led the campaign, knew all this to be entirely untrue. Yet at every point, and by means of every deceit and subtlety, they urged their people to reject every advance that would ease their lives and improve their condition.

The object of such Kikuyu leaders, understandably enough no doubt, was to shake off European rule and achieve unrestricted self-government. But obviously, self-government based upon a prosperous peasantry and a productive agriculture would have better prospects than self-government based upon a degenerate tribalism in whose ambit no one could plant so much as a banana tree without fearing that someone else would dig it up or bring an action about it. The origins of Mau Mau, however, were not logical, they were rooted in a deep, emotional hatred not merely of Europeans but of all they represented, of the whole Western world, the whole twentieth century. They belonged to a perverted romanticism blindly hoping to restore a lost tribal simplicity, and to do so by means of murder, torture and obscenity, the Black Mass up to date.

Until the defeat of Mau Mau, every attempt to tackle at its source the worsening land position of the Kikuyu met with a stubborn, sullen resistance due mainly to fear of being at the least branded as a traitor, at the worst having one's hut burnt down and one's cattle hamstrung. The bulk of the people simply held back and kept mum. Bolder spirits who defied the prevailing wind of politics suffered for their nonconformism. In the years just before Mau Mau a great many cattle-dips were sabotaged, terraces broken, stores burnt and crops destroyed. As matters worked towards a climax, the attacks advanced from property to people, and men who had listened to the Europeans were strangled in the darkness and burnt alive in their huts. It needed a very bold man, in those days, to walk into the mounting gale and openly collaborate with officers of the Government.

IV

Such a man was Chief Muhoya, certainly one of the bravest living Kikuyu, a dauntless loyalist all through the Emergency and so contemptuous of Mau Mau terrorists that he refused to live—as most chiefs did, on official orders—in a garrisoned post behind a moat full of stakes, and refused to take even reasonable precautions, dashing off to the scene of many 'incidents', revolver in hand, to engage gangs in battle with his enthusiastic Home Guard.

He does not look a fire-eater, but seems a quiet, reserved, courteous, modest man of middle age and plain intelligence. It was in his location of North Tetu that the land consolidation movement started, before Mau Mau, and on the initiative of the people, not the Government. This was in 1948.

Indirectly, the movement arose partly because many of the Kikuyu from Tetu, a region that had always taken great pride in its cattle, had worked on nearby European stock farms, and subsequently bought exotic cattle which gave much higher yields than their own. This led to a demand for dips, and then to the spontaneous paddocking of grazing land so as to keep Better Cows free from ticks. So popular did paddocking become that the Veterinary department established nurseries from which those who dipped their cattle could take kei-apple seedlings free of charge—the kei-apple is a prickly, straggling plant that will make a good stock-proof hedge.

So enclosure started in the Nyeri district, and brought with it a whole crop of new troubles. The boundaries of grazing land had never been clearly defined. The clan elders settled boundary disputes as best they could, but it soon became clear to everyone that some more permanent arrangement would have to be made. The whole idea of individual tenure on the European pattern, of one family owning one piece of land, had taken root.

It was here, in North Tetu, that land exchanges between heads of families began to take place, encouraged by Chief Muhoya. Under his resolute leadership, North Tetu is still in the van: nearly half the landowners work to farm plans, the highest proportion anywhere in the country. Then came Mau Mau, and all progress stopped for three years.

A state of emergency was declared on 20th October, 1952. By this time gangs of oath-takers were abroad, killing anyone who refused to join Mau Mau. Huts and schools went up in flames, no one's life was safe, crops went unplanted or were smuggled out to feed the gangs, cattle were mutilated, killed or impounded as fines, and every available European was drafted in to the administration or police, or to help form a Home Guard of Kikuyu loyalists. These men lived in moated forts under tall watch-towers in constant danger of attack, and were called out at frequent intervals to protect threatened points or chase terrorist gangs.

The turning-point was possibly the decision, taken in 1954, to put the whole scattered population into villages. Since time immemorial, families had lived in homesteads apart from each other, each little cluster of huts screened by a thorn or split-log fence and approached by a winding path through bush or forest. From each homestead, women would emerge every morning to plod off to their various fragments of *shamba*, babies on back and *pangas* in hand. Privacy was the normal condition for Kikuyu families.

Now every family had to leave its private homestead for a barrack-like assemblage of huts set out in rows on a hill-top. Although in his heart everyone must have hated it, for the moment many were thankful because, for the first time since Mau Mau had started, they were able to sleep safely in their beds. By October, 1955, nearly a million men, women and children had moved from their homesteads into a total of 845 new villages.

This broke the back of the Emergency. The matter then became one of hunting down terrorist gangs who, while they still emerged to murder and pillage, had retreated to the forest and were gradually eroded away by fighting, desertion and surrender. With the capture of the leading forest gangster, Dedan Kimathi, in October, 1956, the fighting was virtually over and normal life in the main restored. Some changes were irreversible: the villages, for instance, remained.

v

Land consolidation was resumed in 1954 on a new basis: the Government stepped in directly and made it an official concern. The agricolas had worked out in detail a system which they hoped could be applied throughout Kikuyuland, and the administration tried it out in several pilot schemes.

It worked so well that in 1955 they took on a small army of surveyors, measurers and clerks and launched major schemes in each of the three Kikuyu districts.

The enclosure and consolidation movement swept the country almost with the momentum and fervour of a religious revival. In each sub-location it started with a public meeting: until the people themselves decided that they wanted to consolidate, nothing was done. When everyone had agreed, the D.C. accepted their decision in open *baraza*. 'Once an area is declared,' reads a directive, 'consolidation takes priority over all other work. It is most important that this point is fully understood as it has been found that some officers will try to maintain their pet schemes.'

Pet schemes abandoned, the next stage was to form a large committee representing all the elders of the *mbari* concerned and to acknowledge it in open *baraza*. This committee proceeded to hear all disputes and to settle all the boundaries, both of the *mbari* land and of every right-holder. A good many individuals were in detention, but their wives or relatives looked after their interests. The committee also listed all the landless *ahoi*.

The Recording Officer then stepped in. He and his teams went forth with pegs and chains to measure every individual fragment and to compile a 'register of existing rights', which became the ground-plan of future developments. 'Fragment-gathering' went on at the same time. Measurers noted in an exercise book, against every right-holder's name, each of his fragments, their acreage, and a sketch of their shapes. In the Fort Hall district one man actually had 108 fragments which added up to 14 acres—a record: the average in the Nyeri district was about eight fragments to a man. The measurers' sketch-books impressed me greatly with their neatness and, one assumed, accuracy.

The committee of elders, at least thirty strong, accompanied the measurers and agreed on the ground the assessment of every man's fragment. All disputes went to an arbitration board, but disputes were rare. The only Kikuyu to suffer loss of land through Mau Mau were a few of the worst terrorists, whose holdings were forfeited: these amounted to 0.02 per cent of the whole. Their land was paid for, and devoted to public purposes, such as schools.

After fragment-gathering, each owner saw the exercise book and registered agreement with his thumb-print or signature; if he was dissatisfied, he took the matter to an arbitration board.

Then came the percentage cut, to ensure that all sacrifices of land needed for public purposes were shared equally by everyone. This system is plainly much fairer than our own. If some public authority wishes to build a nuclear power station on Mr. Smith's land, or run an arterial road through Mr. Brown's garden, it does so, and Smith and Brown are out of luck. But among the Kikuyu, all losses are equally shared.

After the percentage cut—generally about five per cent— a demarcation team took over. Their job was like fitting together a jigsaw puzzle whose pieces were the acreages of each landowner, and the completed puzzle a map of the sub-location. They had to mark out all the *shambas* on the ground. At the end, if demarcation teams had done their work successfully, each individual was left with his original acreage less the percentage cut, and a lot of pegs in the ground agreed with maps in the office. Probably none of this could have been done had the Kikuyu not moved into villages : no one would have agreed to leave his homestead. As it was, all the homesteads had been shifted, and it was a matter of dividing so many acres among so many people, according to the amounts they had before.

After demarcation came the planting of hedges, and then the holdings were registered. The final stage will be an aerial survey of the whole countryside and registration of title-deeds—an individual freehold title to land. The first issue of these permanent titles began in Kiambu on 15th October, 1959.

VI

Administrators dread a landless population, and consider a smallholder with an acre or two to be a more stable citizen

29 A landscape transformed: terraced and consolidated farms in the Fort Hall district, and a new village on a ridge

30 Kikuyu women still
carry wood for the
homestead on their backs;
but in a canning factory (*above*)
at Thika they are taking
to a new way of life

than a man with no land at all. Moreover he will have somewhere to go when he is old, and so will not become a charge on the community.

Agricolas, on the other hand, calculate that a given district will support more people, not less, if it is farmed properly, because, in order to achieve his larger output, the farmer will employ men. Mr. Roger Swynnerton has given this example to illustrate the point.

'If half the Nyeri district had twelve-acre holdings, the farmers would need to employ something of the order of 51,000 labourers. That is based on our experience of planned farms. If half the Nyeri district were developed to this extent, it would produce an income of about £64 per acre net—that includes coffee and cash crops—and the total net income of this district would be about £6 million, or thirty times as much as it is at present.

'If the other half of Nyeri were to be in six-acre holdings, it could be expected to produce an income of the order of £1.25 million, but it would not employ much labour. This is based on an output of £18 an acre. If the Nyeri district were divided into four-acre holdings, about £6 per acre would be about the best one could expect, without employing any labour at all. The total income would then be about £1.25 million at best. To summarize: with half the district in large holdings and half in economic holdings, the total income would be approximately £8 million; whereas if it was split into four-acre holdings, it would be about £1.25 million.

'Nyeri district is about 322 square miles. Were half of this to be in twelve-acre holdings and half in six-acre holdings, together with employment for about 50,000 families, this district could carry something of the order of 460,000 people. If the district were to be in four-acre holdings, each supporting a family of eight, the population would be about 412,000— that is, about 50,000 less.

'One of the objects of our exercise at the present time is to provide means by which the population can live and produce economically. We cannot take the population too rapidly into industry and commerce, or into rural trades, because we have to wait for that development to take place, and it will be slow. We have no minerals behind us. So in the first instance we must aim at supporting the people on the land economically, while at the same time they contribute the most they can to the wealth of the country.'*

I visited one of the twelve-acre farms working to a plan in the Nyeri district, on which such calculations are based. The owner employed five regular workers and nine casuals, and sold off his holding quantities of coffee, bananas, potatoes, milk, pork and beans. Using the ratio of three casual workers to one regular, these twelve acres provided a livelihood for eight families, and yielded, as well, £550 worth of produce to feed others, and to swell the country's wealth.

Had these twelve acres been split into two-acre plots, said the agricolas, they would have supported six instead of eight families, and produced very little surplus as a contribution to the general economy. Were all the land in the Kikuyu districts to be fully developed, labour (they calculate) would actually be drawn into the area and the unemployment problem vanish—that is, if all the unemployed would agree to work on the land.

VII

Were economic facts the only ones, the authorities would have refused to register any fragment below four acres, or whatever was thought to be the minimum, in each ecological zone, on which a family could make a decent living.† But the Government, as we have seen before, takes the view that, in the last resort, it cannot go against the people's wishes in

*Kenya Legislative Council proceedings, 23rd April, 1959.
†Agricolas have divided Kikuyu country into four ecological zones, depending on altitude, viz.: (1) High bracken zone, with acid soil, suitable for sheep, dairying, pyrethrum and tea; (2) Kikuyu grass zone, suitable for dairying, pigs, potatoes and coffee; (3) Star-grass zone, suitable for a wide range of crops, the main coffee belt; (4) Grass woodland zone, suitable for ranching, pineapples and tobacco. The size of the minimum economic unit varies in each zone. In (1) it is generally 12 acres, in (2) six acres, in (3) four acres and in (4) 15–20 acres. In all zones, half the acreage should generally be under grass at any given time. Over-cultivation leads (among other things) to serious losses due to eelworm.

regard to their own land. The Kikuyu have wished for land consolidation, and the Government has provided a system by which it has been brought about; they have wished for individual tenure, and the Government has registered their holdings. But at present they do not wish either to abolish small, uneconomic holdings, or to prevent the breaking up of larger ones on the owner's death.

On this last point, the Kikuyu are somewhat uncertain. Many realize that to allow fragmentation to arise again, as it certainly will if they do not themselves change drastically their whole system of inheritance, would undo all the good that has been done in the last five years. They are against this: but not yet, with individual exceptions, quite prepared to prevent it where their own children are concerned. They are rather like British Socialists who send their own sons to public schools. They are against the system, but so long as it is there want their own children to enjoy its benefits.

On their decision in the next few years, the ultimate outcome of this revolution will depend. Unless they bring their system of inheritance into line, the great potential of their country will never be realized. Agricolas hope that enough of their number have grasped the magnitude of the opportunity to swing the balance against the break-up of the new registered holdings into fragments through inheritance. They hope, but they cannot be sure.

If all the Kikuyu districts were properly developed and farmed, agricolas reckon, their output could be increased twentyfold. This seems a fantastic figure, but I was assured it was a sober estimate. Twenty times as much wealth coming from a smiling and a stabilized land, employment for everyone and to spare, a secondary population living off and serving the farmers. . . . The agricolas have all the best arguments, but whether they will be able to put them across remains to be seen. A directive issued from headquarters at Nyeri reads: 'No success can be expected if the farmer is made to do something against his will. Often it is necessary for a field or a house to be put in the wrong place owing to a whim of the African farmer—i.e. "grandfather died here", or "the spirits

of my ancestors say that no food must be planted in this area".
This we come across all the time. If we act against these
customs we may be sure of failure. Farm plans and farm
layouts are essentially voluntary and at all costs must remain
that way.'

Most agricolas have grappled their missionary spirit to
some pet project in which they see salvation. With Mr. Storrar
in the Rift Valley it is sheep; with Mr. Graham Gamble at
Nyeri it is tea. Not until thousands of acres of this table-topped,
glossy-leaved little shrub cover the fertile ridges of Kikuyuland, not until factories rise in dozens along the forest's edge,
not until a network of roads humming with leaf-transporting
lorries rings the mountain, will he be satisfied. And the
generating power of his single-minded energy has already
made the wheels begin to turn.

Nyeri is the first district to have a factory, built at a cost
of £85,000 from Swynnerton plan funds, entirely for African-
grown leaf. You still need a Land-Rover to reach it up the
slippery steep hills of the high bracken zone with its cold air,
clear streams and big mauve clumps of *vernonia*, and it was
just as well we had one with us, for when we reached the
large impressive factory, standing all by itself under the
forest, the machinery had been silenced by a power cut. An
agricola removed our Land-Rover's battery and connected it
to a dynamo, and in a few minutes everything was revolving
again.

A tea factory smells clean and bitter and it is here that,
given good leaf, the mysteries of quality are wrought. The
Indian manager brewed for us specimen cups of his own
product and of various other teas, and challenged us to select
the one with the best flavour. Anxious as I was to be tactful,
I plumped for quite the wrong one: but the London market
knows better and just before my visit had paid six shillings a
pound for this Ragati tea, the top price for East Africa. Only
fifty acres are as yet in bearing out of 700 planted, but the
programme calls for annual plantings that will first supply

this factory, and then others due to be erected if the money can be found.*

Will it catch on? 'It's an exacting crop,' Mr. Gamble admitted. 'You must pay a lot of money for your stumps, wait four years, and when it's in bearing you can never leave it. Plucking goes on most of the year round and even when it lets up, there's the pruning. So tea will mean a lot more work, more *regular* work, than peasant farmers normally reckon on. But it pays. If they look after it properly they should get 1,200 pounds to the acre and this brings in about the same as coffee. One man has grown 1,400 pounds of made leaf an acre, higher than the European average at Kericho. The question is, whether they can keep it up.'

At present, leaf comes to this Ragati factory from as far as fifty miles away. There had just arrived a lorry designed to meet this unusual situation, fitted with a fan to start the withering process before the leaf reached the machines.

Quality is all: Mr. Gamble preaches this with a prophet's fervour. Quality starts on the third-of-an-acre plots where the Kikuyu must at present take everything on trust from instructors. The plucking of the leaf is all-important. Mr. Gamble dins in the maxim 'two-leaves-and-a-bud' at every *baraza*, and his instructors are trained to say to every plucker: 'The tips only—two leaves and a bud . . .'

IX

A tough, stern old chief called Murigo used to rule over this moist, green country where the Ragati tea factory now stands. He had led his fellow-warriors against the Masai, kept a retinue of wives, owned large herds of cattle, lived largely off beer and stood no nonsense. I met two of his many sons. One, also a chief, inhabits with three wives a white-washed house surrounded by oranges, limes and two acres of tea, planted as long ago as 1950 and protected from Mau

*Annual plantings should bring the area under African-grown tea to 12,000 acres by 1969. This will call for six to eight new factories. Up to 70,000 acres have been licensed on European estates, of which about half has been planted. Tea is now Kenya's second most valuable export, worth about £3 million a year. Coffee is worth over £10 million.

Mau by a guard post nearby. The other is an up-and-coming
instructor with an eight-acre Better Farm planned according
to the book.

Although, from his holding, a superb view of the mountain
could be seen, Mr. Gari Murigo's tidy white house, set
among salvias and cabbages, faced in the other direction—a
break with tradition, for it used to be a custom universally
observed to build your homestead with its door towards
Mt. Kenya, the seat of God.

'There is too much wind in that direction,' Mr. Gari
Murigo explained, but one might suspect a deeper signifi-
cance. Jomo Kenyatta gave the title 'Facing Mount Kenya'
to his eulogy of the old Kikuyu ways he sought to revive in
a perverted fashion. Many battles were fought out on these
ridges and many loyalists killed, including some of the
Murigo family. In the siting of his house this loyalist son
demonstrated his break with a tradition that had brought
so much grief to his people. Sixteen of old Murigo's sons
are now farming round about their father's resting-place.

One can understand a little of the Kikuyu feeling towards
their mountain: it dominates every ridge and valley, wherever
you look it is there, mighty and magnificent. You can easily
imagine gods and heroes dwelling in its secret caves, and
even conducted donkey-trips to the snow-line have not quite
destroyed its mystery. Above a gathering of Better Farmers
and their wives on the greensward in mild sunshine, beside a
neat row of model pigsties thatched with banana leaves,
it indifferently presided over our mundane talk of loans,
prices and markets.

All these progressive farmers worried about markets; they
had worked up their pigs and then prices had collapsed, as
pig prices appear to do all over the world, and they did not
understand it. No farmer, of course, ever does, but they felt
they had been let down by the Government. And here is the
big danger in positive official action to enrich the citizens:
if things go wrong, latent suspicions come flooding back,
bearing on their crest rumours of deliberate tricks to hold
back the people. A collapse in coffee prices would lead
inevitably to political unrest.

A young man in a green shirt who acted as spokesman for this group was an ex-Mau Mau detainee, of whom over 70,000 have been rehabilitated and reabsorbed in orderly fashion in the last two years—one of those achievements that no one applauded when it went smoothly, but everyone condemned when, at the very end, a blunder was made among the scrapings of the human barrel at Hola.

It is remarkable how quietly so many oath-takers and gangsters have settled back into normal life, and how little open friction there has been between them and the loyalists. But many bitter feuds lie only just beneath the surface and could erupt if the control of chiefs and District Councils were relaxed. It was a piece of good timing that, as the flow of detainees from the camps gathered momentum, so did the tempo of land consolidation and planning. The man from the camp returned to find a new spirit of hope abroad and new opportunities of employment—if he returned to the land. Those who drifted back to the overcrowded cities found few such opportunities, and it is from them that the restlessness has spread.

x

More girls of the Kikuyu people than of any other pass through the secondary schools, some to continue to Makerere college, some to British and American universities; there is a Kikuyu woman Legislative Councillor; in general the women, when they overcome their diffidence, seem at least as alert and intelligent as the men. Yet nowhere in modern Africa, except among still-primitive tribes who have so far kept out of the way of Progress, do you see women used as beasts of burden quite as Kikuyu women are.

To carry things upon one's head is a custom universal in Africa, but Kikuyu women toil along like snails bent double under heavy loads of firewood, water, grain and potatoes borne on their backs, climbing hills most Europeans could barely get themselves up, let alone a hundredweight of maize or a forty-gallon drum of water. I saw a furniture removal headed by an old grandmother carrying an enormous table

247

on her back—a light load, probably, in her estimation. Little girls of six or seven practise with a gourd of water or a bundle of sweet potato tops to feed the goats.

You never see a woman on a bicycle. Their working dress is generally a length of cotton cloth dyed earth-colour with ochre, like an old sack, caught in round the waist by a belt. Their heads are clean-shaven and rings of beads hang from their ears. The very steepness of their ridges holds them back, for tractors are ruled out, everything must still be done with hoe and *panga*, and that is the woman's task. Not that they need driving: they take a peasant's pride in their strength and capacity for toil and would not have it otherwise.

Most of the wives of Better Farmers, on the other hand, wear shapeless but often bright cotton dresses made by tailors who sit behind their treadle sewing-machines on the verandas of their shops in every trading centre. Many of these women belong to Maendeleo clubs, and quite a number have taken courses at one of the Farm Institutes.

'I did not want my husband to get rid of the old cows,' the wife of a Better Farmer said to me as we admired four Guernseys her husband had bought. 'Then I went to Wambugu, and that persuaded me.' Wambugu is one of the outstanding Farm Institutes, thanks largely to its former principal, Mr. Paul Thiongo, whom I met at Embu. Here men and women take their courses separately, a hundred at a time. And here there is a pool of Guernseys issued at cost price to Better Farmers when they first arrive, so that man and cow spend three weeks together under supervision, and then go off together to their farm. Wambugu has the only African-owned herd to be a member of the breed society, and last year the herd average was over 700 gallons. So the best Guernsey blood that can be had is being spread about the Nyeri district and a main preoccupation of vets and agricolas is to see that the resulting progeny is properly reared.

I remember especially a very old, toothless individual, his chin fringed with grey bristles, leading a calf on a string and stroking it possessively—his first by A.I., which he thought a splendid invention, but too expensive; and an elderly, polite, thin man who had worked for fifteen years in Nairobi as a driver, saved money and bought his holding bit by bit, who showed me with tremendous pride three contented high-grade heifers, hand-fed with Napier grass and lucerne, who were giving between them seven gallons a day which he sold for £8 a week to a local tea-shop. About 300,000 cattle are dipped or sprayed every week—a contrast from the Mau Mau times, when all dipping ceased.

Unless there is a set-back, the old humped Zebu will eventually vanish from the Nyeri district to be replaced by Guernseys. The success of this bold experiment depends entirely on the people's ability to keep up a high standard of management. If they grow slack about spraying, about careful calf-rearing, about bull-calf castration, these fine-looking animals will deteriorate into weedy, degenerate beasts without either the hardiness of the Zebu or the high yields of the exotic. It is a gamble on Kikuyu common sense and energy, and on political stability.

In the last three years, this countryside has been transformed. Every hillside is terraced; almost every field lies on the contour; gullies are sealed; coffee trees stand like soldiers on parade, pruned and mulched. Butter-yellow cattle graze on emerald pastures; blue-shirted children swarm in the innumerable schools. Gone are the mushroom huts lurking behind groves of bananas, the higgledy-piggledy *shambas*, the goat-browsed aromatic bush.

Gone too are the moated guard-posts, the high watch-towers, the armed patrols, the barbed-wire barricades of only five years ago. What had become, I asked, of those deep moats bristling with pointed stakes, like a mouthful of wicked fangs? Stripped of the stakes, many of them had been used to grow bananas. Swords into ploughshares, knives into pruning-hooks, moats into banana-trenches.

CHAPTER 16

Towards Subtopia

I

THE oldest living chief in Kenya is Njiri, who was appointed to his office in 1912. Such men, who grew to manhood in a world unchanged for centuries, are almost legendary; soon the last will be gone, and it is a tragedy that no one has taken down from their own mouths recollections which are a part of history.

It was evening when I called on Senior Chief Njiri at his home just below the forest, nearly 8,000 feet up and very cold; he had not been well, but came out to see me on his veranda, muffled in an army greatcoat, and while we talked one of his wives stood motionless behind his chair, a silent sentinel. The old man's bronze, leathery face was lined like the map of a watershed, and there was no mistaking the rock-like character, the habit of command, the force of personality. His eyes were sharp, there was nothing doddery about his quiet and cogent answers to the few questions I put. All through the Mau Mau revolt he kept his district loyal and, although it borders on the forest, the gangs failed to draw from it their expected quota of recruitment, food and support.

I asked his views on the great changes that had come to his country. 'They are good,' he said, 'except for two things: they oblige people to move away from their fathers' homesteads, leaving the inheritance of their ancestors; and there is too much bribery among the staff, among recorders and measurers. And this bribery goes against the loyalists; they resisted Mau Mau and now, in many cases, the Mau Mau have taken some of their land.'

How much truth is there in this? Administrators are inclined to discount it; many loyalists, they say, expected to be rewarded for their staunchness to the Government by receiving forfeited land. But it has not been the Government's policy to confiscate land, except from a very few of the gang leaders, and detainees have been treated in exactly the same way as loyal Home Guards.

This is a policy that men of the older generation, like Njiri, cannot understand. Their code holds that loyalty should be rewarded and rebellion punished. So they feel aggrieved when loyalists are not rewarded in this obvious way—or indeed in any other way, except for a few medals: and even medals do not seem to mean much, for a man from this district who received one for gallantry, and risked his life many times in defiance of Mau Mau, was subsequently imprisoned for two years because he assaulted a detainee who had defied him in a camp in which he exercised some authority. British justice, as so often happens, did not in this instance accord with Kikuyu ideas. Here is an example of a fundamental cleavage in outlook between the races that goes much deeper than questions of constitutions, electoral rolls and social benefits: it strikes at the very roots of trust and respect.

As to bribery, most administrators admit that it goes on in spite of every precaution they can think of to prevent it, but on a scale which does not materially affect the final distribution of land.

Customs must change, Chief Njiri agreed; old ways were dying; did he think that, on balance, the new ways were better for his people?

'Old customs were good,' he said, looking back to days of order, simplicity and adventure, 'but education is good also, because it will teach a man how to speak alike to Europeans and to Kikuyu; it is a bridge between the two. There was no bridge in the old days. We must understand each other.' Although he was born into a world in which no woman could address a man as an equal, he has given some of his own land and money to start a girls' school nearby. One of his many sons returned the other day from America with a university degree and a wife.

II

Njiri spoke in Kikuyu, and the Kikuyu agricola who interpreted had not long returned from eleven years' study at the University of Allahabad. Here were old and new personified: the quiet elder with his enormous dignity, a tree rooted in the deep, stable soil of tribalism, and the well-educated, intelligent young graduate with his air of puzzled diffidence, his roots groping through the shallow soil of transition. Perhaps, when he is old, he will regain that calm certainty of which he has been robbed by the onset of a thousand possibilities and doubts swarming round him and his fellows like angry bees.

'The poverty of India!' he exclaimed, and shook his head despairingly. 'We have nothing like that here. But we must be careful—it is something that could happen, if we fail to take care of our land.'

Now a confirmed agricola, he had been at school with some of the Kikuyu political leaders and one, he said, had come to visit him the other day. 'I tried to tell him what we are doing here, but he wouldn't listen. He stood in the middle of one of the villages and said: "Are there any complaints against the Government? Is anyone not satisfied?" There are always people who are not satisfied. A fortnight after he left, the D.C. had to close the coffee factory in that area because the people were refusing to obey the rules. How can this help the Kikuyu people? All this man was doing was to try to make a position for himself. We used to be friends, but now we have agreed to go in different ways.'

He spoke sadly, for no Kikuyu of his generation could repudiate the aims of nationalism. It is the methods that divide men of the cities from men of the land, who need security. As yet there is no leader able to combine the two.

III

About half the adult males of the Fort Hall district are away at any given time either at work, or seeking it. On farms and at markets you see mostly women and elders, and of course children in swarms. Apart from farming, there is little work for younger men. Fort Hall above all needs industries, but there seems nothing much to found them on. Such industries as exist cluster round Nairobi or, at the farthest, Thika, which is connected by tarmac with the capital.

Here an up-to-date factory exists to deal with pineapples. Unloaded from lorries on to endless belts, they vanish into a large, airy building where they are set on by an army of Kikuyu girls, neatly attired in overalls and rubber gloves, presiding over machines which peel, slice, core and pack the fruit into tins. I wondered what Chief Njiri would have thought if, as a Masai-fighting, painted warrior guarding his father's cattle, a vision of the future had flashed into his mind—a future within his own lifetime containing independent, wage-earning Kikuyu girls feeding strange fruit into incomprehensible machines while dance music from a loud-speaker tickled their ears, and going home with their own pay-packets at the end of the week. This work is very popular, the manager told me, and the girls, although anxious to learn, are as yet only one-quarter as efficient as their counterparts in the factory he had previously managed in Essex. But they are the pioneers.

The factory's intake could be doubled if more pineapples could be sold. They go all over the world, to Britain, Switzerland, Sweden, Germany, the Middle East; but competition is severe, and they start with the disadvantage of a 350-mile railway journey before they reach the sea. The local company that owns the factory has ploughed everything back and has not declared a dividend for ten years.

One of the directors and moving spirits is Mr. Bob Harries, who has lived on the same farm at Thika for fifty-five years. Roughly half the fruit dealt with in the factory comes from European and half from African farms. Mr. Harries assured me that African production was founded mainly upon suckers stolen from Europeans. 'Only one lot of suckers was bought, and that was fifty sold to an African in 1949,' he said. 'I lost five acres of newly-planted suckers in one night—

a clean sweep. Lorries came in and 75,000 plants were ripped out before daylight, a very well organized operation. That founded most of the pineapple industry in Kiambu.' Some of the European farmers on the border of the African area have given up pineapple growing because of thefts.

Whatever the origin and ethics of the pineapples, in they roll at one end and out at the other to a railway siding where I saw men loading trucks with 2,000 cases for Hamburg—not only pineapples but also tomato juice, chutney, peas, baked beans and other appetizing vegetables and juices. Next door, another factory assembles the tins, and in Nairobi an all-Israeli firm designs and prints the labels. International, inter-racial, it seems to work smoothly and to the advantage of all.

IV

The inter-district race for complete consolidation was won by Kiambu in August, 1958, with 83,645 registered holdings and plots, covering 238,000 acres. Here you may see the pattern of the future squarely laid. The old Emergency villages are going or have gone: over 300 of them, in the Kiambu district, are in process of reduction to 120 permanent towns, each holding anywhere from 2,000 to 10,000 people and to be equipped with water and light. The density has been fixed at eight houses to the acre. Every one of the *ahoi* in the district, and every Kikuyu whose fragments added up to less than four acres, has been allocated a quarter of an acre in one of the towns.

Right-holders in Kiambu were found to average ten fragments each, now consolidated into holdings which average seven acres and vary from the minimum of four to 273 acres. The Kiambu district, shared between Africans and Europeans, is packed with people and, when everyone is living on his farm, three-quarters of the population will be in towns. Kiambu provides a clear example of the population increase that is going on. In 1950 it had an estimated 43,000 males. A count in 1955 revealed 59,454 adult males, and by 1958 this figure had risen to an estimated 63,000.

From the air, Emergency villages look like rows of straw-coloured halma pegs stuck in a green board, each cluster filmed by a soft haze of smoke. They are depressingly basic and symmetrical, but were temporary expedients and one may hope that the new towns, although they can scarcely aspire to beauty, will at least offer more variety, and the shade of trees. Urbanization is a result of Mau Mau that will endure.

It is from the air that one can best observe the footprints of Progress; the clustering villages, the contoured terraced hillsides, the gleaming tin roofs, the cattle-sheds, the grey-green strips of pineapples, the coffee trees like pins stuck on to squares of canvas, pale with mulch. I flew with Mr. Dick Henderson, who planned many of the farms. He picked out his favourite holdings from above, his eye critically directed towards their progress, or the reverse. 'Mwangi hasn't mulched his new coffee properly; I shall have to tackle him . . .' 'I see Gitu's started on his new dairy . . .' 'Stephen Ndwega's planted that Napier grass at last below his pines . . .' The Better Farmers' wives, little bright dots below us, did not pause to look up at this keen-eyed but benign Big Brother overhead, checking up on their farm plans. Infants in blue danced in circles round their teachers, cycles sped along new red roads, roofs winked up at us, the patchwork fields were like a part of Kent.

Back on the ground, to stand in a Kiambu valley was like being on the stage of a Greek amphitheatre, so narrow are the bench terraces that rise like tiers of steps all round you to meet a clear blue sky. They are intersected by fences, or euphorbia hedges, running straight up and down to divide the narrow farms, which normally extend from the crest of a ridge down to a river at the bottom.

Cultivation still is, and must be, done by hoe, because the terraces are too narrow for tractors. This leads, fortunately, to a heavy rate of employment. One of the Better Farmers I visited had fourteen acres, every bit bench-terraced, had invested £500, all savings, and employed eighteen men; one can see the force of the argument that the landless will find work on developed farms. Many of these Kiambu holdings are in fact market gardens rather than farms, and supply Nairobi with vegetables and flowers. One man I visited had a quarter of an acre of carnations, neatly layered and staked; he had learnt his craft from a skilled European horticulturalist. Specialists in all fields have made their appearance. I saw a poultry farm with 500 hens in sawdust deep litter, fed on poultry mash bought in Nairobi, to which the owner takes the eggs in his car.

v

In the Kiambu district office are shelves full of large black ledgers in which each landowner has a page bearing details of his holding, and of all transactions that ensue. Every transfer of land must be registered. Sales are taking place freely and prices reach £100 for quarter-acre plots in the towns. All the ledgers are duplicated in Nairobi, in case of local accidents.

The system was explained to me by Mr. John Golds, a farmer and cheese-maker who joined the administration in the Emergency and stayed on to play a major part, with Mr. Tony Sutton, in carrying out the system which has now reached its full development in Kiambu. Consolidation in this district has cost about £110,000, of which half has already been recovered from the landowners who are charged a fee of ten shillings an acre up to twenty acres, and five shillings an acre after that. Now the main headaches are the question of inheritance, and the prevention of corruption. On the larger holdings, most farmers will probably divide the land among their sons, and are free to do so provided that no portion falls below the four-acre minimum.

A complicated system has been devised to allow men with smaller holdings to divide their value fairly among their sons without dividing the acres.* Whether this will work remains to be seen. The same may be said of the system devised to

*On a man's death, his holding is valued by the Government. One son gets the land, and he must pay to each of the others an equal share of the value within five years. If he fails to do this, the land is auctioned and the proceeds divided among the sons.

31 Chief Kasinga of the Kitui district. Drawing water at a rock dam, Kitui

32 Old and new co-exist: Suk spearmen herd their flocks but, in Nyanza, young men take their brides with Christian ritual

record transfers and to prevent people falsifying the value
of the land, on which the Government collects stamp duty,
or subdividing it unofficially. A local Land Board must
approve every transaction, and each transfer must be signed
by a European registrar. I was told that European control
at some stage was essential, or bribery would proliferate.

'Now that consolidation is over,' said Mr. Terence
Gavaghan, the D.C., 'a tremendous surge forward in farming
is about to begin—if only we have peace.' He meant local
political peace and, having to control matters on the fringes
of Nairobi, was none too optimistic. Unrest is everywhere,
and one-third of all Kiambu men had been Mau Mau
detainees.

We drove to the *mbari ya Igi*, where Kiambu consolidation
began. This *mbari*, before consolidation, had always imported
food. For the first time this year its people fed themselves
and sold 2,000 bags of maize and 500 bags of potatoes and
beans. Now they are beginning to keep Guernsey cattle;
ideas are coming to the boil; they may double their production
next year. Multiply this by all the other ridges in Kiambu,
and then in Fort Hall, Nyeri, Embu, Meru—there is no limit
to what the high potential land of the Kikuyu could produce.
'If we have peace!'

VI

Ngecha is one of the new towns that are growing out of
Emergency villages. Huts are disappearing and nearly all
the houses—all bungalows—are made of stone, concrete
blocks or bricks. They will not be imposing, but they will
have space around them and should not turn into slums.
Water is laid on to stand-pipes, and electricity available to
anyone who wants it and will pay a flat-rate of ten shillings
a month for three lights, with no meters. Only about thirty
householders have taken up this offer so far, but Ngecha is
one of the first towns to be put on the main. All are equipped
with shops, schools and churches. They are something wholly
new—so new that the *mbari* round Ngecha, all forest then,
was still in process of being bought from the Aathi by the

Kikuyu when the first Europeans arrived. Holes in the ground made by the Aathi to store honey are found to this day in parts of the district.

On the outskirts of the town every inch is cultivated, and houses with corrugated iron roofs are going up on every plot. Pyrethrum blooms in white and grey arcs along the terraces, there are food crops, coffee, vegetables, and pastures with Jerseys in them for a change. This is indeed a smiling countryside that breathes a rising prosperity, and no one who knew it even five years ago, when it was beleaguered, gang-ridden and untended, would credit the changes that have come about unless he saw them with his own eyes.

And so, at last, to Nairobi, by way of one of the satellite towns, the latest in planned development, that soon will ring the capital. Near Dagoretti, sixty years ago a dangerous outpost established to protect caravans, and subsequently railway surveyors, from suspicious, arrow-firing, skin-clad Kikuyu warriors, there is now arising a town to house up to 10,000 people who will travel daily by bus, car and cycle to their work in Nairobi. Riruta is a child of the Kiambu District Council, who will build for any applicant one of five types of stone house, ranging from a grand six- or seven-roomed affair, plus servants' quarters, suitable for company directors and future Ministers, to smaller ones for Civil Servants, shopkeepers and the like.

The most popular type costs £650 and all are equipped with light, running water and sanitation. The District Council will not only build the house but advance the money to pay itself back, subject to a down payment. The town was not far advanced when I was there, but building was going on apace by African contractors; the District Council public works and transport departments were busy, and prospective householders were inspecting electric and gas cookers, refrigerators, radios, kettles and other appliances in a showroom maintained there by a big Nairobi firm. Just across the boundary lay the Duke of York's, one of the two European secondary schools for boys.

Riruta will soon be in use as a thriving dormitory town for the new and relatively well-to-do African middle class, complete, no doubt, with garages, filling stations, drive-in cinemas, tea-shops, brothels, nursery schools, television aerials and many other amenities of modern life. Rapidly, with gusto, vigour and hideous sprawl, Subtopia advances on the shoulders of Progress into the green hills of Africa.

CHAPTER 17

The Nationalist Stand

I

THIS ends our tour: not of the whole of Kenya, but of most of the African land units, covering some 52,000 square miles—England totals just over 50,000 square miles—where probably about 5½ million out of 6½ million people live.

Of the remainder, about a quarter of a million Africans live in the two big cities, and a quarter of a million in the so-called white highlands, which for half a century have been reserved for Europeans, just as other sections of the highlands were reserved for the Kikuyu, Abaluhya, Kamba, Masai, Nandi and so on. The end of this policy was envisaged by a Government statement at the end of 1959.

An impression has prevailed for many years that white settlers took nearly all the best land and left only the dregs for Africans, to whom it all rightfully belongs. Anyone who has read as far as this will know by now that this is untrue. Most of the best land, in an agricultural sense, is still in African ownership, where it has always been. Kenya's Ministry of Agriculture, Animal Husbandry and Water Resources has made a study of the distribution of what is called 'land of high potential'—good land—which they roughly define as land lying in a rainfall belt where thirty inches or more can be depended on annually, and where the soil is suitable for cultivation under a system of mixed or plantation farming.

In round figures, they estimate that there are about 32,300 square miles of high potential land in existing African areas, and 8,460 square miles of it in the hands of Europeans. In other words, that Europeans own about one-fifth of the high potential land in Kenya, and Africans four-fifths.

There are, of course, millions of Africans in occupation

of it as against thousands of Europeans, but this does not alter the fact that to say that Europeans have most of the best land in the highlands is inaccurate. They have 20 per cent of it, a different thing altogether. Anyone can see this for himself if he goes round. It is remarkable how often you will find that a change from well-watered, deep-loamed, fertile-looking country to a region much less favoured and more dry will correspond with your passage from an African to a European area.

There is, of course, nothing surprising in this. By and large, African tribes had either occupied the most fertile areas, or were beginning to do so, before the Europeans arrived, and an official policy was pretty well adhered to that all land in use by Africans was to be reserved for their benefit.

II

The first leases issued to Europeans from about 1903—very little was allocated before then—covered, in the main, three types of country. First was land either altogether unoccupied, like the Mau escarpment and the Trans Nzoia, or used intermittently for pasture by the Masai, who had at their disposal such enormous areas, and were themselves so few and scattered, that they sometimes left whole stretches of country alone for five or even ten years. At other times internecine battles almost wiped out entire sections of the tribe, leaving their plains deserted: this happened to the Uasin Gishu and to the Laikipia sections, whose abandoned grazing grounds were in due course leased to Europeans.

A second category consisted of chunks of forest, too high and cold for African settlement, where glades ran like tongues into thickets of cedar, olive and other indigenous trees. Finally, buffer regions between hostile tribes, left unoccupied for safety, were leased to Europeans in order to discourage tribal war. These contained some of the best agricultural land to be found in the erstwhile white highlands, such as the tea-producing areas of Kericho, Kaimosi and Nandi.

All these scattered, oddly assorted types of land were

combined into the so-called white highlands, an area about twice the size of Yorkshire. They are mainly pastoral, not agricultural, in their ecology. Of the 11,579 square miles actually leased to Europeans, about two-thirds are classified as mainly pastoral land, where cultivation is inhibited by shallow or infertile soils, or by uncertain rainfall. Such land could not lend itself to smallholdings of the type I have described in these pages, although no doubt it could be used for grazing schemes. These, however, would absorb no extra population, and would certainly not increase the present output of meat.

In two areas, however, some land that did, in fact, belong to African clans or families was mistakenly leased to Europeans. This was in Kiambu and in Nandi. Kiambu district today consists of 733 square miles and about one-third of it belongs to Europeans—this is where most of the coffee plantations are—as against two-thirds to the Kikuyu. When the leases were made, the Kikuyu had been much reduced in numbers by a terrible outbreak of smallpox, and several years of famine, that had devastated the country at the end of the nineteenth century. Land in the ownership of certain *mbaris*, which had reverted to bush, was thought to be unoccupied, and some of it was made over to Europeans.

All this was gone into in 1933 by the Morris Carter Land Commission, which compensated the Kikuyu with more land elsewhere. But this did not remove a sense of grievance that has festered over the years. By very much exaggerating their grievances, the Kikuyu have succeeded in creating a wholly false impression that most of their land was taken away, and now many members of the younger generation are not even aware that much of what they believe is part of a myth.

This sense of grievance springs from an even deeper feeling of resentment against the very presence of an alien race whose members, encased in a conviction of their own superiority, not only bring Africans material benefits but often press, drive, badger and patronize them. Materialist as most human beings are, there are still instincts that materialism does not satisfy; and it is these that have been roughened and bruised by the presence of Europeans. Chafed by continued pressure, these feelings of the Africans ooze a pus of bitter racialism, as much an outcome of their inflamed condition as is a discharge from a physical injury. As with the body, it is a symptom, not a cause; to treat it by itself is vain. Can the causes of bitter racialism be removed without amputation? That is the question on which all else now depends, and its discussion lies outside the scope of this book.

III

A word, however, needs to be said about the economics of the matter. If it was not for that, the problem could be solved with comparative simplicity by conceding outright to the nationalists all they desire, as has been done in so many other countries—Ghana, Nigeria, Guinea, the Sudan, Somalia, the Cameroons, Mali, the Union of Benin, the Central African Republic—the list is long and the very names of some of these new states unfamiliar. In Kenya, it is not merely a question of abandoning to their fate a handful of Europeans—the total white population is about 68,000—and a much larger, but perhaps more adaptable, population of Asians, in the hope that they would either find their own feet or move elsewhere. It is a question of whether the country's economy could, and would, survive and expand under such a drastic and experimental change of management.

About four-fifths of Kenya's wealth comes from the produce of the land. Industries are growing—tourism is one with great potentialities—but they are still very small compared with the products of agriculture. Kenya is handicapped by having no minerals of importance, and no oil. Power is expensive, markets patchy and mainly poor. It is hard to develop prosperous industries when the average citizen can only spend a few pounds a year. Nor is there any reservoir of skilled labour to draw upon.

These problems are shared by most countries emerging from the pre-industrial revolution stage into the age of nuclear fission. They are not insuperable, but they do make things difficult and, if they are to be overcome, there is one absolute essential: incoming capital. And no capital, whether private or public, ventures into stormy waters. Political stability is a condition of favourable investment everywhere.

If the potentialities of the African lands, released by consolidation, registration and the Swynnerton plan, are to be fully realized, large injections of capital will be needed. This provision, which cannot be beyond the capacity of the Western nations, would seem to be the quickest, most efficient and indeed perhaps the only way to raise the living standards of the people. Small individual loans which will enable families to do things for themselves, as they really want, would seem more sensible than large, expensive schemes to do for them things that may raise their living standards, but will not give them the satisfaction and the independence they seek.

Of the agricultural exports on which Kenya depends for its existence, £26,300,000 worth came, in 1958, from the European sector of the country, and £5,900,000 worth from the African. As the developments I have outlined proceed, the African share will rise year by year until eventually it overtakes the share of the Europeans. For instance, if the coffee programme proceeds as it should—and the big threat here is a break in the market—African production should catch up European by 1970, and thereafter surpass it. And there is reckoned to be twice as much land suitable for tea in the African areas as is at present planted in the European.

This lies in the future: at present it is mainly European production that supports the country's economy, and provides the bulk of the revenue on which all progress depends. And so no conscientious government could surrender control until it was satisfied on at least two counts: that Africans would run things efficiently, and that they would not, through inflamed racial soreness, wreck the European sector of the economy, at any rate before they were themselves in a position to take it over with a good chance of success. It is a matter of timing: but a wide gulf separates the African and the European estimate of the necessary time.

IV

Politics, as I have said, lie outside the scope of this book, but nowhere in Africa, or indeed in the world, can major changes in peoples' ways of life be separated from the art and practice of government. In the wider sense, this bold attempt to change the basis of the Africans' relation to their land is a part of politics; in the narrower sense in which the word is often used, politics keep intruding, if only through the attempts of African nationalists to oppose this movement of agrarian reform.

If you hate someone—really hate them—you refuse to see good in any of their actions, even those genuinely meant well; and it is the same with nationalists. They hate colonialism in any form, even when it tries its hardest to do good; the better its actions, indeed, the more repugnant these actions must seem, since they are likely to win over to a tolerant view of colonialism some of the very people who are supposed to be groaning under its yoke.

If African nationalists are to get rid of colonialism immediately, they must enrol all Africans behind a militant and united front. A contented peasant making money out of his land and depending, like every farmer, on a stable market, will seldom prove himself so ardent a nationalist as the unemployed and frustrated young man of the town. Smallholders, in fact, who have never had it so good, and hope to have it better still, will not join marches in Nairobi to demand the release of Jomo Kenyatta, who did everything he possibly could to wreck the land reforms which have brought about their prosperity.

The nationalist position is therefore quite understandable, and not so illogical as would at first sight appear. African nationalism is everywhere an urban movement which spreads outwards to the mass of the people, who are not urban at all. This, of course, has nearly always been the case throughout history, in the political field; religious movements, on the other hand, seem more often to emerge from a rural or pastoral background, and to impose themselves on the towns.

In the long run, there is no doubt that the interests of African nationalism could best be served by the success, at the earliest possible moment, of the so-called agricultural revolution. Only this success can provide an economic base for independence, and create the wealth on which all future progress must depend. However understandable in human terms, it is therefore short-sighted of the nationalists to oppose it; and, as a result, a deep division of opinion has arisen among the African population. There seems very little doubt that a majority of Africans, the farmers and pastoralists, wish to see the land reforms pushed on with and extended; and I found a good deal of resentment, as I have suggested here and there, against the attitude of African nationalists in opposing these reforms.

The majority, however, are at work on their farms and are largely voiceless; the minority who live in towns monopolize the ways of getting heard. They edit and write to newspapers, organize and go to meetings, parade with banners, draw up petitions, assemble in headline-provoking crowds, stand for parliament and do all the other things that attract attention and publicize their point of view. An overseas newspaper correspondent will report a political meeting in Nairobi and interview Mr. Mboya, but he will not travel round remote regions talking to smallholders; so it is only the voices of people who go to meetings that are heard in London, Moscow, Washington and New York.

Even were spokesmen for the smallholders to appear in Nairobi, they would not get very far. Of the technique of politics they are quite ignorant; and, besides, the pressure of opinion organized by nationalists is formidable. It takes a very bold man, and a very strong one, to stand up against the sweeping nationalist current, and in any country there are few men with the moral courage of, say, Chief Muhoya, or of the Minister of Housing, Mr. Musa Amalemba, who have done so. On a lower level, intimidation may take shape in acts of violence, or at least in threats, which make defiance impossible for anyone but martyrs, and to be a martyr in the neutral cause of moderation is very rare indeed.

For these reasons, among others, the future of the land

reforms described in these pages is by no means assured. Experts have planned them on the whole soundly, the people on the whole desire them, administrators and technicians are carrying them through competently. But these reforms need, say, ten years of stability to hoist the economy on to an altogether higher plane, and to become themselves irreversible. Ten years' stability of two kinds: of markets, and of politics. Either a market collapse or a severe political upheaval could bring the programme to a halt and undo most of the good that has been achieved.

V

At this stage in human history, every truth has become a platitude or a cliché. In spite of having, therefore, to repeat one as a final observation, I must remark that nothing can be done without teamwork and united effort, and the outstanding impression that remained with me from this tour was of the amount of genuine teamwork that is going on: between Europeans and Africans, between different kinds of African, and between different kinds of European.

District and provincial committees composed of officials, European farmers and Africans, plan and advise upon the work in every area. District teams unite the various officials who have often, in the past, been at loggerheads—and occasionally are today—in a local command. African District Councils' by-laws and money underpin all the Better Farming; a hierarchy of headmen and chiefs works under district officers and commissioners; and all the technicians, whether agricolas, vets, administrators or African instructors, whether levellers, veterinary scouts or foresters, conspire together for the common end. A growing body of Better Farmers and their wives patiently follow plans and lay-outs, invest their life's savings and do a lot of exacting and often rather mysterious work largely on trust. It is teamwork between all these, and many others, that has made the agricultural revolution possible.

I have mentioned, as I went along, the names of various people engaged in this work: the people that I happened to meet, and who were often kind enough to entertain and instruct me. This was a matter of luck; and I hope no one will feel he has been ignored through lack of interest in his story, or appreciation of the work he is engaged upon. All are stitches in a tapestry, but the beholder's eye can take in only the pattern and the general effect.

However, it would be wrong to end an account of a campaign without even mentioning the names of the commander-in-chief and of his principal Generals. The whole scheme of land reform and development, although no doubt it had for years been gestating in various files, memoranda and conferences, was formulated and launched during the Governorship of Sir Evelyn Baring. It was he who, grasping the need both to offer the people an objective after the strain and turmoil of Mau Mau, and drastically to reform the country's economy, adopted and pushed through the land consolidation programme and the Swynnerton plan, twin bases of the whole project. Thanks to Sir Evelyn Baring's patient, enthusiastic and firm advocacy of its principles, it won the highest priority as an aspect of rehabilitation and recovery from civil war.

Before he left the Ministry of Agriculture to become Speaker of the Legislative Council, Sir Ferdinand Cavendish-Bentinck laid down the general strategy, and his successor, Mr. Michael Blundell, was the Minister in charge of the campaign. It was he who planned, guided and supported the scheme through its many vicissitudes. He did much more than that, however; he gave up the political leadership of Kenya's Europeans, which he exercised at the time without serious challenge, in order to take over the Ministry of Agriculture. Land reform has been his special baby, and only when it seemed to be over its first troubles, and well established in a lusty infancy, did he hand it over to his successor, Mr. Bruce Mackenzie, and resume the thankless task of political leadership in a community by then considerably divided and confused.

Throughout this period Mr. R. O. Hennings, in his twin capacity as Permanent Secretary for Agriculture and Chairman of the Board of ALDEV, used his abundant energy and knowledge to keep the giant Progress—to go back to our original metaphor—supplied with sustenance and weapons. And finally there is the present Director of Agriculture, Mr. Roger Swynnerton, whose name on the plan is an indication of his part as its progenitor. When the time comes for its final assessment, whatever its political and economic future may be, there will be nothing but admiration for the thoroughness and imagination of the technical aspects, which were conceived and shaped in his brain, and for the staff work in its execution. As a modest man he would no doubt prefer others to have most of the credit— Mr. C. M. Johnston, for instance, then Minister for African Affairs, who saw land consolidation launched among the Kikuyu, where its failure would have wrecked everything; Sir Ernest Vasey who, as Minister of Finance, secured the money; Mr. MacOwan, chief of the veterinary services; Mr. Leslie Brown, second-in-command to Mr. Swynnerton; and many others it is impossible to name.

Men at the top make plans; people at the bottom accept or reject them. By and large, these plans have been accepted by the people of Kenya, to whom they offer their first real opportunity to leave behind a tribal way of life and, for good or ill, become full members of the twentieth century. That they would like these plans to continue and to come to fruition is unquestionable. Whether this will happen remains to be seen. The plan's fate depends on many factors but most of all, perhaps, on the condition named by the District Commissioner of Kiambu—'If we have peace.' Peace is always possible, but it is a lot to ask for in the world of men.

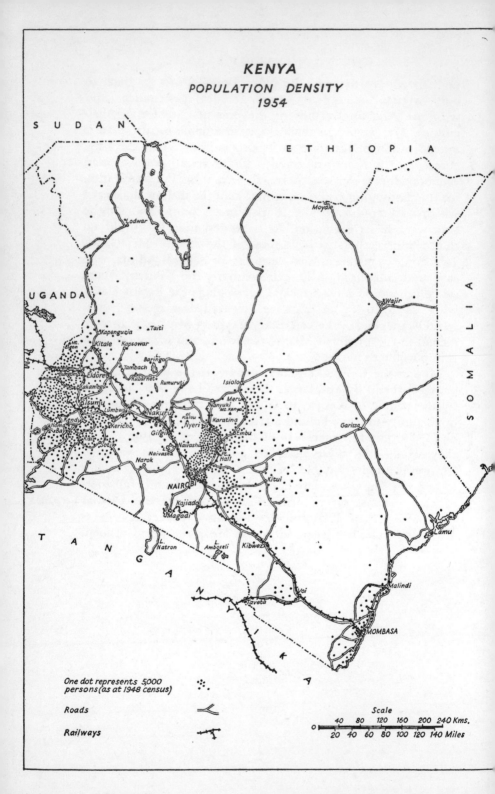

KENYA
POPULATION DENSITY
1954

One dot represents 5,000
persons (as at 1948 census)

Roads

Railways

Scale

0 40 80 120 160 200 240 Kms.

20 40 60 80 100 120 140 Miles

KENYA
LAND DIVISION

SUDAN

ETHIOPIA

UGANDA

SOMALIA

Lake Rudolf

Mandera

Moyale

Lodwar

Marsabit

Wajir

Kapenguria

Kitale

Marakwet

Tororo

Eldoret

Baringo

Bungoma

Kakamega

Kapsabet

Isiolo

MERU

Kisumu

NORTH POKOMO

Garissa

Nakuru

Kericho

Nyeri

Embu

Homa Bay

Fort Hall

Kisii

Lake Victoria

Narok

NAIROBI

KIBUI

Musoma

Machakos

COAST

Magadi

Lamu

TANGANYIKA

Tsavo

Malindi

Moshi

Arusha

COAST

COAST

Mombasa

Crown land	
African land	
European land	
Other alienated land	
National forest	

Scale

0   40   80   120   160   200   240 Kms.

20   40   60   80   100   120   140 Miles

APPENDIX A

LAND POTENTIAL IN KENYA

1. The whole, or nearly the whole, of Kenya tends to have its rain in two seasons separated by a more or less sharp drought. Not less than 15 inches of rainfall is normally needed to bring a crop to maturity: hence 30 inches a year is the bare minimum. It would be preferable to put the lowest sound minimum at 35 inches. Putting it, however, at 30 inches, and excluding the Northern Frontier District, the following facts emerge:

Land Classification	Area in Square Miles		
	Over 30″	20–30″	Under 20″
European . . .	8,459	4,025	337
African: (1) Land Units .	25,883	16,798	4,073
(2) Masai .	3,025	5,905	3,446
(3) Crown Land .	3,398	14,918	19,372
Total African . .	32,306	37,621	26,891

2. The above is a classification purely on rainfall. A classification worked out on ecological grounds (also excluding the N.F.D.) arrived at the following estimates:

Potential	European Highlands	African Land Units and Crown Lands
1. Highest . . .	2,500	12,000
2. Fair	5,000	20,000
3. Extensive ranching . ' .	4,000	37,000
4. Nomadic Pastoral or game .	321	21,000
Totals	12,821	90,000

3. The total area of the European Highlands, including National Forest, was 16,196 square miles. The area actually alienated to Europeans and Asians is 11,724 square miles. The difference mainly consists of forest reserves, national parks, craters and lakes.

APPENDIX B

KENYA: AREA AND POPULATION

Note.—There has been no population census since 1948. Since then, the population has risen sharply but the rate is conjectural. It has been suggested that the population may be doubling itself every 25 to 30 years. An arbitrary, but possibly conservative, increase of 25 per cent in the last twelve years has been assumed, in the fourth column, to give a rough guide to present population figures. This has been applied bluntly to all districts: in fact, of course, population in some districts will have risen more than in others, and various population shifts may have taken place.

Administrative District	Area in square miles	African Population	
		1948	Estimated 1960
Nairobi .	187	109,428	137,000
CENTRAL PROVINCE:			
Thika .	877	66,475	83,000
Kiambu .	733	258,085	323,000
Fort Hall .	724	303,646	380,000
Nyeri .	689	183,057	229,000
Embu .	1,615	202,125	253,000
Meru .	3,773	312,917	391,000
Nanyuki .	2,710	32,784	41,000
NYANZA PROVINCE:			
Elgon Nyanza .	1,610	231,286	289,000
North Nyanza .	1,062	402,282	503,000
Central Nyanza .	1,847	462,772	578,000
South Nyanza .	2,958	545,284	682,000
Kericho .	2,101	212,608	266,000

Administrative District	Area in square miles	African Population	
		1948	Estimated 1960
RIFT VALLEY PROVINCE:			
Trans Nzoia	1,137	61,424	77,000
Uasin Gishu	1,691	79,492	99,000
Nakuru	2,618	182,179	228,000
Nandi	711	80,562	101,000
Elgeyo/Marakwet	1,031	64,455	81,000
Baringo	3,838	72,034	90,000
Laikipia	2,461	33,926	42,000
West Suk	1,978	42,777	53,000
Naivasha	1,563	17,000	21,000
SOUTHERN PROVINCE:			
Kajiado	8,108	28,987	36,000
Narok	7,148	37,444	47,000
Machakos	5,776	356,545	446,000
Kitui	11,975	210,788	263,000
COAST PROVINCE:			
Mombasa	81	55,438	69,000
Kwale	3,027	115,136	144,000
Kilifi	4,916	181,425	227,000
Tana River	9,168	19,331	24,000
Teita	5,939	61,463	77,000
Lamu	2,583	15,465	19,000
NORTHERN FRONTIER PROVINCE	123,154	212,500	266,000
TOTALS	219,789	5,251,120	6,565,000

EUROPEAN POPULATION 1960 estimate Approximately 68,000

ASIAN POPULATION 1960 estimate Approximately 220,000

APPENDIX C

KENYA: AFRICAN LANDS AND TRIBES

1. The land pattern of Kenya is complicated. There are three main categories: Crown land, Alienated land, and African Land Units. Broadly speaking, Crown Lands are unscheduled areas without permanent settlements; Alienated land consists of leaseholds and freeholds held by Europeans or Asians; African Land Units, once called Reserves, are the inalienable property of the main tribes, protected until this year by the Native Lands Trust Board. There are, in addition, smaller categories such as Native Reserves, Native Leasehold Areas, Native Settlement Areas and Communal Reserves.

2. The matter is further complicated by the fact that administrative districts (one might very roughly compare these with English counties) do not correspond with African Land Units, which often overlap several districts. The following table shows the main African Land Units with their areas, the administrative districts they embrace, the total population in 1948 and the same rough estimate of 1960 populations, reached by adding 25 per cent, as in Appendix B.

Land Unit	Area in square miles	District (Whole or Part)	African Population 1948	Estimated 1960
NYANZA	7,191	Elgon Nyanza	231,286	289,000
		North Nyanza	402,282	503,000
		Central Nyanza	462,772	578,000
		South Nyanza	545,284	682,000
	7,191		1,641,624	2,052,000
MERU	3,425	Meru	312,917	391,000

Land Unit	Area in square miles	District (Whole or Part)	African Population	
			1948	Estimated 1960
NANDI	738	Nandi	80,562	101,000
KIPSIGIS	997	Kericho	212,608	266,000
KERIO	6,460	West Suk	42,777	53,000
		Baringo	72,034	90,000
		Elgeyo/Marakwet	64,455	81,000
	6,460		179,266	224,000
MASAI	14,931	Kajiado	28,987	36,000
		Narok	37,444	47,000
	14,931		66,431	83,000
KAMBA	8,266	Machakos	356,545	446,000
		Kitui	210,788	263,000
	8,266		567,333	709,000
KIKUYU	2,718	Nyeri	183,057	229,000
		Embu	202,121	253,000
		Fort Hall	303,646	380,000
		Kiambu	258,085	323,000
	2,718		946,913	1,185,000
COAST	4,835	Kilifi	181,425	227,000
		Kwale	115,136	144,000
		Teita	61,463	77,000
		Tana River	34,796	43,000
	4,835		392,820	491,000

Land Unit	Area in square miles	District (Whole or Part)	African Population	
			1948	Estimated 1960
NORTH POKOMO	119	Northern Frontier	186,500	233,000
RESERVED AREAS	2,519			
TOTALS	52,271		4,586,974	5,735,000

3. The principal tribes with actual numbers in 1948 and estimated numbers (1948 plus 25 per cent) in 1960, are as follows:

Tribe	1948	Estimated 1960
Kikuyu . . .	1,026,341	1,283,000
Luo . . .	757,043	946,000
Baluhya . . .	653,774	817,000
Kamba . . .	611,725	765,000
Meru . . .	324,894	406,000
Nyika . . .	296,254	370,000
Kisii . . .	255,108	319,000
Embu . . .	203,690	255,000
Kipsigis . . .	159,692	200,000
Nandi . . .	116,681	146,000
Others . . .	845,918	1,058,000
TOTAL . .	5,251,120	6,565,000

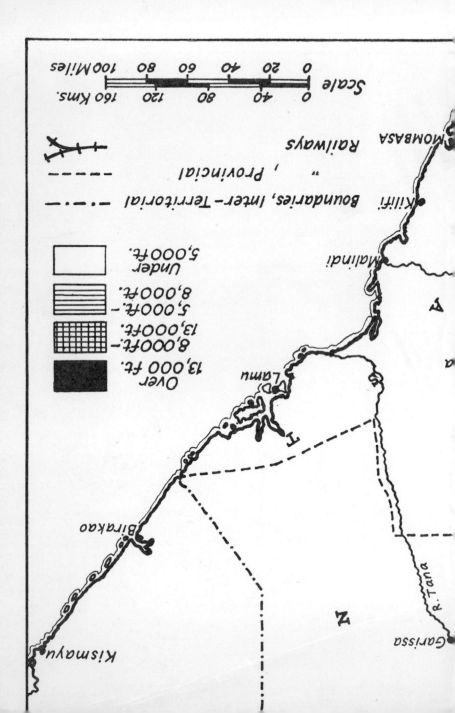

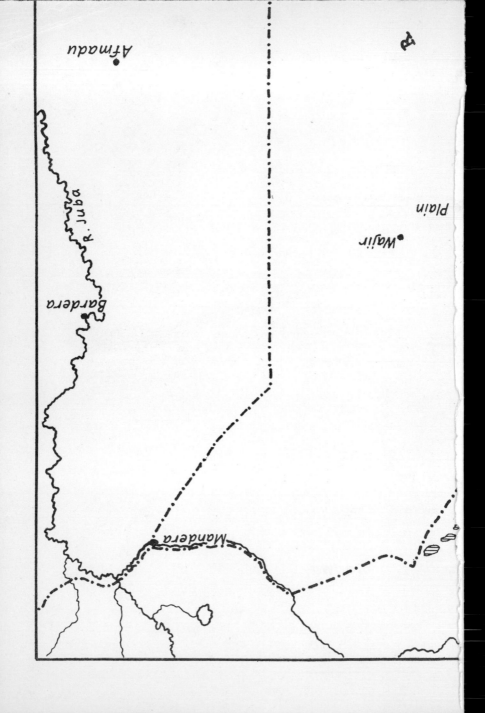

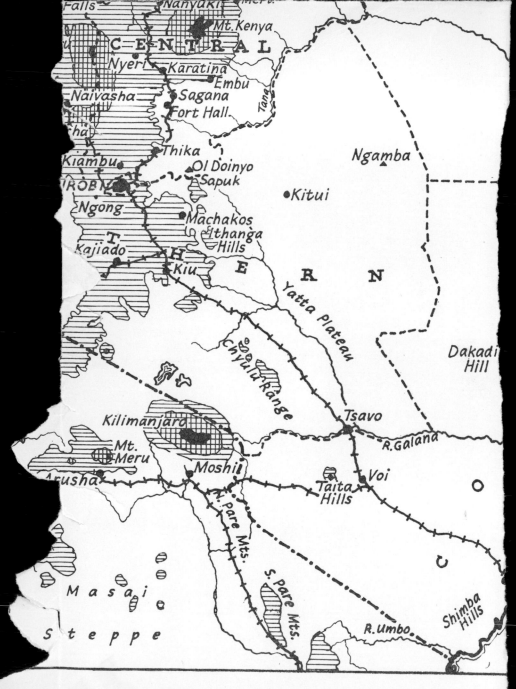

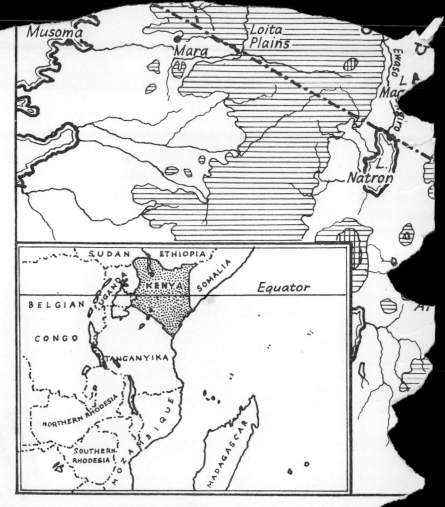

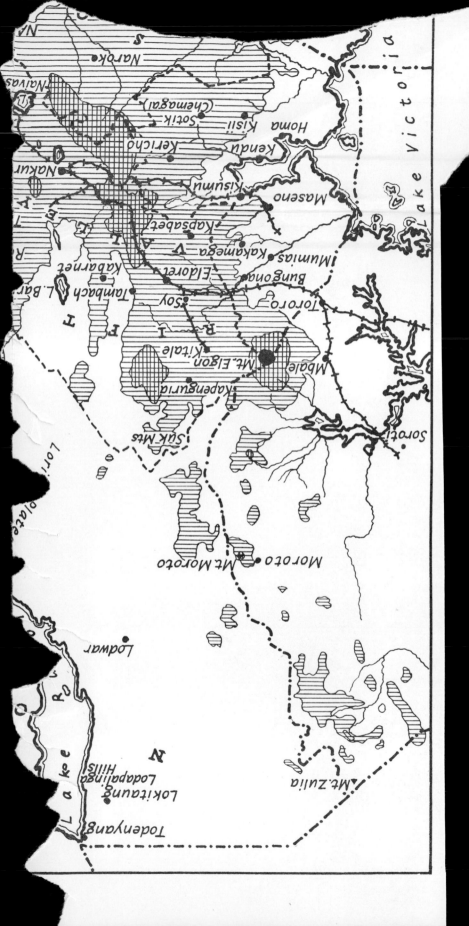